Trust, Power and Public Relations in Financial Markets

T0384260

The public relations profession positions itself as experts in building trust throughout global markets, particularly after crisis strikes. Successive crises have tainted financial markets in recent years. Calls to restore trust in finance have been particularly pressing, given trust's crucial role as a lubricant in global financial engines. Nonetheless, years after the global financial crisis, trust in financial markets remains both tenuous and controversial. This book explores PR in financial markets, posing a fundamental question about PR professionals as would-be 'trust strategists' – if PR promotes its expertise in building and restoring trust, how can it ignore its potential role in losing trust in the first place?

Drawing on examples from state finance, international lending agencies, trade bodies, financial institutions and consumer groups in mature and emerging financial centres, this book explores the wide-ranging role of PR in financial markets, including:

- State finance and debt capital markets
- Investor relations, M&A and IPOs
- Corporate communications for financial institutions
- Product promotion and consumer finance
- Financial trade associations and lobbying
- Consumerism and financial activism.

Far reaching and challenging, this innovative book will be essential reading for researchers, advanced students and professionals in PR, communication and finance.

Clea Bourne is a Lecturer in Public Relations, Advertising & Marketing, at Goldsmiths, University of London, UK. Her research on communication in financial markets has appeared in *Culture and Organisation, Public Relations Inquiry, Journal of Public Relations Research* and *New Media and Society*, and in edited collections.

Routledge New Directions in Public Relations and Communication Research
Edited by Kevin Moloney

For a full list of titles in this series, please visit www.routledge.com

Current academic thinking about public relations (PR) and related communication is a lively, expanding marketplace of ideas and many scholars believe that it's time for its radical approach to be deepened. *Routledge New Directions in PR &Communication Research* is the forum of choice for this new thinking. Its key strength is its remit, publishing critical and challenging responses to continuities and fractures in contemporary PR thinking and practice, tracking its spread into new geographies and political economies. It questions its contested role in market-orientated, capitalist, liberal democracies around the world, and examines its invasion of all media spaces, old, new, and as yet unenvisaged. We actively invite new contributions and offer academics a welcoming place for the publication of their analyses of a universal, persuasive mind-set that lives comfortably in old and new media around the world.

Books in this series will be of interest to academics and researchers involved in these expanding fields of study, as well as students undertaking advanced studies in this area.

Trust, Power and Public Relations in Financial Markets
Clea Bourne

International Public Relations
Perspectives from deeply divided societies
Edited by Ian Somerville, Owen Hargie, Maureen Taylor and Margalit Toledano

Nation Branding, Public Relations and Soft Power
Corporatizing Poland
Pawel Surowiec

Public Relations and Participatory Culture
Fandom, social media and community engagement
Amber Hutchins and Natalie T. J. Tindall

Social Media and Public Relations
Fake friends and powerful publics
Judy Motion, Robert L. Heath and Shirley Leitch

Trust, Power and Public Relations in Financial Markets

Clea Bourne

Routledge
Taylor & Francis Group

LONDON AND NEW YORK

First published 2017 by Routledge

2 Park Square, Milton Park, Abingdon, Oxon OX14 4RN
605 Third Avenue, New York, NY 10017

Routledge is an imprint of the Taylor & Francis Group, an informa business

First issued in paperback 2021

Publisher's Note

The publisher has gone to great lengths to ensure the quality of this reprint
but points out that some imperfections in the original copies may be apparent.

British Library Cataloguing in Publication Data
A catalogue record for this book is available from the British Library

Library of Congress Cataloging in Publication Data
A catalog record for this book has been requested

ISBN: 978-0-415-71921-6 (hbk)
ISBN: 978-0-367-34072-8 (pbk)

Typeset in Bembo
by Apex CoVantage, LLC

To Ron, my finance sherpa. And to all those who know life on the financial periphery.

Contents

Tables

Abbreviations

ABI	Association of British Insurers
AFME	Association for Financial Markets in Europe
AIFA	Association of Independent Financial Advisers
AIMA	Alternative Investment Management Association
BBA	British Bankers Association
BSA	Building Societies Association
BVCA	British Venture Capital Association
CBI	Confederation of British Industry
CSR	Corporate Social Responsibility
ECB	European Central Bank
EFAMA	European Fund and Asset Management Association
ELSA	European Life Settlements Association
Eurozone	European Monetary Union
GDP	Gross Domestic Product
IA	Investment Association
IFA	independent financial advisers
IFC	international financial centre
IMF	International Monetary Fund
IR	investor relations
ISDA	International Swaps and Derivatives Association
M&A	mergers and acquisitions
MFA	Managed Funds Association
NAPF	National Association of Pension Funds
NGO	Non-Governmental Organisation
PR	public relations
RBS	Royal Bank of Scotland
S&P	Standard & Poor's
SME	small and medium-sized enterprise
SPVs	Special Purpose Vehicles
TA	trade association
UK	United Kingdom
US	United States of America

Preface

Financial markets have transformed so dramatically in recent decades that they are considered to be one of the wonders of our age. But wonderment cannot mask the power shift in society's relationship with financial markets. Where once bankers were at the beck-and-call of companies wanting to make capital investments, companies now march to the tune of investment bankers and hedge funds. The general public and CEOs alike feel intimidated by their everyday interactions with finance.

Global financial markets employ thousands of public relations (PR) professionals in diverse roles. Some of these professionals have the most powerful, lucrative communications roles available. Despite an abundance of professional communicators working in financial markets, most citizens cannot claim to understand finance very well. This is not helped by the astonishingly scant number of books or articles published on public relations in the world of finance, particularly in the twenty-first century. The few exceptions among academic publications focus on stock market communication, corporate governance and corporate responsibility. While these are important pursuits, they represent only a tiny portion of the strategic PR programmes in global finance.

This book attempts to remedy this oversight by conducting an intensive exploration of PR activity from the very apex of financial markets down to grassroots activism in the streets. The object of my exploration is 'trust', which has become rather an obsession in mature financial centres of Europe and North America. Perhaps this is not surprising. After all, the world's biggest financial centres have played host to innumerable financial scandals in the past 40 years. Maybe it is even less surprising that an entire 'trust restoration industry' has emerged, offering to 'solve' the problem of trust. It is definitely not surprising that the global PR industry has played a leading voice in this discourse.

However, having worked as a PR professional through two major financial crises in different parts of the world, what *does* surprise me is the lack of self-reflection exhibited by the PR sector as it eagerly proffers its trust restoration skills. PR's mantra is 'we need to move forward', without ever learning lessons by reflecting on what went before. Scholars of public relations have done little to address this failure. In fact, the majority of PR scholarship ignores finance altogether. As a result, PR professionals and scholars have ceded important ground to other disciplines. Put simply: if you are looking for a good book or article examining the role of communications in financial markets, then bypass public relations research and head to disciplines such as management studies, marketing, sociology, anthropology, linguistics, economics, media studies or journalism.

I have been inspired by work from all of these disciplines and have included them where I can throughout this book. As a result, you can expect interdisciplinary perspectives throughout the following chapters. In addition, I have drawn on my own previous empirical work on public relations in financial markets. Finally, there has been plenty of room for practitioner voices, reflected in stimulating debates published by think tanks, not-for-profit organisations and the specialist trade press.

I hope this book will prove useful to researchers and students who want to think more critically about how trust is organised in commercial markets, and particularly financial markets. It is also a book for the many PR professionals who work in every corner of finance. Their voices are rarely heard and, I fear, poorly represented by some of the 'exposés' written about public relations in recent years.

Finally, I feel it important to mention that my entire working life has been defined by the financial sector. During that time, I have been lucky enough to work with many financial professionals who are dedicated to making finance work better for customers and the wider society. Some of them still soldier on. I am forever grateful for all they have taught me.

1 PR and trust 'booms and busts'

> In today's increasingly global world of business, there is a clear … pressing agenda for public relations … our profession is uniquely positioned to help further the global business interests of multinational organisations. … The agenda is all about the critical components of reputation that have to do with values and trust – trustworthiness being the ultimate condition of public approval that we seek for our companies, our clients and our profession – on a global scale and wherever in the world we operate.
>
> 'The Character of Public Relations' (Nielsen 2006)

Global PR firms and associations have done much to position trust as a pressing agenda for public relations. This agenda has been precisely tailored to establish a need, then offer a solution to global business in an era when trust is portrayed as a crisis, while public trust has never seemed more urgent or consequential (Rottger and Voss 2008, Arthur W. Page Society 2009). Before economies grew into complex, globalised systems, people did business with people they knew and trust was given in situations they could monitor. Today, consumers are often called upon to put their trust in corporations via faceless, automated and electronic transactions (Giddens 1990). Abstract trust in financial systems has characterised the era of financialisation, during which time financial markets have grown in significance as a result of market deregulation and intensified financial and technological innovation.

Financialisation has also been marked by successive trust 'booms and busts' in global financial markets, in which scores of financial institutions earned disrepute – global investment banks, retail banks, credit rating agencies, hedge funds, asset managers and more. These trust 'booms and busts' are typically accompanied by increasing public demand for transparency and accountability, as financial institutions 'compete' with each other through performative acts designed to produce the impression of trustworthiness (Beckert 2005). Meanwhile, consulting professions, including PR, compete to provide 'early warning systems' and trust remedies, giving rise to a lucrative growth industry in trust restoration (Hilton 2004).

Trust plays a part in PR's positioning to client-organisations. PR has even been defined as trust-building – equated at various points with 'advertising for trust'[1] (Bentele and Wehmeier 2003, p. 203) and 'strategies for generating trust'[2] (Rojas 2012). Trustworthiness is understood to be the ultimate condition of public approval that PR seeks for companies, clients and the profession (Valin 2004, Nielsen 2006), and the main aim of international public relations when mobilising political or material support from other nations (Kunczik 2003).

Persistent promotion of PR's 'trust restoration' capabilities can be traced to the dot-com 'bust' in 2000, and the later collapse of widely admired companies, Enron and Worldcom, generating a 'crisis of trust'. The response from the global PR industry included a series of conferences, 'think tanks' and other remedies designed to restore trust in the corporate world. Edelman, the world's largest PR firm, launched its Trust Barometer in 2000. Edelman's Trust Barometer became an annual marketing event staged at the World Economic Forum, the 'annual healing moment' for corporate trust abuse (Phillips 2015, p. 47). The site and scope of the launch highlights Edelman's trust strategist credentials with global power elites who purchase PR services. More than a decade later, the Trust Barometer is still regularly cited in research and the popular media (e.g. CIPD 2012, Foroohar 2016). Levick, a US-based PR firm, trademarked the strapline *Communicating Trust*. For years, GolinHarris, a global PR firm,[3] promoted the phrase *Building Trust Worldwide* as its corporate strapline. Company founder Al Golin claimed to be the first to the describe PR practitioners as 'trust strategists' in his 2004 book, *Trust or Consequences*, promoting PR's trust-building expertise. In 2007, Kathy Bloomgarden, CEO of the international firm Ruder-Finn, published *Trust: The Secret Weapon of Effective Business Leaders*. Her book presented a portfolio of trust-building strategies for targeting chief executives as key decision-makers for Ruder-Finn's high-value, senior PR consultancy.

The 'trust strategist' title connotes a certain professional anxiety. 'Strategists' devise intentions, designs and plans; they take risks, are responsible autonomous agents of change, attempting to master their environment, even future (Knights & Morgan 1991). For the PR profession, becoming 'strategists' first meant defining PR as a management discipline with boardroom representation. Managers are defined by the object they manage; something measurable, ideally correlated to corporate profit. For PR, that 'object' encompasses relationships, reputation and trust. However, PR's desire for domain over trust has never been formalised. Trust is too nebulous a concept – it is not a management target, not a balance sheet, not even regularly discussed in boardrooms (Golin 2004). The arguably immodest term 'trust strategist' remains an implied *positioning* rather than a job title wielded on PR practitioners' business cards. As a result, a range of professionals have been free to stake their claim to expertise in trust restoration (see Table 1.1).

The PR profession has had plenty of competition in the trust arena from various experts positioning themselves as 'trust strategists'. The fields of human resources (HR) and management consulting have aligned trust with organisational productivity, focusing on rebuilding employee trust in organisations and their employers. HR consultants WatsonWyatt[4] published the widely cited trust survey, WorkUSA, in 2002. Pennington Performance Group published its study on 'trust factors at work' soon after even trademarking the phrase. Leadership

Table 1.1 'Trust Restoration' Industry: Surveys and Reports

Organisation	Sector	Survey/Report	Region	Year
Accenture	Management Consultancy	*The Business of Trust*	US	2003
Arthur W. Page Society	Public Relations	*Building Trust: Leading CEOs Speak Out*	US	2004
Arthur W. Page Society; Institute for Corporate Ethics	Public Relations/ Business Leaders	*The Dynamics of Public Trust in Business*	US	2009
Association of British Insurers	General Insurance	*The Insurance Industry – Building Confidence in Europe*	UK	2009
Association of Independent Financial Advisers	Financial Advisers	*Restoring Trust in Financial Services*	UK	2009
Auth0	IT Security	*What Consumers and Developers Think of IoT Security*	US	2015
BBC	Media	*BBC Trust Survey*	UK	2008
Big Brother Watch	Civil Liberties	*A Breach of Trust: Local Authority Data Loss*	Civil Liberties Campaign	2015
Charity Commission	Voluntary Sector	*Public Trust and Confidence in Charities*	UK	Intervals since 2002
Chartered Institute of Insurance	General Insurance	*What We Talk about When We Talk about Trust*	UK	2010
Chartered Institute of Personnel Directors	Human Resources	*Where Has All the Trust Gone?*	UK	2012
CFA Institute	Financial Services	*From Trust to Loyalty: A Global Survey of What Investors Want*	US	2016
Development Dimensions International	Human Resources	*Survey of Trust in the Workplace*	US	1999
Digital Catapult	Information Technology	*Trust in Personal Data: A UK review*	UK	2015
Echo Research; International Business Leaders Forum	Market Research/ Business Leaders	*A World in Trust*	UK	2010
Economic & Social Research Council	Research Council	*People's Trust: A Survey-Based Experiment*	UK	2008

(Continued)

Table 1.1 (Continued)

Organisation	Sector	Survey/Report	Region	Year
Edelman	Public Relations	*Annual Trust Barometer*	Global	Annual since 2001
Ethical Corp	Specialist Media	*Reputation and Financial Services – Regaining Trust through Transparency*	UK	2006, 2007
European Commission	Public Policy	*Eurobarometer*	Europe	Annual since 1973
Financial Services Compensation Scheme	Financial Services	*Mind the Gap: Restoring Consumer Trust in Financial Services*	UK	2015
Financial Services Research Forum	Financial Services	*Financial Services Trust Index*	UK	Annual since 2005
Gallup	Market Research	*Annual Honesty & Ethics Poll*	US	Since 1976 (Annually since 2000)
Golin/Harris	Public Relations	*Golin/Harris Trust Survey*	US	2002, 2003
Great Place to Work	Human Resources	*Trust Index*	US	Offered since 2001
Guardian Media; First Direct	Media/ Insurance	*Trust in the Digital Age*	UK	2010
Harris Research	Market Research	*Restoring Faith in Products and Services*	UK	2006
IABC Research Foundation	Public Relations	*Measuring Organisational Trust*	US	2000
Information Sciences Institute	Information Technology	*A Survey of Trust in Computer Science and the Semantic Web*	US	2007
Institute for Public Relations	Public Relations	*Guidelines for Measuring Trust in Organisations*	US	2003
Institute of Internal Communication/Top Banana	Public Relations/ Internal Communications	*Building Trust in Companies through Effective Leadership Communication*	UK	2015
Institute of Leadership and Management	Management/ Executive Coaching	*The Truth about Trust: Honesty and Integrity at Work*	UK	2014
Interaction	Human Resources	*Building Trust in Business*	US	2009
Involve	Human Resources	*Trust: All is not Lost*	UK	2009
IPSOS MORI	Market Research	*Public Trust in Professions*	UK	Annual since 1983
John Hancock/ Manulife	Life Insurance	*John Hancock Trust Survey*™	US	2012

Organisation	Sector	Survey/Report	Region	Year
Lansons Communications	Public Relations	*UK's Most Trusted Companies*	UK	2010
LMAX Exchange	Financial Services	*Restoring Trust in Global FX Markets*	UK	2015
McKinsey	Management Consultancy	*What Consumers Expect from Companies*	Global	2006
NatCen Social Research	Public Policy	*British Social Attitudes Survey*	UK	Annually since 1983
New Philanthropy Capital (NPC)	Charity/Third Sector	*Matter of Trust: What the Public Thinks of Charities*	UK	2014
Nfp Synergy	Charity/Third Sector	*Charity Awareness Monitor*	UK	2015
Nielsen	Media	*Global Trust in Advertising and Brand Messages*	US	2013
OECD	Public Policy	*Measuring Trust in Official Statistics*	FRANCE	2015
OFCOM	Media	*Children's Online Behaviour: Issues of Risk and Trust*	UK	2014
PBS	Media	*UK Trust Report*	UK	2011
Pennington Performance Group	Human Resources	*Trust Factors At Work Study*	US	2004
Pew Research Center	Political Research	*Beyond Distrust: How Americans View Their Government*	US	2015
PRSA Foundation	Public Relations	*National Credibility Index*	US	1999
Public Affairs Council	Public Relations/ Public Affairs	*Public Affairs Pulse Survey*	US	Annually since 2011
Razor Public Relations	Public Relations	*Food Supply Chain*	UK	2005, 2007
Readers' Digest	Consumer Media	*European Trusted Brands*	Europe	Annual since 2001
ResPublica	Public Policy	*In Professions We Trust: Fostering Virtuous Practitioners in Teaching, Law and Medicine*	UK	2015
Watson Wyatt	Human Resources	*WorkUSA*	US	2002

Source: The Author.

consultant Stephen Covey Jr set out his stall via the popular business book, *The Speed of Trust* (2006). In his book, Covey expressed organisational trust as an equation, with rising trust driving up productivity while driving down costs. The 2000s were filled with an unprecedented flow of trust surveys, books, conferences and productivity models. Yet, while professional trust strategists were presumably dedicated to their cause, they could not prevent trust from draining out of financial markets in 2007, eventually leading to the 2008 global financial crisis.

Global financial crisis

The global financial crisis features prominently throughout this book, not just because it was the single largest economic crisis since the Great Depression of the 1930s, and the first major global crisis to be triggered by financial markets. The global financial crisis also figures in the ensuing chapters because this particular crisis was, at its core, a crisis of trust (Yandle 2008), leading to a series of systemic failures, beginning in the credit markets, spreading to global equity markets, and resulting in estimated losses of US$19.2 trillion in lost household wealth (US Treasury 2012). Banks were the most heavily implicated financial institutions. Central banks and regulators were criticised for 'light touch' regulation and poor oversight. Insurers were censured for underwriting dodgy financial instruments, and credit rating agencies for not rating the instruments accurately. Governments were accused of propping up over-inflated troubled domestic financial sectors. While many financial players vowed to change future conduct, the post-crisis years yielded further market transgressions, including international money laundering, and manipulation of Libor inter-bank lending rates.

Predictably, trust restoration efforts intensified after the crisis. HR and management consultants churned out more trust expertise across various areas of public life where trust was supposedly being eroded. In the UK, the Financial Services Compensation Scheme focused on surveying consumer trust (FSCS 2015); while foreign exchange traders surveyed trust in currency markets following the Libor scandal (LMAX Exchange 2015). The UK's legal profession used a trust survey to launch professional reform following high-profile misconduct cases (SRA 2015). NGOs surveyed public trust in charities, again following major scandals in the sector (NPC 2014, NfpSynergy 2015). Public trust in UK media was surveyed after a major phone-hacking scandal (PBS 2011). In both the UK and the US, surveys on trust in safekeeping of personal data appeared after well-publicised data-hacking scandals (Auth0 2015, Digital Catapult 2015). At the government level, long-standing annual surveys refocused their interest in public trust in government and society (Johnston 2015, Pew Research 2015), while other surveys were commissioned to measure trust in national statistics (OECD 2011) or in the European Union (Stylianou 2014).

Trust surveys, rankings and reports are all examples of calculative regimes designed to establish the authority of the experts behind their publication. Trust surveys also have powerful symbolic effects, particularly when their results are repeated over and over in popular media. The media frenzy accompanying survey results transforms trust surveys into media rituals that rouse public emotions, enhancing solidarity among 'us' (the general public) against 'them' (the rich and powerful) (Pixley 2012, citing Collins 1975, p. 58). If the 'trust strategist' role is a source of professional anxiety for corporate advisers, then the corporate obsession with trustworthiness reveals a broader anxiety in Anglo-Saxon societies where there is the evidence that societal trust levels are falling and that Western culture is somehow in peril.

Trust surveys remain an important marketing tool for PR advisers (see Table 1.1). Lansons, the British PR consultancy, published a ranking of the UK's most trusted companies in 2011. Edelman stimulated renewed interest in its Trust Barometer. Public affairs consultants measured trust in big business lobbying in Washington DC (Public Affairs Council 2015). Trust restoration is a recurring theme at PR industry conferences (IPR 2010, CICOM 2012, IPRA 2012, CMC 2016). *Building the High-Trust Organization*, an industry-sponsored tome, described the global financial crisis as a 'trust crash' fracturing relationships for years to come (Shockley-Zabalak et al. 2010, p. 5), offering leaders an 'internationally recognised' model for building organisational trust. Years after the global financial crisis, 'trust strategist' claims remain part of PR's vernacular. Writing in *Campaign* magazine in January 2013, marketing professional Roisin Donnelly argued that communicators had 'an important role to play in rebuilding trust' in the year ahead. Former Edelman UK head, Robert Phillips, also described 2013 as a 'watershed year for PR', marked by better measurement systems for quantifying trust.

The 'trust strategist' paradox

The 'trust strategist' role may be one route to building PR's influence in corporate boardrooms, but it presents a curious paradox for PR theory and practice. On the one hand, PR practitioners are keen to promote their expertise in restoring trust following corporate failures. On the other hand, the PR field remains silent on how it may have contributed to a loss of public trust in the first place, or how its 'manipulative engineering of consent' has engendered a climate of public distrust in many countries (McKie 2007, p. 106). Three veteran practitioners concede that PR is part of the problem. George Pitcher singles out PR practitioners in financial markets as complicit in selling 'perceived value as a fundamental value', becoming 'hubristic architects' of a message that was 'only ever about boom – and to hell with bust' (2008, p. 69). Robert Phillips, once responsible for Edelman's Trust Barometer in the UK, now denounces PR as a 'moribund' profession which has used the 'calamitous state of world business' as an opportunity for professional revival (Phillips 2015, p. xvi). Richard Edelman, chief spokesperson for the Trust Barometer, argues that PR is not a primary contributor to corporate malaise, but it has facilitated a cult of personality around business leaders, particularly those in financial services sector, lost the transparency wars to the lawyers and failed to convince management to shift from shareholder to stakeholder value. Edelman laments PR's inability to increase public trust in business by communicating the central role of business in society. Despite these mixed acknowledgements, the PR profession has been largely content to gloss over its potential misdemeanours, instead profiting from advising organisations on how to fix and/or manage poor levels of trust (Seaman 2010), by moving forward and 'setting things to rights' (PRSA 2003, Nicholas 2005). For the PR profession, this glaring oversight is the 'elephant in the room' (Callaghan 2003).

This book will acknowledge that 'elephant in the room', focusing on the highly contested arena of financial markets. My aim is to disrupt beliefs of PR professionals as 'trust strategists' – by problematising the generalised trust placed in global financial systems. In line with Berger and Reber (2006, p. 5), I contend that power is the number one issue in public relations. Anxiety over power is the reason trust management has gained such traction in the highly competitive world of senior-level PR consulting. I maintain that if PR is to adopt the 'trust strategist' mantle, it should focus first on understanding *who* enacts the techniques and practices that lead to the loss of trust, and *how* such practices are enacted, *before* turning attention to how trust can be restored. I argue that public trust in financial systems is deliberately produced, and therefore a mechanism for power created through discursive and material practices. I further contend that in the case of financial systems, PR works to produce trust by discursively translating financial discourses into trust discourses, in order to gain public consent for material financial practices. This positioning draws on Giddens' (1990) understanding of system trust, and uses Foucauldian (Foucault 1981, Faubion 1994) approaches to locate PR within a circuit of discursive relations linking trust and power. By uncovering deliberate strategies used to produce trust communicatively, my purpose is to reframe trust, power and public relations. The next section of the chapter focuses on trust relations in financial markets, and sets the scene for the rest of the book.

Trust in financial markets

The role of trust in financial services is neither new nor even a modern phenomenon. Trust has always been a central element wherever credit (lending) takes place (Kincaid 2006). Purely commercial credit has its roots in simple circulation where money developed as a means of payment. The act of offering credit is itself closely related with trust, and banks and insurers often choose brand names that include words evoking trust, such as 'fidelity', 'guardian', 'guaranty', 'prudential' or, 'equitable' (Shapiro 1987). Hence, financial services is 'the business of trust', (Knights et al. 2001); this is even more so in modern times when daily turnover on the world's foreign exchange markets far exceeds the annual level of world exports (Held and McGrew 2000); and when more people engage with financial services through bank accounts, credit cards, personal loans, savings and investment products. Strategic trust production has long been integral to organisational techniques in highly competitive financial markets. However, an organisation's production of the appearance of trustworthiness demands 'ever more polished strategies' as intended publics become used to existing trust strategies, inspecting their signals 'suspiciously' (Beckert 2005, p. 15).

The need to produce system trust in financial markets became more urgent after Western economies were deregulated in the 1980s, releasing money to move more freely around the globe. International finance became the nodal point of economic globalisation (Vestergaard 2009), through the dramatic growth in the world's tradable financial value, made possible by advanced mathematical models, powerful computer systems and a constant supply of information transmitted instantly and electronically (Castells 2000). Cross-border mergers and acquisitions proliferated among large financial institutions (Berger et al. 2000). Financial markets expanded rapidly in size, complexity and distribution channels as more companies turned to the capital markets for finance, issuing bonds or shares, merging with or acquiring other companies. For more than 20 years, developed countries and most developing countries experienced faster growth in their financial sectors than in their actual economies. In the largest of these markets, domestic and international financial institutions competed aggressively for business. However, finance remains so homogenised, its corporate messages so similar, that the sector's main route to differentiation has always been to imbue financial brands with trust.

PR in financial markets

PR is an important means of building credibility in and shaping attitudes toward financial markets. In the largest financial centres, PR has developed various financial specialisms for promoting financial experts and an array of financial products offering safety and protection from risks, as well as building compelling narratives about financial markets as places of hidden financial opportunities. In the UK, home to one of the largest international financial centres, 20 per cent of in-house PR practitioners in the private sector work in financial services/corporate PR. Of those working for PR firms, 26 per cent rank financial services/corporate among the clients they are most likely to represent (CIPR 2015). Some PR advisers focus on wholesale financial markets (the factory floor of financial services). Others spend more time in retail finance (the 'shop window') (Bourne 2013). Of the various specialisms, Financial PR is arguably the best-known: addressing the communication needs of companies accessing finance from capital markets through mergers and acquisitions (M&A), initial public offerings (IPOs) and the marketing of shares and bond issues, dealing with the financial media, 'sell-side' analysts at brokerage firms, as well as investor relations, communicating relevant information about a company's valuation to existing and potential shareholders, and their advisers. Financial *Services* PR is another specialism, promoting financial products and services for investment banks, asset managers, private equity firms, retail banks, credit card companies, 'supermarket banks', insurance companies, building societies, wealth managers, stockbrokers, mortgage specialists and financial advisers. Financial Services PR also supports the professional services firms which serve financial markets, including law firms, accountancy firms, actuarial firms, management consultants and other intermediaries. Still other PR advisers are public affairs specialists and lobbyists. They work in public affairs departments in large financial institutions, or for specialist consultancies based in Washington DC or Brussels, while some work for financial trade associations and think tanks.

Financial media and communication issues

PR specialisms are also defined by the financial media, which has a symbiotic (if uneasy) relationship with the PR profession, particularly in an era of shrinking news rooms and journalistic resources. This symbiotic relationship has resulted in higher levels of PR content in the financial media than in other sectors (Davis 2007), further problematising PR's role in organising trust in financial markets. Financial media covers a broad spectrum, from global financial news agencies to national media houses with strong business and finance coverage, to specialist financial titles, including websites and blogs. Global financial media – from *CNBC, Bloomberg, Reuters* and *Dow Jones*, to the *Financial Times, Wall Street Journal* and *International Business Times* – cater to more financially educated publics and wield substantial influence over market players, for example, helping to drive share prices up and down, or giving greater visibility to bond market trading. National media, including dedicated TV and radio money programmes, act as 'choice editors' (FSA and Henley Centre 2005), helping consumers to navigate the range of personal finance opportunities on offer. Some have been influential in campaigning against mis-sold products, in getting customers to surrender insurance policies or funds or to avoid financial products or company shares altogether (Pixley 2004).

Journalists working for regional and national titles often cover finance as part of a broader remit to cover business news, and will avoid in-depth financial coverage in case it bores their audience (Doyle 2006). Editors prefer financial stories that are entertaining, or that align with audience's typically middle-class interests. PR practitioners are therefore tasked with simplifying financial news, making it more 'interesting' or controversial (Doyle 2006). Alternatively, PR practitioners develop stories supporting news frames of a 'middle class in peril', with worries over pensions, high taxes, lack of job security and 'holding on by a thread' (Kendall 2005). These editorial concerns leave inadequate room for forensic analysis of poor financial products and practices in the mainstream media, while the specialist financial media has little visibility with the general public.

Unlike the PR profession, the media industry has examined its own role in successive financial 'booms and busts' of trust (See Chakravartty and Schiller 2010, Tambini 2010, Schiffrin 2011, Schifferes 2014). The PR industry's focus has included remedial work for financial markets, not least evangelising their societal and economic contributions. PR has also engaged in remedial work for consumer finance through financial education and 'life skills'. This is troubling, considering the financial sector's ongoing reputational issues. In the decade since the 2007 credit crunch, negative public perception of banks and other financial institutions has topped the list of challenges faced by PR practitioners (Makovsky and Company 2012). Since the global financial crisis, there has been repeated mis-selling of inappropriate financial products to unsuspecting customers, and declining banking support for small-to-medium enterprise, which forms the backbone of many economies. Attempts to rebuild trust seem futile when financial institutions repeatedly engage in questionable activity.

Perhaps the most crucial issue for PR in financial markets, arising from the global financial crisis, is the issue of global inequality. Globalisation was once heralded as the 'new knight to fight poverty' (Koku & Acquaye 2011, p. 354), yet after decades of market freedom, an astounding volume of wealth is now controlled by a small proportion of the world's citizens, many of whom are successful bankers, hedge fund managers and other financial professionals. A complex global debate has emerged, with PR playing a visible role in promoting different viewpoints. In one corner of this debate are groups promoting greater equality by enabling more people to access financial services. In developing countries, 90% of people lack access to financial services from institutions, either for credit or savings, further fuelling a 'vicious cycle of poverty' (Hinson 2011, p. 320). NGOs such as Accion (accion.org) actively employ PR to promote financial inclusion. Interestingly, this same financial inclusion agenda has been adopted and promoted by financial institutions aiming to sell products and services in developing markets. In another corner are activist groups campaigning against financial capitalism, and the damage wrought on many lives. The Occupy movement achieved high visibility in the summer of 2011, staging sit-ins, teach-ins and other street activities, crystallising many cities around the world, and engaging in varying degrees of PR activity. The Robin Hood Tax campaign backed a tax on the transactions of big banks, to be rerouted to fight poverty. The Jubilee movement has campaigned for the cancellation of unjust or unpayable debts since the 1990s, renewing its efforts to tackle debt inequality during and after the global financial crisis (see Chapter 8 for an in-depth discussion).

Guide to the book

In the next chapters, I will explore the production of trust and mistrust across retail and wholesale financial markets, uncovering PR's role in such activity. While public relations scholarship on financial markets is limited, the book is largely shaped by the rich variety of interdisciplinary scholarship exploring the impact of financial market communication. I have drawn on fields such as anthropology (e.g. Ho 2009, Holmes 2014); economics (e.g. Blinder et al. 2008); linguistics (e.g. Smart 2006); media sociology (e.g. Davis 2007); organisational and management studies (e.g. Knights et al. 2001, De Cock et al. 2011); political geography (e.g. Leyshon and Thrift 1997); politics (e.g. De Goede 2005); and sociology (e.g. Pixley 2004, 2012, McFall 2014). The book also draws on financial media coverage; as well as PR and marketing documents issued by financial institutions, including annual reports, corporate advertising, press releases, speeches and websites. The book also draws on internal communications documents now in the public sphere thanks to government investigations of financial sector misconduct, together with documents published via industry consultations and public inquiries. Finally, *Trust, Power and Public Relations in Financial Markets* is also informed by my two decades spent as a communicator working in public relations, advertising and marketing in different markets, and through several financial scandals and crises.

Chapter 1 has set the scene for modern PR activity in financial markets, against a background of successive 'booms and busts' of trust in financial markets, including the 2008 global financial crisis – at its core, a crisis of trust. Since the collapse of Enron in 2001, successive 'booms and busts' of trust have been a catalyst for a lucrative 'trust restoration' industry, which has seen various experts – including PR professionals – position themselves in the role of 'trust strategists', targeting organisations coping with lost trust and reputational damage. **Chapter 1** also pointed to the problematic and paradoxical nature of PR's trust strategist positioning, while highlighting the importance of financial markets as a site of study for contemporary PR activity. **Chapter 2** reframes trust, power and PR, first, by shifting the trajectory of PR research to focus on system trust: an abstract, impersonal form of trust which differs from individual and organisational trust. This contrasts with previous PR studies, which focus primarily on individual and organisational trust relations, ignoring the broader impact played by PR in contributing to generalised trust in systems. Second, I establish the link between system trust relations and power relations through the Foucauldian notion of discourses as systems of knowledge informing the practices that constitute power in society (Wetherell et al. 2001). PR is defined here as one such system of knowledge, but so too is trust. The chapter also sets out my trust practice framework which emerges from the discussion of the strategies and practices used to organise trust in financial markets.

Chapters 3 through **9** provide a series of in-depth explorations of trust, power and public relations activity in various areas of financial markets. **Chapter 3** looks at the well-oiled PR machines of central banks and global financial institutions comprising the international financial architecture. These include the International Monetary Fund and the World Bank, as well as global credit rating agencies, which provide a voluntary system of trust regulation in financial markets. State finance has been governed by 'radical transparency' since the 1990s, creating an increased role for PR at the apex of financial markets. **Chapter 4** moves to another layer of voluntary 'regulation' provided by financial trade associations, exploring controversial efforts to fend off restrictive policies over the banking industry, hedge funds and other financial sectors. **Chapter 5** looks at equities markets, and financial communication in international financial centres where PR is often employed to construct exciting narratives of financial exploration and conquest. The chapter considers the role PR plays in assigning trust to the designated value of financial instruments, triggering daily ebbs and flows in consumer retirement savings etc.

Chapter 6 explores the banking system, the area of finance most demonised for its role in triggering the global financial crisis. While the chapter includes investment banking activity, the meat of the discussion focuses on 'everyday' retail banking. In particular, Chapter 6 highlights the disconnect between the trust restoration programmes built around 'everyday banking', despite the fact that the traditional model of everyday banking no longer exists. **Chapter 7** moves on to an equally large area of finance, and arguably a more complex one – the companies offering insurance, pensions and investment services. Many of these services are sold through 'middlemen', who acted as consumers' traditional trust access point to financial services. These middlemen could soon be replaced by 'robo-advisers', which might reduce the financial losses associated with flawed human advice, but only for those able to afford it. **Chapter 8** gives voice to areas of financial markets less likely to be featured in PR texts – the large numbers of citizens who are 'unbanked' and financially excluded. The chapter covers PR's role in promoting financial education and inclusion, as well as the highly controversial microfinance industry. Chapter 8 closes with a discussion of PR's role in grassroots financial activism, and movements such as Occupy which attempted to capitalise on post-crisis mistrust in the banking system, in order to bring about meaningful change to global finance.

Chapter 9 focuses on 'hidden spaces' in financial markets, exploring the various ways PR is used to 'organise silence' on behalf of financial elites. The chapter considers industries that have long cultivated exclusivity and opacity, while considering new hidden spaces, including 'dark pools' of equities trading inside global banks. Silence is discussed as a discursive strategy that may wield even more power and influence than strategies to produce trust. **Chapter 10** concludes the book. Here, I return to the notion of PR as 'trust strategist', proposing that while the global financial crisis triggered unprecedented debates over trust, trust itself remains an amorphous concept, unquantifiable for financial decision-makers who are increasingly swayed by experts claiming to manage risk. I do not discount associations between PR and trust altogether, arguing instead that the profession's future role could lie in stimulating healthy doses of *mis*trust not just in financial markets but all those areas which are governed by state and market power.

Notes

1 This was how PR was originally translated in German.
2 The definition once used by Spain's main professional body for PR.
3 Now owned by IPG.
4 Now part of Willis Towers Watson.

References

Arthur, W. Page Society. (2009). *The Dynamics of Public Trust in Business*, New York, NY: Arthur W. Page Society and the Business Roundtable for Corporate Ethics.

Auth0. (2015). *What Customers and Developers Think of IoT Security*, Bellevue, Washington: Auth0. Retrieved from: https://auth0.com/blog/2015/11/06/surprised-turns-out-consumers-dont-trust-iot-security/

Beckert, J. (2005). 'Trust and the performative construction of markets', *MPIfG Discussion Paper 05/8*, Max Planck Institute for the Study of Societies.

Bentele, G. and Wehmeier, S. (2003). 'From literary bureaus to a modern profession'. In Sriramesh, K. and Verčič, D. (eds) *The Global Public Relations Handbook*. Mahwah, NJ: Lawrence Erlbaum Associates, pp. 199–221.

Berger, A.N., DeYoung, R., Genay, H. and Udell, G.F. (2000) 'Globalisation of financial institutions: evidence from cross-border banking performance'. In Litan, R.E. and Santomero, A.M. (eds) *Brookings-Wharton Papers on Financial Services Vol III*, pp. 23–56.

Berger, B.K. and Reber, B.H. (2006). *Gaining Influence in Public Relations: The Role of Resistance in Practice*, Mahwah, NJ: Lawrence Erlbaum.

Blinder, A., Ehrmann, M., Fratzscher, M., De Hann, J. and Jansen, D. (2008). 'Central bank communication and monetary policy: A survey of theory and evidence', *NBER Working Paper*, No. 13932, April.

Bloomgarden, K. (2007). *Trust: The Secret Weapon of Effective Business Leaders*, New York: St. Martin's Press.

Bourne, C.D. (2013). 'Public relations in the world of finance'. In Tench, R. and Yeomans, L. (eds) *Exploring Public Relations* (Third Edition). London: Pearson Education, pp. 381–394.

Callaghan, T. (2003). 'Repent professional sins', *Public Relations Strategist*, April, p. 2.

Castells, M. (2000). *The Rise of the Network Society, Vol 1: The Information Age: Economy, Society and Culture*, Oxford, UK: Wiley Blackwell.

Chakravartty, P. and Schiller, D. (2010). 'Global financial crisis, neoliberal newspeak and digital capitalism in crisis', *International Journal of Communication*, 4, pp. 670–692.

CICOM. (2012). 'Building trust through communication in times of crisis', *The 27th International Conference of Communication (CICOM)*. Available at: http://www.unav.es/comunicacion/cicom/english-version-cicom/cicom.html.

CIPD (Chartered Institute of Personnel Directors). (2012). *Where Has All the Trust Gone?* London: Chartered Institute of Personnel Directors.

CIPR (Chartered Institute of Public Relations). (2015). *State of the PR Profession Research Report*, London: Chartered Institute of Public Relations.

CMC (Corporate and Marketing Communications). (2016). 'Integrated communications and branding: Past, present and future', *21st International Conference on Corporate and Marketing Communications*, Middlesex University, 7–8 April 2016.

Collins, R. (1975/7?). *Conflict Sociology: Toward and Explanatory Science*, New York: Academic Press Inc.

Covey, S.M.R. (2006). *The Speed of Trust*, New York: Free Press.

Davis, A. (2000). 'Public relations, business news and the reproduction of corporate elite power', *Journalism*, 1, pp. 282–304.

De Cock, C., Baker, M. and Volkmann, C. (2011). 'Financial phantasmagoria: Corporate image-work in times of crisis', *Organization*, 18, pp. 153–172.

De Goede, M. (2005). *Virtue, Fortune and Faith: A Genealogy of Finance*, Minneapolis: University of Minnesota Press.

Digital Catapult. (2015). *Trust in Personal Data: A Review*, London: Digital Catapult.

Donnelly, R. (2013). 'The year ahead for . . . marketing', *Campaign*, 10 January, p. 11.

Doyle, G. (2006). 'Financial news journalism: A post-Enron analysis of approaches towards economic and financial news production in the UK', *Journalism*, 7, pp. 433–452.

Faubion, J.D. (1994). *Michel Foucault: Power. Essential Works of Foucault 1954–1984*. 2002 Reprint ed., London: Penguin.

Foroohar, R. (2016). 'The 1 thing on everybody's mind at Davos 2016', *Time*, 20 January. Retrieved from: http://time.com/4186599/davos-2016-technology-jobs/?iid=sr-link2

Foucault, M. (1981). 'The order of discourse'. In Young, R. (ed) *Untying the Text: A Poststructuralist Reader.* London and Boston: Routledge and Keegan Paul, pp. 51–77.

FSA. (2005). 'Towards understanding consumers' needs'. *Consumer Research 35.* London: FSA.

FSCS (Financial Services Compensation Scheme). (2015). *Mind the Gap: Restoring Consumer Trust in Financial Services,* London: Financial Services Compensation Scheme.

Giddens, A. (1990). *The Consequences of Modernity,* Oxford, UK: Polity Press/Blackwell.

Golin, A. (2004). *Trust or Consequences.* New York: American Management Association.

Held, D. and McGrew, A. (eds) (2000). *The Global Transformations Reader: An Introduction to the Globalisation Debate,* Cambridge: Polity Press.

Hilton, A. (2004). 'Lack of return is key', *Evening Standard,* 24 November, p. 35.

Hinson, R.E. (2011). 'Banking the poor: The role of mobiles', *Journal of Financial Services Marketing,* 15 (4), pp. 320–333.

Ho, K. (2009). *Liquidated: An Ethnography of Wall Street,* Durham, NC: Duke University Press.

Holmes, D.R. (2014). *Economy of Words: Communicative Imperatives in Central Banks,* Chicago: University of Chicago Press.

IPR (Institute for Public Relations). (2010). *Trust and Recovery.* Retrieved from: http://www.instituteforpr.org/events/colloquiums/

IPRA (International Public Relations Association). (2012). *20th Public Relations World Congress, Dubai 2012.* Retrieved from: http://www.ipra.org/secciones.php?sec=8&nid=70

Johnston, I. (2015). 'Half the British public . . . don't trust the British public, survey finds', *Independent.co.uk.* Retrieved from: http://www.independent.co.uk/news/uk/home-news/half-the-british-public-dont-trust-the-british-public-survey-finds-10452928.html

Kendall, D. (2005). *Framing Class: Media Representations of Wealth and Poverty in America,* Plymouth: Rowman & Littlefield.

Kincaid, J. (2006). 'Finance, trust and the power of capital: A symposium on the contribution of Costas Lapavitsas. Editorial Introduction', *Historical Materialism,* 14, pp. 31–48.

Knights, D. and Morgan, G. (1991). 'Corporate strategy, organization and subject: A critique', *Organization Studies,* 12 (2), pp. 251–273.

Knights, D., Noble, F., Vurdubakis, T. and Willmott. H (2001). 'Chasing shadows: Control, virtuality and the production of trust', *Organization Studies,* 22 (2), pp. 311–336.

Koku, P.S. and Acquaye, H.E. (2011). 'Who is responsible for rehabilitating the poor? The case for church-based financial services for the poor', *Journal of Financial Services Marketing,* 15 (4), pp. 346–356.

Kunczik, M. (2003). 'Transnational public relations by foreign governments'. In Sriramesh, K. and Vercic, D. (eds) *The Global Public Relations Handbook.* Mahwah, NJ: Lawrence Erlbaum, pp. 399–424.

Leyshon, A. and Thrift, N. (1997). *Money/Space: Geographies of Monetary Transformation,* London: Routledge.

LMAX Exchange. (2015). *Restoring Trust in Global FX Markets,* London: LMAX Exchange.

Makovsky and Company. (2012). *2012 Makovsky Reputation Study,* New York: Makovsky Press.

McFall, L. (2014). *Devising Consumption: Cultural Economies of Insurance, Credit and Spending,* London: Routledge.

McKie, D. and Munshi, D. (2007). *Reconfiguring Public Relations,* Abingdon: Routledge.

NfpSynergy. (2015). *Charity Awareness Monitor,* London: NfpSynergy.

Nicholas, K. (2005). 'Rebuilding reputations in financial services'. *PR Week White Paper.* London, pp. 1–8.

Nielsen, B. (2006). 'The singular character of public relations in a global economy', *International Distinguished Lecture at Institute for Public Relations,* Reform Club, London.

NPC (New Philanthropy Capital). (2014). *Matter of Trust: What the Public Thinks of Charities and How It Affects Trust*, London: New Philanthropy Capital.

OECD (Organisation for Economic Cooperation and Development). (2011). *Measuring Trust in Official Statistics: Cognitive Testing*, Paris: Organisation for Economic Cooperation and Development.

PBS (Public Broadcasting Service). (2011). *UK Trust Report*, Arlington, VA: Public Broadcasting Service.

Pew Research Center. (2015). *Beyond Distrust: How Americans View Their Government*. Retrieved from: http://www.people-press.org/2015/11/23/beyond-distrust-how-americans-view-their-government/

Phillips, R. (2013). 'Ex Edelman chief Robert Phillips: Trust can't be restored by taking one action', *Management Today*, 12 April. Retrieved from: http://www.management today.co.uk/features/1177911/ex-edelman-chief-robert-phillips-trust-cant-restored-taking-one-action/

Phillips, R. (2015). *Trust Me, PR Is Dead*, London: Unbound.

Pitcher, G. (2008). 'Financial PR is no scapegoat', *Profile*, December/January, p. 69.

Pixley, J. (2004). *Emotions in Finance: Distrust and Uncertainty in Global Markets*, Cambridge: Cambridge University Press.

Pixley, J. (2012). *Emotions in Finance: Booms, Busts and Uncertainty* (Second Edition), Cambridge: Cambridge University Press.

PRSA (Public Relations Society of America). (2003). 'A discussion on public trust', *Public Relations Tactics*, September, pp. 31–33. Public Affairs Council. (2015). 'Can big companies be trusted?' *Public Affairs Pulse Survey*, Washington, DC: Public Affairs Council.

Rojas, O.I.O. (2012). *Relaciones publicas: la eficacia de la influencia* (Third Edition). Madrid, Spain: ESIC Editorial.

Rottger, U. and Voss, A. (2008). 'Internal communication as management of trust relations'. In Zerfass, A., van Ruler, B. and Sriramesh, K. (eds) *Public Relations Research: European and International Perspectives and Innovations*. Wiesbaden: VS Verlag fur Sozialwissenschaften, pp. 163–178.

Schifferes, S. (ed) (2014). *The Media and Financial Crises: Comparative and Historical Perspectives*, Abingdon: Routledge.

Schiffrin, A. (ed) (2011). *Bad News: How America's Business Press Missed the Story of the Century*, New York: The New Press.

Seaman, P. (2010). 'How PR sells firms and trust short'. In Whittle, P. (ed) *A Sorry State: Self-Denigration in British Culture*. London: The New Culture Forum, pp. 3–21.

Shapiro, S.P. (1987). 'The social control of impersonal trust', *American Journal of Sociology*, 93, p. 623.

Shockley-Zalabak, P.S., Morreale, S.P. and Hackman, M.Z. (2010). *Building the High-Trust Organization*, San Francisco, CA: IABC/Wiley & Sons.

Smart, G. (2006). *Writing the Economy: Activity, Genre and Technology in the World of Banking*, London: Equinox.

SRA (Solicitors Regulation Authority). (2015). '*A Question of Trust*' Survey Opens, News Release. Solicitors Regulation Authority, 21 July. Retrieved from: https://www.sra.org.uk/sra/news/press/question-trust-survey-launch.page

Stylianou, N. (2014). 'Trust in EU at an all time low latest figures show', *Daily Telegraph*. Retrieved from: http://www.telegraph.co.uk/news/worldnews/europe/eu/10586961/Trust-in-EU-at-an-all-time-low-latest-figures-show.html

Tambini, D. (2010). 'What are financial journalists for?', *Journalism Studies*, 11 (2), pp. 158–174.

US Treasury. (2012). *The Financial Crisis Response*, Washington, DC: US Department of the Treasury.

Valin, J. (2004). 'Overview of public relations around the world and principles of modern practice'. Remarks by Chair of the Global PR Alliance, *CONFERP Conference*, Brasilia, Brazil, October.

Vestergaard, J. (2009). *Discipline in the Global Economy*, New York: Routledge.

Wetherell, M., Taylor, S. and Yates, S.J. (2001). *Discourse as Data*, London: The Open University/Sage Publications.

Yandle, B. (2008). 'Lost trust: The real cause of the financial meltdown'. In George Mason University (ed) *Mercatus Center Working Papers*. Working Paper No. 09-02, February. Fairfax, VA: Mercatus Center, pp. 1–21.

2 Reframing trust, power and PR

Introduction

This chapter reframes trust, power and PR, first, by shifting the trajectory of PR research in order to understand how trust is produced through strategic communication techniques in global markets. I position PR as a societal phenomenon, in which trust production is a systemic rather than an organisational process – part of a series of global discourses. In the first section of the chapter, I review existing research on trust in the PR discipline. I contend that in focusing on individual and organisational trust relations, much of this research ignores the broader impact played by PR in contributing to generalised trust in systems. Although there are different layers of trust in financial markets – interpersonal, professional, organisational – I make the case that the primary form of trust enabling modern financial markets to thrive is system trust, an abstract form of trust that co-exists alongside other forms of trust, and is unable to emerge without them (Giddens 1990). The first part of the reframing therefore shifts the focus of PR research toward system trust which, unlike individual and organisational trust, is both faceless and impersonal. In the second section of the chapter, I establish the link between system trust relations and power relations through discourse. The chapter then presents a framework revealing trust strategies and practices used to produce trust in financial markets. In the final section of the chapter, I locate PR activity within discursive moments of trust/ mistrust production in financial markets.

Trust and public relations have been closely linked as research concepts in the PR discipline (Watson 2005, Rawlins 2008). Since public trust is extended to actors such as PR professionals, who enact and advocate the resulting trust narratives, much of the trust-related research in the PR field has framed trust either in terms of PR professionalism or from the perspective of client-organisations served by PR. Earlier models of public relations imagined PR as 'publicity' or 'public information', focused on delivering a message to key audiences through mass media. In these models, trust is critical to gaining credibility with the media, and ultimately, the audiences they reach (Rawlins 2008). Hence, the first trajectory of trust research in the public relations discipline involved framing trust as a question of professional conduct within the PR profession, focused on credibility and truth-telling by those operating in and with the media (Harrison 1997, Jempson 2005, Larsson 2007, Bentele and Seidenglanz 2008). In focusing on public relations' interaction with the public via the media, this initial research trajectory has been reinvigorated in the digital age, by concerns with PR's digital interactions with the public via Facebook, Twitter and other forms of social media (Yang et al. 2009, Bekmeier-Feuerhahn 2010, Kim et al. 2015, Painter 2015).

The first research trajectory also encompasses Bentele's (2008) public trust theory, which explores the central role played by PR and the media in gaining and losing trust. Bentele differentiates generalised, public trust from individual or interpersonal trust as follows:

> Public trust is a communicative mechanism for the reduction of complexity in which public persons, institutions and the general social system take on the role of the 'object of trust'. Public trust is a process moderated by the media in which the 'subjects of trust' have future-oriented expectations that are heavily influenced by past experiences.
>
> (Röttger and Voss 2008, p. 166 translated from Bentele 1994, p. 141)

Bentele carves out a specific role for public relations actors in trust production as 'trust mediators' or 'trust intermediaries' between organisations and specific publics (Bentele and Seidenglanz 2008). Bentele's public trust theory also spans the second trajectory of trust research in PR by encompassing both the 'public information' model of public relations and the 'organisational-public' relationship model, which casts PR as symmetrical communication, and relationship/reputation management (Kent and Taylor 2002, Welch 2006).

The relationship management model of public relations, now central to normative research, positions public relations as a management function on behalf of organisations intent on good reputation. Trust is identified as a key dimension of organisational relationships, central to leadership, work design and organisation within companies (Maclagan 1998, Welch 2006). Trust is the lens through which an organisation's behaviour is interpreted, determining how and whether others will interact with it (Lerbinger 2013, p. 67). Trust and reputation are closely linked, since fulfilled expectations generate trust and trust generates reputation. Equally, a loss of reputation leads to a collapse of trust, destabilising action, increasing complexity and delegitimising the organisation's hierarchical structures (Eisenegger and Imhoff 2008, Lerbinger 2013). PR is characterised as the means for negotiating, building and maintaining mutually beneficial relationships upon which the organisation depends (Kent and Taylor 2002, Gregory 2006).

This second trajectory of trust research in the PR discipline has a particular motivation – organisational legitimacy, survival and success. Its founding concept is that companies should gain trust, then profit by maintaining it (Harris and Wicks 2010, Kramer 2010). PR's organisational trust imperative mirrors similar scholarship on the value and operation of trust in disciplines such as organisational behaviour and business management, during the 1990s (Rawlins 2008). PR's growing focus on organisational trust yielded different ways to measure and manage organisational trust levels (Delahaye Paine et al. 2003), as well as models and frameworks for restoring organisational trust once lost (Poppo and Schepker 2010). The 1992 *Excellence in Public Relations* study, led by James Grunig, was a call-to-action for trust measurement in organisational-public relationships. Several PR studies on organisational trust followed, including *Guidelines for Measuring Trust in Organisations*, commissioned by the Institute for Public Relations (Delahaye Paine et al. 2003), a US-based think tank and research institute. However, PR's concern with organisational trust gathered genuine urgency after the collapse of Enron in 2000.

Enron's collapse was associated with a generalised loss of trust in large corporations. It triggered a spurt of trust surveys as PR scholars and practitioners collaborated on organisational solutions for a supposed crisis in lost trust. Research findings typically advised organisations to 'articulate a set of ethical principles', 'create a process for transparency' and establish a formal means to measure organisational trust (Delahaye Paine et al. 2003, p. 2). Formal trust measurement isolated variables such as organisational competence, integrity, reliability, openness and honesty, shared goals and norms, the willingness to be vulnerable, and 'control mutuality' – agreement on the appropriate (im)balance of power between parties (Delahaye Paine et al. 2003). The increasingly managerial perspective of public relations forming in PR scholarship bolstered efforts to position PR practitioners as 'trust strategists'.

Critiques of PR's alignment with trust

Critical perspectives have challenged attempts to position PR as a trustworthy pursuit, or even a key facilitator in organising trust. These critiques are in line with evolving research perspectives of public relations and its relationship with struggles for power. L'Etang (2003) maintains that PR's imagined role as the organisation's conscience or 'ethical guardian' is an occupational myth. Moloney (2005) contends that trust and PR are strange bedfellows, distanced both by practitioners' agency role and by the competitiveness of organisations employing PR services. Far from being about the communication of trust, says Moloney, public relations is actually the communicative expression of conflict, discord and stasis. Lawniczak (2007) and Bourne (2013, 2015) directly question whether PR has *itself* contributed to repeated corporate scandals, and whether it can lay claim to the role of trust strategist, with Bourne's work providing a cross-section of PR activity in trust/mistrust production. Meanwhile, Demetrious (2015) contextualises these perspectives, arguing that the growing cynicism toward PR – whether from journalists, political activists or academics – reflects a broader erosion of trust in experts in modern society.

The current bias toward organisational trust in normative PR scholarship is governed by a prevailing notion of PR as an organisational pursuit. This narrow perspective has prevented PR research from getting to grips with mistrust (Welch 2006), while limiting its examination of the relationship between trust and power. (Exceptions include Bourne and Edwards 2012, Bourne 2013, 2015, Demetrious 2015.) The trust-power nexus is crucial when considering the strategic value organisations give to trust-building in their struggle for market dominance. It also reconfigures PR's ambition to be the 'trust strategist'. Rather than a desire for ethical responsibility (Bowling and Truitt 2003, L'Etang 2003), the trust strategist role reflects a longing for professional authority and power. In this book, I deconstruct PR's efforts to align itself with organising and restoring trust. I position PR not as an organisational pursuit but as a social phenomenon, a mechanism through which local, national and global power can be sustained and contested through discursive struggles (Edwards 2010). The book focuses on PR in financial markets, social and economic constructions where different layers of trust exist but where system trust has come to dominate.

Applying system trust in public relations research

The authors most closely associated with theories of system trust are Niklas Luhmann (1979) and Anthony Giddens (1990, 1994). Both theorists characterise modern society by its increasing reliance on system trust as an effective strategy for managing new forms of complexity. Luhmann's work took a bottom-up approach, seeking to define the function of trust in society, arguing that a social system or systems can be either the source or the object of trust (Misztal 1996, Bentele and Seidenglanz 2008). In his 1975 essays later translated into English as *Trust and Power*, Luhmann emphasised that while interpersonal trust lies at the root of everyday trust, helping us to overcome an element of uncertainty in other people, system trust is not a constant. Instead, interpersonal trust *evolves* into system trust, as complexity grows, allowing people to renounce simple 'wary indifference' or even a more acute need for 'continuous control of results' (Luhmann 1979, p. 18). Luhmann argued that system trust is easier to acquire than personal trust, but more difficult to control (Luhmann 1979).[1]

Giddens's approach to system trust is top-down, beginning with an interest in the changing nature of modern society, and problematising the question of how social systems 'bind' time and space (1990, p. 4). Giddens's perspectives on system trust emerged, in part, as response to Luhmann's earlier thesis. His work, published after financial market deregulation in the 1980s, enabled Giddens to incorporate greater observation of global markets' relentless expansion and interconnection than Luhmann, writing in the 1970s. Consequently, his work is more relevant to my theorising of trust, power and public relations in financial markets. Giddens proposed system trust relations as a solution to the modern condition of risk and danger because of trust's ability to compress space and time. He presents system trust as a faceless, impersonal form of trust placed in money and, increasingly, in expert systems of technical, educational, scientific or financial knowledge. Since much of the knowledge and information circulating in globalised systems is specialist and difficult to trade, trust reduces the uncertainty of others' actions (Korczynski 2000). System trust entails the sort of watchful suspicion applied when making decisions. More importantly, it switches between trust and distrust as validating evidence emerges (Pixley 2004). Both Luhmann and Giddens explore the role of money in modern trust relations. However, Giddens's work encompasses detailed explorations of trust, risk and expert systems (see Giddens 1990, 1991, 1994, 1999, 2000).

Giddens (1990) positions expert systems as 'disembedding' mechanisms which lift social relations out of their local context and restructure them across indefinite spans of time–space. System trust emerges as a consequence of the loss of this local context. By putting our trust in systems, we implicitly trust the experts who populate those systems. Their expert status, articulated in the form of specialist knowledge, becomes a source of power for the system and the actors within it. Experts in financial markets leverage their specialised financial knowledge by assuming risk on customers' behalf, then packaging that risk into financial products and services. Consumers employ system trust in order to reduce the uncertainty and risk of buying these financial products (Rendtorff 2008).

Because system trust is a way of managing risk, the validity of claims to expert status depends on the extent to which the expert's specialist knowledge can be used to identify, calculate and manage risk (Gilbert 2005). In this sense, trust, knowledge and power are inextricably linked. However, while system trust may be a way of managing risk, it is inherently uncertain. The possibility always exists that experts will not deliver on expected outcomes – a situation that would challenge their claims to expert status, the validity of their knowledge and the trust in the system as a whole. Consequently, any form of system trust co-exists with system *mis*trust, which Giddens defines as a degree of scepticism or an actively negative attitude to the system's claims to expertise (Giddens 1990). As a result of this uncertainty and the likelihood that people could switch from trust to mistrust, experts have developed techniques for deliberately producing trust. This is not just true of experts' relations with the public; the reality of finance is that a great many market transactions take place not with the public but *between* experts. System trust increasingly applies between experts, for while personal relationships remain vital, financial market relationships are far less rooted in the old-fashioned discourse of the gentleman's club (Leyshon and Thrift 1997). Intra-market relations are increasingly distant or faceless, so trust *between* financial experts must be worked at too. If financial actors must work harder to establish trust with each other, as well as with the public, then they will invest less time in looking for signs of actual trust, choosing to construct trust more deliberately instead (Leyshon and Thrift 1997).

Giddens emphasised that 'expert' and 'professional' are not synonymous terms. An expert is any individual who can successfully lay claim to either specific skills or types of knowledge which the layperson does not possess (Giddens 1994). Financial services and public relations are *both* knowledge systems and areas of professional expertise forming power in modern society, yet they are very different. Financial knowledge fulfils two main criteria of professional jurisdiction. First, market control: financial knowledge controls which new and existing financial products and services are offered. Second, social closure: financial expertise requires regulatory approvals, licences and examination, conferring elite status (Larson 2012). Public relations, on the other hand, is an 'entrepreneurial profession' (Muzio et al. 2008), with no formal professional credentials or independent sources of knowledge, remaining largely open and governed by market mechanisms (Muzio et al. 2008). In fact, PR expertise is so 'open', it is not always performed by PR professionals.

As an entrepreneurial profession, PR is highly responsive to the organisations and cultures it serves, continually developing new forms of knowledge and radically different strategies as needed (Muzio et al. 2008). Lury and Warde (1997) argue that the constant shifting and changing of professions like PR is a response to producer anxiety, where 'producers' are the clients of PR services. In mature financial markets, producer anxiety is acute, because most consumers who want financial products already have them. Financial producers and intermediaries struggle not just to find sufficient willing consumers for products and services (Lury and Warde 1997), they must often switch consumers from a competitor's product to their own, typically by transferring trust from the competitor to themselves. This has resulted in perpetual contesting of expert claims by competing groups intent on proving each other's untrustworthiness (Vassilev and Pilgrim 2007) by questioning theoretical viewpoints, personal values, extent of knowledge and experience. Marchand (1998) argues that many PR initiatives undertaken by client-organisations have been a quest to create a 'corporate soul', encompassing a pressing need to produce trust. For corporate and financial PR, trust production is a form of expertise that helps define this niche area of PR. Meanwhile, Falkheimer (2009, p. 111) positions the *entire* PR profession as a 'typical late modern expert system' whose *specific* function is to create 'trust and legitimacy' (p. 114). PR techniques are therefore used to promote one group of experts in a field while simultaneously debunking their competitors.

Expert systems are just one disembedding mechanism identified by Giddens. Money is the other disembedding mechanism crucial in producing system trust, both presuming and fostering the time–space distanciation it promotes. It is in money that the unique link between finance and trust is truly forged. Money works to reduce complexity and manage expectations, when traditional symbols of trust and authority have given way to competence in risk management and the capacity for reflexivity (Gilbert 2005). It is money which truly enjoys trust, more so than individuals or organisations with whom monetary transactions are carried out (Giddens 1990). Money needs constant 'feedback' but does not require specific built-in guarantees; it is used on the presumption that others whom we never meet will honour its value. Trust in money is therefore incomparably easier to acquire than trust placed in encounters with new and different people. Anyone who trusts in the stability of the value of money and the continuity of opportunities for spending it assumes that a system is functioning and places trust in that function.

According to Hardin (2004), society is exhibiting not just rising trust relations, but rising mistrust relations too. If system trust is produced through disembedding mechanisms such as money and expert networks, how is mistrust produced? Luhmann (1979) maintains that trust and mistrust are functional equivalents, while Giddens (1990) emphasises that trust and mistrust are not polar opposites, though he does not tackle mistrust in great detail. Yet a logical explanation for mistrust production is implicit in Giddens' thesis. If trust serves as a disembedding mechanism in modern relations, lifting these relations out of space and time, then I submit that mistrust production works in the reverse manner. In other words, mistrust is likely to be produced through *re-embedding* mechanisms, because society's mistrust in modern systems often arises through the information provided by local and cultural contexts, interactions and discourses. System trust and mistrust are not the antithesis of each other; systems may even be able to produce trust without ever witnessing any countermove to produce mistrust, and vice versa. Competing experts may choose to produce mistrust in each other, or even in the state, while the state may do the same to selected experts. Since all of these actors engage in public relations activity, PR professionals almost certainly play a role in supporting the production of system mistrust, just as they do with trust. The implication here is that both trust and mistrust are produced in response to agency, the act of exerting power (Seligman 1997).

Connecting trust, power and discourse

Several authors assert that trust and power are both social mechanisms which can be used to coordinate expectations (Luhmann 1979, Lane and Bachmann 1998). Trust is often produced as a rational response to power wielded by institutions and authorities forming collective agency within systems (Shapiro 1987, Rendtorff 2008). The form of power associated with trust production is non-coercive, helping to reduce conflict and foster satisfaction, thus facilitating system trust (Lane and Bachmann 1998, Leonidou et al. 2008). Institutions and authorities able to enhance trust in this way may enhance their own power within systems (Young and Wilkinson 1989). Whatever balance is achieved between trust and power within systems, the literature suggests that this balance may be unstable, even imaginary. According to Korczynski (2000), any perceived balance shifts when systems become volatile; power becomes an awkward means for achieving cooperation, so trust steps in as substitute. Korczynski's argument implies a strategic decision on the part of actors within systems to *switch* from producing power to producing trust as the appropriate means to an end. Möllering (2005) leans toward a more organic shift, arguing that trust can gradually gain a control-like quality, as actors within a system become embedded in it. Power then produces trust whenever actors refer to and maintain social structures within the system (Möllering 2005). A third view maintains that trust may actually be produced as a way to conceal power (Harriss 2005). This facade is then deliberately exploited in order to consolidate trust, promoting vested interests by manipulating and capitulating weaker actors (Hardy et al. 1998).

I submit that system trust production is not so much a facade but a mechanism for power, created through discursive and material practices. I also submit that the production of system mistrust is a similarly potent mechanism. Specifically, I propose that both system trust and mistrust are among the power strategies used by dominant actors in financial markets. Through system trust/mistrust production, these dominant financial actors convey knowledge and ensure their survival under a 'mask of knowledge' and perceived expertise (Holtzhausen 2000). Giddens himself argues that system trust production is a modern strategy for governing systems. However, Giddens does not explore the practices employed by system actors in order to produce trust. A more applicable lens for exploring such practices comes from post-structural Foucauldian views of discourse and power. In his extensive body of work, the French philosopher Michel Foucault was concerned primarily with power produced through discourse (e.g. Foucault 1969, 1976, 1981, 2008).

Incorporating discursive perspectives of system trust

Like Giddens, Foucault establishes a direct link between power and expertise, but Foucault makes expert systems the primary source of power, contending that discursive strategies are forms of expert knowledge (Foucault 1981). Foucault defined society by its multiplicity of fields of knowledge – e.g. banking, insurance, investment and all specialist fields in financial services – highlighting the production of meanings, the strategies of power and the propagation of knowledge (Motion and Weaver 2005). Discourse is everything written or spoken about a specialist practice/knowledge, 'controlling' those who lack the specialism. Experts produce statements about their specialist practice, 'regimes of truth' defined by the discursive rules of their field (Faubion 2002[1994]). Everything written or spoken about a specialist practice/knowledge controls those who lack specialist knowledge inasmuch as it excludes them from the 'regime of truth' defined by discursive rules of the field (Foucault 1981, Faubion 2002[1994]). Hosking (2002) argues that much of what Foucault describes as power could be better explained through trust (Hosking 2002). Although Foucault assigned little attention to trust practices (Luxon 2015), he did question the shift in the trust-power nexus from states to markets. Foucault (2008) argued that, following the rise of neoliberalism, the state 'because of its defects, is mistrusted by everyone' (p. 117).

I argue that trust and power are joined through discourse, particularly in financial markets, where some of the most powerful discourses persist – those grounded in scientific, rational expertise (Holtzhausen 2000, Hook 2001). In line with Giddens' view of system trust and mistrust, a Foucauldian presentation of discourse makes equal room for both, regarding them as co-existing rather than dichotomous. Just as system trust can be deliberately produced through discourse, so too can system mistrust. Trust discourses are equally discourses of mistrust, and must be so 'always, already, simultaneously and in a plurality of ways' (De Goede 2005, p. 172). One may, for example, trust an investment house to generate high returns, but not trust it to be completely open about how it does so. Similarly, one may mistrust the ability of regulatory bodies to effectively carry out their role in relation to powerful financial institutions – but one may trust the authenticity of their intent to regulate. The nuanced production of both trust and mistrust may be central to the protection of a dominant actor's position in the financial system. When a Foucauldian approach is applied, public relations becomes much more than a benign managerial activity, and is instead closely linked with power and influence.

Trust practice framework

Having positioned trust production as a discursive process, following Foucault (1969, 1976, 1981), I have also isolated practices which produce trust or mistrust in financial markets, exploring how and where these practices might be deployed through PR. I draw on a range of fields where trust has been explored discursively as a managerial strategy (Grey and Garsten 2001), as a locally meaningful performative act (Carolan 2006) or as self-legitimising discourses (Gilbert 1998, Biltereyst 2004). The resulting framework (see Table 2.1) has been applied to empirical studies on trust in credit rating agencies, hedge funds, insurers and global investment banks (Bourne 2012, 2013, 2015, Bourne and Edwards 2012). The next chapters build on this previous work by conducting a vertical and horizontal exploration of wholesale and retail financial markets. The framework isolates five sets of practices – protecting, guaranteeing, aligning, opening up (making transparent) and simplifying – to explain how trust and mistrust are produced. Financial actors can enact trust practices, or by failing to enact them, generate mistrust. Similarly, when experts contest the trust practices of other experts, they open up a discursive space for mistrust. The more material (therefore powerful) the failed trust practice, the more likely trust is to be destroyed.

The first trust practice is the act of protecting customers' assets, reflecting the crucial role protecting and safeguarding play in building trust (Baier 1986, Cook 2005). In financial markets, protecting and safeguarding includes the ability to produce a reasonable financial return (Shapiro 1987, Hilton 2004, Arthur W. Page Society 2009). This first trust practice is both discursive and material, and is the most important trust practice engaged in by financial institutions. Banks and investment houses, covered in Chapters 6 and 7, hold an important role in safeguarding deposits and investments, as do central banks in shoring up national currencies. The second trust practice is the act of guaranteeing: here financial actors must show evidence of certainty that they can produce concrete, measurable results in a specific timeframe. This second trust practice is further linked with honouring contractual obligations (Casson and Della Giusta 2006). Guarantees are also implicit in high-quality products that deliver on customer promises (Arthur W. Page Society 2009), discursively represented through symbolic 'trust marks' such as warranties, guarantees, seals of approval

Table 2.1 Trust Practice Framework

1. Protecting	2. Guaranteeing	3. Aligning	4. Making visible
'We represent our stakeholders' interests since they bear the risk'	*'We are certain of delivering set results in a set time frame'*	*'We associate with other trust codes and systems'*	*'We are truthful, open and detailed about our expert practices'*
• Building wealth or reducing debt • Managing risk while providing customers with exit strategies • Assigning high/low trust actors, e.g. custodian to look after funds • Respecting property, e.g. installing and monitoring customer data protection • Treating all customer groups fairly • Adopting the role of industry or consumer' 'champion'	• Keeping promises, honouring contracts, repaying money • Producing certification of competence, expertise • Monitoring system soundness • Assessing effectiveness of policies • Enlisting third party endorsement, recommendation, ratings, warranties, seals of approval	• Adopting standards and codes of 'best practice', e.g. auditing • Complying with law and regulation • Foregoing competitive imitation • Recognising and supporting customer loyalty • Negotiating against stated expectations, with willingness to compromise • Supporting socially responsible behaviour	• Making and pricing accessible, transparent products and services • Making transparent contract terms • Measuring financial performance, reporting frequently, honestly • Submitting or subscribing to monitoring and assessment • Giving customers a voice, listening to and acting on complaints • Apologising for failings; making amends

◄──────► *5. Simplifying* ◄──────►

'We are expert enough to explain what we do in plain terms'

Codifying products and practices. Delineating 'good' from 'bad', 'opinion' from 'fact', 'myth' from 'reality'. Selecting and omitting messages, explaining technical material or jargon, ranking product providers, clarifying arguments or positions. Supported by PR through communication tools such as websites, fact sheets, brochures, press releases, speeches, commentary, case studies, surveys etc.

Source: The Author.

and league tables (Zucker 1986, Yandle 2008). Guarantees operate in many parts of financial markets – from central banks guaranteeing the rest of the banking system, to credit rating agencies assigning a Triple-A rating to a country's debt, to investment institutions applying for third party rankings for their funds or 'wrapping' their products with an insurance policy to make investments appear more secure. Audit procedures are also important in guaranteeing trust in financial institutions, as with other sectors.

The third trust practice involves aligning: 'performing' trust by obtaining certification and codification from other trust systems and codes. Individuals can align by completing approved licensing and examinations, while institutions can align by joining formal trust networks such as professional and/or trade associations (Shapiro 1987), or by complying with audit and regulatory mechanisms (Zucker 1986, Yandle 2008). Those financial institutions appointed as 'trust guardians' institutionalise trust codes by setting standards and scrutinising industry actors (Shapiro 1987). One significant means of alignment for financial institutions is via recognised trade and professional associations – trade association activity is examined in Chapter 4. Similarly, international players often align with established global expertise in order to promote their global reach (Bourne 2015). Finally, many financial institutions produce trust by aligning with state regulatory or legislative mechanisms, while others reject visible trust mechanisms altogether, as discussed in Chapter 9.

The fourth trust practice is that of opening up or making transparent by showing evidence of truth-telling and transparency (Carolan and Bell 2003, Bentele and Seidenglanz 2008). Such techniques include expressing ideas freely, while maintaining accountability. Investment institutions, for example, might emphasise their commission-free sales process, banks might publish their internal codes of conduct, or open up third party relationships that would not normally be apparent to clients. Interestingly, while many areas of finance make much 'hay' of transparency, successive crises have emphasised just how fundamentally opaque finance often is, based on complex probabilities with densely written contract terms. Similarly, financial institutions may choose to be transparent about *certain* company practices, using PR techniques to promote these so as to direct attention away from activity behind the scenes (see Chapter 9). Crises often bring to the fore opaque practices which conceal poor decision-making or hidden risks on their balance sheets, thus negating any transparency and trust achieved through PR.

Finally, there is the trust practice of simplifying – here a financial institution demonstrates expertise by explaining the way it conducts business in simple terms. Simplifying is a highly communicative strategy, often involving PR. As a means of trust production, simplifying involves providing accurate, timely and useful information (Fann Thomas et al. 2009); disseminating organisational messages consistent in quality, clarity and mode of delivery (Green 2006). By contrast, organisations that generate discrepancies – intentionally or unintentionally – are more likely to produce mistrust (Bentele and Seidenglanz 2008). Organisations produce trust when they make complex products or ideas simpler to understand, even when such products and concepts are not simple to implement (Allen and Santomero 2001). Simplifying strategies also includes the ways an organisation articulates its position on an issue to affected stakeholders (Fisher et al. 2010): by standing up for fairness and procedural justice (Cook 2005), or demonstrating that they are acting in stakeholders' best interests (Farrell 2004) by simplifying, as well as protecting. Certain independent experts, media houses and pundits play this role in financial markets, positioning themselves as customer champions by naming and shaming bad products, services and providers. As I will demonstrate throughout this book, simplifying is the most legitimate role for PR, yet PR is not always required to simplify at all. Many wholesale market financial institutions liberally use exclusionary jargon, suggesting that simplifying may not be an important trust strategy for persuading *expert* publics.

Some qualifying points on the trust framework

A few points to highlight before I begin my exploration of trust, power and public relations across financial markets. First, in focusing on system trust, I do not downplay other forms of trust production. System trust co-exists alongside interpersonal and organisational trust, and would never emerge if individual or organisational trust were not present first (Korczynski 2000, Gilbert 2005, Rendtorff 2008). Nor should Giddens's notion of system trust be confused with organisational trust, which is neither truly faceless nor abstract (Rawlins 2008). In exploring trust as a discursive strategy, I also make ample room for non-discursive practices, understanding that trust is not only produced through discourse but through material acts. Furthermore, like Foucault, I acknowledge the presence of structural hierarchies within discourses (Risse 2007). Trust discourses may be constantly in motion, yet structural hierarchies of trust exist (Lapavitsas 2007), together with institutional trust roles and access points (Giddens 1990), most notably 'trust guardians' such as central banks (see Chapter 3) and regulators who oversee financial markets (Shapiro 1987).

The second point to make is that while much of the book's discussion is located in Anglo-Saxon markets, system trust operates distinctively in different markets (Fukuyama 1995, Tyler and Stanley 2007). Moreover, cultural bias applies to portrayals of trust. For example, the Western media often stigmatise countries through issues of trust, claiming that 'country x' is high (or low) in trust (Marková and Gillespie 2008). (Promotional tools such as the Edelman Trust Barometer contribute to such stigmatisation.) I therefore acknowledge the influence of local realities, historical rather than modern trust frameworks, the link between trust, finance and faith (De Goede 2005), and even the complete absence of trust relations where applicable (Beckert 2005). The next chapters unpack PR's role in organising trust in parts of different financial markets – from the dizzying heights of inter-state communication to grassroots financial campaigning – in order to determine where PR's influence truly lies in trust relations, if at all.

Note

1 Ronneberger and Rühl (1992) produced a comprehensive theory of PR based on Luhmann's work, including his views of system trust. Their German-language study has not been translated yet, but a translated version would help it receive wider recognition.

References

Allen, F. and Santomero, A.M. (2001). 'What do financial intermediaries do?' *Journal of Banking & Finance*, 25, pp. 271–294.

Arthur W. Page Society. (2009). *The Dynamics of Public Trust in Business*, New York: Arthur W. Page Society.

Baier, A. (1986). 'Trust and antitrust', *Ethics*, 96, pp. 231–260.

Beckert, J. (2005). 'Trust and the performative construction of markets', *MPIfG Discussion Paper 05/8*, Max Planck Institute for the Study of Societies.

Bekmeier-Feuerhahn, S. and Eichenlaub, A. (2010). 'What makes for trusting relationships in online communication?' *Journal of Communication Management*, 14 (4), pp. 337–355.

Bentele, G. (1994). 'Öffentliches Vertrauen – normative und soziale Grundlage für Public Relations'. In Armbrecht, W. and Zabel, U. (eds) *Normative Aspekte der Public Relations*. Opladen: Westdeutscher Verlag GmbH, pp. 131–158.

Bentele, G. and Seidenglanz, R. (2008). 'Trust and credibility – prerequisites for communication management'. In Zerfass, A., van Ruler, B. and Krishnamurthy, S. (ed) *Public Relations: European and International Perspectives and Innovations*. Wiesbaden: VS Verlag Fur SozialWissenschafeten, pp. 49–62.

Biltereyst, D. (2004). 'Public service broadcasting, popular entertainment and the construction of trust', *European Journal of Cultural Studies*, 7, pp. 341–362.

Bourne, C. (2012). 'Rating agencies as a corporate governance mechanism: Power and trust production in debt capital markets'. In Tench, R., Jones, B. and Sun, W. (eds) *Corporate Social Irresponsibility: Issues, Debates and Case Studies*. Bingley: Emerald Books, pp. 135–156.

Bourne, C. (2013). 'Reframing trust, power and public relations in global financial discourses: Experts and the production of mistrust in life insurance', *Public Relations Inquiry*, 2 (1), pp. 51–77.

Bourne, C. (2015). 'Thought leadership as a trust strategy in global markets: Goldman Sachs' promotion of the 'BRICs' in the marketplace of ideas', *Journal of Public Relations Research*, 27 (4), pp. 322–336.

Bourne, C. and Edwards, L. (2012). 'Producing trust, knowledge and expertise in financial markets: The global hedge fund industry 're-presents' itself', *Culture and Organization*, 18 (2), pp. 107–122.

Bowling, J.C. and Truitt, R.H. (2003). 'Public relations in post-bubble America', *Public Relations Quarterly*, 22 March.

Carolan, M.S. (2006). 'Sustainable agriculture, science and the co-production of 'expert' knowledge', *Local Environment: The International Journal of Justice and Sustainability*, 11, pp. 421–431.

Carolan, M.S. and Bell, M.M. (2003). 'In truth we trust: Discourse, phenomenology, and the social relations of knowledge in an environmental dispute', *Environmental Values*, 12, pp. 225–245.

Casson, M. and Della Giusta, M. (2006). 'The economics of trust'. In Bachmann, R. and Zaheer, A. (eds) *Handbook of Trust Research*. Cheltenham, UK: Elgar Publishing, pp. 332–354.

Cook, K.S. (2005). 'Networks, norms, and trust: The social psychology of social capital', *Social Psychology Quarterly*, 68, pp. 4–14.

De Goede, M. (2005). *Virtue, Fortune and Faith: A Genealogy of Finance*, Minneapolis: University of Minnesota Press.

Delahaye Paine, K., Hon, L. and Grunig, J. (2003). 'Guidelines for measuring trust in organisations'. Gainesville, FL: Institute for Public Relations, p. 13.

Demetrious, K. (2015). 'Sanitising or reforming PR? Exploring 'trust' and the emergence of critical public relations'. In L'Etang, J., McKie, D., Snow, N. and Xifra, J. (eds) *The Routledge Handbook of Critical Public Relations*. Abingdon, Oxfordshire: Routledge, pp. 101–116.

Edwards, L. (2010). 'Critical perspectives in global public relations: Theorising power'. In Bardhan, N. & Weaver, C.K. (eds) *Public Relations in Global Cultural Contexts: Multiparadigmatic Perspectives.* New York: Routledge, pp. 29–49.

Eisenegger, M. and Imhof, K. (2008) 'The true, the good and the beautiful: Reputation management in the media society'. In Zerfass, A., van Ruler, B. and Sriramesh, K. (eds) *Public Relations Research: European and International Perspectives and Innovations.* Wiesbaden: VS Verlag fur Sozialwissenschaften, pp. 125–146.

Falkheimer, J. (2009). 'On Giddens: Interpreting public relations through Anthony Gidden's structuration and late modernity theory'. In Ihlen, O., van Ruler, B. and Fredriksson, M. (eds) *Public Relations and Social Theory.* New York: Routledge, pp. 103–118.

Fann Thomas, G., Zolin, R. and Hartman, J.L. (2009). 'The central role of communication in developing trust and its effect on employee involvement', *Journal of Business Communication*, 46, pp. 287–310.

Farrell, H. (2004). 'Trust, distrust and power'. In Hardin, R. (ed) *Distrust.* New York: Russell Sage Foundation, pp. 85–105.

Faubion, J.D. (1994). *Michel Foucault: Power. Essential Works of Foucault 1954–1984*, 2002 Reprint ed., London: Penguin, p. 528.

Fisher, J., van Heerde, J. and Tucker, A. (2010). 'Does one trust judgment fit all? Linking theory and empirics', *The British Journal of Politics and International Relations*, 12, pp. 161–188.

Foucault, M. (1969). *The Archaeology of Knowledge,* Abingdon: Routledge Publications.

Foucault, M. (1976). *The History of Sexuality (Volume 1): The Will to Knowledge,* London: Penguin Books.

Foucault, M. (1981). 'The order of discourse'. In Young, R. (ed) *Untying the Text: A Poststructuralist Reader.* London and Boston: Routledge and Keegan Paul, pp. 51–77.

Foucault, M. (2008). *The Birth of Biopolitics,* London, Palgrave Macmillan.

Fukuyama F. (1995). *Trust: The Social Virtues and the Creation of Prosperity,* New York: Free Press Paperbacks.

Giddens, A. (1990). *The Consequences of Modernity,* Oxford, UK: Polity Press/Blackwell.

Giddens, A. (1991). *Modernity and Self-Identity: Self and Society in the Late Modern Age,* London: Polity Press.

Giddens, A. (1994). 'Living in a post-traditional society'. In Beck, U., Giddens, A. & Lash, S. (eds) *Reflexive Modernization: Politics, Tradition and Aesthetics in the Modern Social Order.* Cambridge: Polity Press, pp. 56–109.

Giddens, A. (1999). 'Risk and responsibility', *The Modern Law Review*, 62 (1), pp. 1–10.

Giddens, A. (2000). 'The globalising of modernity'. In Held, D. & McGrew, A. (eds) *The Global Transformations Reader: An Introduction to the Globalisation Debate.* Cambridge: Polity Press, pp. 92–98.

Gilbert, T.P. (1998). 'Towards a politics of trust', *Journal of Advanced Nursing*, 27, pp. 1010–1016.

Gilbert, T.P. (2005). 'Impersonal trust and professional authority: Exploring the dynamics', *Journal of Advanced Nursing*, 49, pp. 568–577.

Green, F. (2006). *Restoring Faith in Financial Products & Services Financial Services.* Research & Insight Forum. London: Harris Interactive.

Gregory, A. (2006). 'The truth and the whole truth?'. In Hobsbawm, J. (ed) *Where the Truth Lies: Trust and Morality in PR and Journalism.* London: Atlantic Books, pp. 98–109.

Grey, C. and Garsten, C. (2001). 'Trust, control and post-bureaucracy', *Organization Studies*, 22, pp. 229–250.

Hardin, R. (2004). 'Distrust: Manifestations and management'. In Hardin, R. (ed) *Distrust.* New York: Russell Sage Foundation, pp. 3–33.

Hardy, C., Phillips, N. and Lawrence, R. (1998) 'Distinguishing trust and power in interorganizational relations: Forms and facades of trust'. In Lane, C. and Bachman, R. (eds)

Trust Within and Between Organizations: Conceptual Issues and Empirical Applications. Oxford: Oxford University Press.

Harris, J.D. and Wicks, A.C. (2010). 'Public trust and trust in particular firm stakeholder interactions', *Corporate Reputation Review*, 13, pp. 142–154.

Harrison, S. (1997). 'Earning trust by telling the truth: How should public relations and media professionals behave when a disaster happens?' *Journal of Communication Management*, 1 (3), pp. 219–230.

Harriss, J. (2005). *Widening the Radius of Trust: Ethnographic Explorations of Trust and Indian Business*, LSE Research Online, London: London School of Economics.

Hilton, A. (2004). 'Lack of return is key', *Evening Standard*, 24 November, p. 35.

Holtzhausen, D.R. (2000). 'Postmodern values in public relations', *Journal of Public Relations Research*, 12 (1), pp. 93–114.

Hook, D. (2001). 'Discourse, knowledge, materiality, history: Foucault and discourse analysis', *Theory & Psychology*, 11 (4), pp. 521–547.

Hosking, G. (2002). *Why We Need a History of Trust*. Retrieved from: http://www.history.ac.uk/reviews/articles/hoskingGA.html

Jempson, M. (2005). 'Spinners or sinners? PR, journalists and public trust', *Journal of Communication Management*, 9 (3), pp. 267–276.

Kent, M.L. and Taylor, M. (2002). 'Toward a dialogic theory of public relations', *Public Relations Review*, 28, pp. 21–37.

Kim, J.Y., Kiousis, S. and Molleda, J. (2015). 'Use of affect in blog communication: Trust, Credibility, and Authenticity', *Public Relations Review*, 41 (4), pp. 504–507.

Korczynski, M. (2000). 'The political economy of trust', *Journal of Management Studies*, 37, pp. 1–21.

Kramer, R.M. (2010). 'Collective trust within organizations: Conceptual foundations and empirical insights', *Corporate Reputation Review*, 13, pp. 82–97.

Lane, C. and Bachmann, R. (eds) (1998). *Trust Within and Between Organizations: Conceptual Issues and Empirical Applications*, New York: Oxford University Press.

Lapavitsas, C. (2007). 'Information and trust as social aspects of credit', *Economy and Society*, 36, pp. 416–436.

Larson, M.S. (2012). *The Rise of Professionalism: Monopolies of Competence and Sheltered Markets*, Piscataway, NJ: Transaction Publishers.

Larsson, L. (2007). 'Public trust in the PR industry and its actors', *Journal of Communication Management*, 11 (3), pp. 222–234.

Lawniczak, R. (2007). 'Public relations role in a global competition "to sell" alternative political and socio-economic models of market economy', *Public Relations Review*, 33, pp. 377–386.

L'Etang, J. (2003). 'The myth of the "ethical guardian": an examination of its origins, potency and illusions', *Journal of Communication Management*, 8, pp. 53–67.

Leonidou, L.C., Talias, M.A. and Leonidou, C.N. (2008). 'Exercised power as a driver of trust and commitment in cross-border industrial buyer-seller relationships', *Industrial Marketing Management*, 37, pp. 92–103.

Lerbinger, O. (2013). 'Public relations in international management'. In Gambetti, R. and Quigley, S. (eds) *Managing Corporate Communication: A Cross-Cultural Approach*. Basingstoke: Palgrave Macmillan, pp. 51–72.

Leyshon, A. and Thrift, N. (1997). *Money/Space: Geographies of Monetary Transformation*, London: Routledge.

Luhmann, N. (1979). *Trust and Power*, Chichester: Wiley and Sons.

Lury, C. and Warde, A. (1997). 'Investments in the imaginary consumer'. In Nava, M., Blake, A., MacRury, I. and Richards, B. (eds) *Buy This Book: Studies in Advertising and Consumption*. London, UK: Routledge, pp. 87–102.

Luxon, Nancy. (2015). *Crisis of Authority: Politics, Trust and Truth-Telling in Freud and Foucault*, Cambridge: Cambridge University Press.

Marchand, R. (1998). *Creating the Corporate Soul: The Rise of Public Relations and Corporate Imagery in American Big Business*, Berkeley: The University of California Press.

Marková, I., Linell, P. and Gillespie, A. (2008). 'Trust and distrust in society'. In Marková, I. and Gillespie, A. (eds) *Trust and Distrust: Sociocultural Perspectives*. Charlotte, NC: Information Age Publishing, pp. 3–28.

Maclagan, P. (1998). *Management and Morality: A Developmental Perspective*, London, Sage Publications.

Misztal, B.A. (1996). *Trust in Modern Societies*, Cambridge: Polity Press.

Möllering, G. (2005). 'The trust/control duality', *International Sociology*, 20, pp. 283–305.

Moloney, K. (2005). 'Trust and public relations: Center and edge', *Public Relations Review*, 31, pp. 550–555.

Motion, J. and Weaver, C.K. (2005). 'A discourse perspective for critical public relations research', *Journal of Public Relations Research*, 17 (1), 49–67.

Muzio, D., Ackroyd, S. and Chanlat, J.-F. (2008). 'Introduction: Lawyers, doctors and business consultants'. In Muzio, D., Ackroyd, S. & Chanlat, J.-F. (eds) *Redirections in the Study of Expert Labour*. Basingstoke, UK: Palgrave Macmillan, pp. 1–30.

Painter, D.L. (2015). 'Online political public relations and trust: Source and interactivity effects in the 2012 U.S. presidential campaign', *Public Relations Review*, 41 (5), pp. 801–808.

Pixley, J. (2004). *Emotions in Finance: Distrust and Uncertainty in Global Markets*, Cambridge: Cambridge University Press.

Poppo, L. and Schepker, D.J. (2010). 'Repairing public trust in organizations', *Corporate Reputation Review*, 13, pp. 124–141.

Rawlins, B.L. (2008). 'Measuring the relationship between organizational transparency and employee trust', *Public Relations Journal*, 2, pp. 1–21.

Rendtorff, J.D. (2008). 'Corporate citizenship, trust and accountability'. *24th Conference of the Nordic Sociological Association*. University of Aarhus, Denmark.

Risse, T. (2007). 'Social constructivism meets globalisation'. In Held, D. and McGrew, A. (eds) *Globalisation Theory: Approaches and Controversy*. Cambridge: Polity Press, pp. 126–147.

Ronneberger, F. and Rühl, M. (1992). *Theorie der Public Relations*, Opladen: Westdeutscher Verlag GmbH.

Röttger, U. and Voss, A. (2008) 'Internal communication as management of trust relations: A theoretical framework'. In Zerfass, A., van Ruler, B. and Sriramesh, K. (eds.) *Public Relations Research: European and International Perspectives and Innovations*. Wiesbaden: VS Verlag fur Sozialwissenschaften.

Seligman, A.B. (1997). *The Problem of Trust*, Princeton, Princeton University Press.

Shapiro, S.P. (1987). 'The social control of impersonal trust', *American Journal of Sociology*, 93, pp. 623–658.

Tyler, K. and Stanley, E. (2007). 'The role of trust in financial services business relationships', *Journal of Services Marketing*, 21, pp. 334–344.

Vassilev, I. and Pilgrim, D. (2007). 'Risk, trust and the myth of mental health services', *Journal of Mental Health*, 16, pp. 347–357.

Watson, M.L. (2005). *Can There Be Just One Trust? A Cross-Disciplinary Identification of Trust Definitions and Measurement*, Gainesville, FL: The Institute for Public Relations.

Welch, M. (2006). 'Rethinking relationship management: Exploring the dimension of trust', *Journal of Communication Management*, 10 (2), pp. 138–155.

Yandle, B. (2008). 'Lost trust: The real cause of the financial meltdown'. In George Mason University (ed) *Mercatus Center Working Papers*. Working Paper No. 09-02, February. Fairfax, VA: Mercatus Center, pp. 1–21.

Yang, S. and Lim, J.S. (2009). 'The effects of blog-mediated public relations (BMPR) on relational trust', *Journal of Public Relations Research*, 21 (3), pp. 341–359.

Young, L.C. and Wilkinson, I.F. (1989). 'The role of trust and cooperation in marketing channels: a preliminary study', *European Journal of Marketing*, 23, pp. 109–122.

Zucker, L.G. (1986). 'Production of trust: Institutional sources of economic structure, 1840–1920', *Research in Organizational Behavior*, 8, pp. 53–111.

3 Promoting state financial power

Creditworthiness as trustworthiness

My exploration of public relations in financial discourses begins at the apex of financial markets, where national financial systems – governments, central banks and state financial institutions – promote trustworthiness by affirming creditworthiness of national investment assets. Since states raise large volumes of funding in global markets, the image of nations has a strong influence on the flow of international capital. Public relations therefore plays an integral role in promoting a nation's creditworthiness both within its borders and internationally, promoting national currencies and debt instruments, and promoting the financial stability behind these instruments.

A state's trustworthiness is governed by a complex apparatus of global and national authority. At the global level, this apparatus includes the Group of 20 most wealthy nations (G20),[1] NATO, the World Trade Organization, as well as international financial institutions such as the International Monetary Fund (IMF) and the World Bank, all of which engage in PR activity as part of strategic campaigns to shape global financial architecture. Within this apparatus, weaker, poorer states are greatly subjugated by the IMF and the World Bank which facilitate borrowing from richer member nations. States convey trust-as-creditworthiness through a complex set of narratives designed principally for international investors in Western markets (Kunczik 2000, Holmes 2014). For international investors, creditworthiness is measured by solvency of domestic businesses, stable monetary policy and a state's capacity to 'tame' inflation (Seabrooke 2014). A state's most influential financial storyteller is its central bank, which guarantees the state's trustworthiness through a carefully crafted monetary story (Lapavitsas 2007). On the strength of this monetary story, states can market their currency, seek endorsement from credit rating agencies and raise funds in debt capital markets. If things go wrong and a state becomes insolvent, markets interpret any subsequent interventions by the IMF as a symbol of *distrust*, handicapping the state's ability to borrow elsewhere.

This chapter explores PR activity at the apex of the financial system in an era of shifting trust relations. To do this, I begin by briefly exploring the opacity that was once the hallmark of state finance. This opacity came to an abrupt end following the Asian Financial Crisis in the 1990s, when an international financial architecture was created, ushering in an era of 'radical transparency'.

State finance mechanisms, and particularly central banks, increasingly focused on transparency as a trust strategy. I then examine the communication fallout posed by recurring financial crises, their impact on 'least trusted' nations, and the power still wielded by the IMF and other lending agencies in determining which economies are 'untrustworthy'. The chapter closes by reviewing developments since the global financial crisis, offering perspectives on trust and public relations in contemporary state finance.

Secrecy in state finance

National borrowing is politically sensitive, and, historically, shrouded in secrecy. State finance is still largely controlled by an elite group of economists, financial and political experts operating in national and international institutions. Within national boundaries, these elites share common kinship, culture, education and social networks (Porter 1995, Riles 2006). Many are part of transnational elites working together at international lending institutions or investment banks, before taking home shared policy ideas or market knowledge to their national treasuries and central banks (Seabrooke 2014). They have an esoteric language, impenetrable to all except professional 'central bank watchers' in the markets and the media (Sweeney 2001, Smart 2006). For decades, this shared kinship and language promoted trust *between* bureaucrats and 'central bank watchers', while preserving public mystique over state finance (Holmes 2014).

Institutional insularity was traditionally maintained through closely controlled communication, illustrated well by the tight-lipped stance once adopted by the IMF and the World Bank (Woods 2006). Historically, the IMF spoke its 'inconvenient truths' to governments behind the scenes, while governments dealt directly with the media (Shafik 2013). Similarly, the World Bank vigilantly guarded information – internal leaks were uncommon. Details of certain loan agreements were even hidden from Bank directors (Caufield 1996). PR's role was primarily defensive, with World Bank PR officers on the ground in developing countries stymying investigations into controversial projects by environmentalists and the press. The Bank eventually launched an openness policy and a Public Information Center focused on its success stories, yet a defensive atmosphere prevailed. In a *Financial Times* op-ed, the Bank's chief spokesperson accused its detractors of condemning the Third World to brutish conditions by their obstruction of World Bank projects (Caufield 1996).

Central banks are 'communicators-in-chief' for national economies, national currencies, and monetary institutions (Holmes 2016). PR's historical role within central banks was to 'translate' monetary policy and economic value to financial markets, while maintaining a high degree of opacity. The accepted approach was to 'say as little as possible and say it cryptically' (Blinder et al. 2008, p. 7). At the Bank of England, the press officer's stated objective was 'to keep the Bank out of the press, and the press out of the Bank' (Lambert 2005, p. 63). Central bankers' mystical utterances were treated like those of high priests. If communications officers attempted to simplify these utterances, they were told that plain language 'dumbed down' texts (Meyersson and Karlberg 2012, p. 119). When information was released it was carefully channelled through the small club of journalists who covered state finance (Irwin 2013). Central bank governors personified the central bank's credibility and trust; journalists considered it prestigious to gain access to them (Meyersson and Karlberg 2012). Unlike government ministers, central bankers rarely made the rounds of TV and radio talk shows, as even 'ducking' a question might invite market intrigue and speculation (Boak 2012). However, the shock of several regional financial crises in the late 1990s ended opacity in central banking communication, created an increased role for PR.

Twenty-first century 'radical transparency'

State finance came under increased scrutiny during the 1990s, enabled by faster media technologies, a 24-hour news cycle and the rise of activist groups able to organise on a global scale. Anti-globalisation protests targeted the World Bank, the IMF and G20 meetings. Institutional investors were disgruntled with Asian and Latin American financial institutions for masking the systemic flaws which triggered 'trust' crises in these markets (Martin 2002). Political activists and financial experts joined in demanding more openness by state lending institutions and central banks (Sweeney 2001). The twenty-first century ushered in a new era of 'radical transparency'. Central banks, treasury departments and international financial institutions formed an 'international financial architecture' (IFA) to supervise state financial relations through consensus (Martin 2002). The IFA's strategy was to produce safe, 'docile', 'proper functioning' economies (Martin 2002, Vestergaard 2009). The accompanying rhetoric implied that *all* economies, regardless of size or location, would be subjected to the same compliance standards and reforms (Vestergaard 2009). Consensus-driven surveillance would supposedly foster trustworthiness through increased visibility and transparency (Resche 2004, Savage 2011). By the dawn of the twenty-first century, extensive communication activity in state finance became a worldwide phenomenon (Blinder et al. 2008). IFA participants were now required to speak clearly, and with 'one voice', instead of relying on 'market watchers' to translate their mystic commentary.

At the global level, PR helped to open up the IMF and the World Bank, hosting annual seminars, and making staff economists, country specialists and other experts available to journalists (Sweeney 2001). Both institutions now publish hundreds of studies and reports, made available on their websites (Sweeney 2001). Today, their greatest performance of 'radical transparency' is the joint meeting of finance ministers. Here, central bankers, diplomats, global financiers and NGO representatives converge to discuss the global economy, providing the perfect platform to launch the international agencies' most 'transparent' tool, the annual World Development Report (Sweeney 2001). At the national level, central banks remain the chief 'trust communicators' in state economic affairs. The locus of central bank transparency is monetary policy, consolidating

credibility through 'inflation targeting'. The IFA compels central banks to produce information on whether inflation targets are being met through fluid, continuous communication with the public (CEMLA 2004). Large gaps between a
central bank's interest rate forecasts and market forecasts indicate faltering trust
in central bank narratives (Meyersson and Karlberg 2012). Hence, the objective
is to recruit the public to collaborate with central banks in achieving monetary
policy objectives (stable prices, confidence in the currency) by opening up the
central bank decision-making process (Lambert 2005, Holmes 2016).

Radical transparency requires everyone inside a central bank to become part
of the communicative apparatus (Holmes 2016). A large group of specialists
operates as the central bank's 'eyes and ears'. This close-knit community-of-
practice gathers information, data, intelligence and experience from all sectors
and levels of the economy (Smart 2006), creating 'scalable narratives' (Holmes
2016, p. 13) from which the central bank's authority emerges. A central bank's
PR team is part of this community-of-practice, working with technocrats to
relay resulting narratives through monthly reports, economic commentaries,
regular bulletins, staged events and, significantly, the Monetary Policy Report –
the key trust symbol in central bank communication. Central bankers put store
in these reports. Journalists do not, particularly when they are given just minutes to peruse thick volumes detailing monetary decisions, while PR officers
act as timekeepers (Irwin 2013). Instead, journalists prefer central banking press
conferences for their plain language and instant access (Holmes 2014). Consequently, radical transparency has been a mixed success. The media continued to
chafe at restricted access to central bankers, while market watchers found radical
transparency produced more noise than clarity (Meyersson and Karlberg 2012).

Promoting state financial brands

Once a nation has developed a positive monetary policy story, it can leverage
this to promote its state 'financial brand' in the form of trust-based products –
sovereign currency, debt instruments and, increasingly, a state's physical location as an international financial centre (IFC). Countries and regions are now
paraded before international investors just like companies. Currencies are the
quintessential state financial brand. A strong currency displays economic power,
stability and confidence in a nation's future, offering safe haven to investor
capital (Cohen 2000, Kunczik 2000). Cross-border currency competition is
increasingly 'Darwinian' as global money markets expand, widening the chasm
between 'hard' and 'soft' currencies. Hard currencies are highly tradable, and
used widely beyond their country of origin as a medium-of-exchange (Cohen
2000). It is 'hard' currencies to which Giddens (1990) refers when describing
money as a disembedding mechanism enabling system trust (see Chapter 2).
The US dollar is a singular trust mechanism, effectively acting as the world's
reserve currency since World War II. 'Soft' currencies, by contrast, are deemed
too risky and volatile to act as disembedding mechanisms for producing system
trust. Soft currencies are usually attached to developing nations, which must

work harder to prop up their financial brands. Yet 'hard currency' regions cannot take their financial brand for granted. The European Central Bank (ECB),
for example, had to campaign assiduously to build trust in the euro when it was
first launched in 1999. Behind the scenes, various groups successfully lobbied to
prevent the euro from launching as a common currency.[2] The single currency
was the resulting compromise. The launch campaign, led by global communications firm Publicis, laid the groundwork through a public information and
'emotional acceptance' campaign (van Ham 2002, p. 259). The euro campaign
successfully integrated the EU into financial globalisation, nearly ousting the
US dollar as the world's primary reserve currency and store of financial trust.

Debt instruments are a vital way for countries, regions, municipalities and
companies to raise money. Investors (the lenders or creditors) tender for 'branded'
promissory notes known as bonds, or for Treasury Bills, collateralised loans or
repurchase agreements, all of which can be traded on to other investors. Debt
capital markets are worth trillions, and governments are their most important
customers. Government-backed institutions were the first to adopt innovative
debt instruments such as CDOs (collateralised debt obligations), decades before
investment banks commandeered this market (Dodd 2014). PR has long played
a role in promoting government's ability to borrow and repay its debts. Early
twentieth-century practitioner Ivy Lee handled loans for Poland, Romania,
France and other countries after World War II (Kunczik 2000 citing Hiebert
1966). Lee advised countries on the importance of national image over statistics, and the need to highlight characteristics valued by Western investors. When
Argentina struggled to attract investors, Lee directed the country to promote
its 'civilised' atmosphere by sending a polo team to the US (Kunczik 2000 citing Hiebert 1966). Today, governments have debt management units dedicated
to promoting debt issuance through investor relations campaigns, including
presentations to banks, investment houses and rating agencies. PR and marketing staff also produce advertisements, public announcements, monthly bulletins,
speeches, conference presentations and articles in financial media (Dooner and
McAlister 2013).

States can also promote their financial brands collectively. The African
Development Bank (ADB) promotes creditworthiness by highlighting its role
in accelerating African development and eradicating poverty (ADB 2009). The
most famous collective state financial brand is arguably the BRICs, a moniker
created by Goldman Sachs, the global investment bank, to represent Brazil,
Russia, India and China as an investment concept. The moniker is counter-
intuitive since the BRICs are not a 'region'. The term typifies global investors' preference for bifurcating the world into 'stable' developed markets and
riskier 'emerging markets'. Goldman Sachs's promotion of the BRICs as an
emerging markets theme helped build credibility in these countries as investment destinations, while simultaneously bolstering trust in Goldman Sachs's
asset management expertise (Bourne 2015). All state financial brands further
rely on credit rating agencies to promote their economic value, by evaluating
and translating a country's ability to repay its debt. Rating agencies provide a

voluntary system of governance based on rating symbols, ranging from AAA (trustworthy) through to DDD (untrustworthy). Through these symbols, rating agencies convert trust into a saleable product, thereby creating an active trust market in sovereign and corporate debt (Zucker 1986, Yandle 2008).

International Finance Centres (IFCs) are a third area of state financial promotion, channelling billions, even trillions, of public and private funds into investment markets. In the marketing of IFCs, politics and finance meet as equals (Hosking 2010) because there is so much at stake for the host city and national government, as well as the global financial interests which choose an IFC for their headquarters. A complex hierarchy of trust relations therefore governs IFCs, extending vertically *within* national boundaries, where financial centres are subject to national legislation, regulation and government policy, and extending horizontally *beyond* national boundaries, where IFCs are part of the self-regulating international financial architecture or IFA (Vestergaard 2009). London, New York, Hong Kong and Singapore are the largest IFCs, aggressively promoting their ability to host to money markets, multiple stock exchanges, and deep, liquid bond markets. But it is London and New York that are most competitive in the battle to wear the crown of world's 'biggest and best' IFC.

Trust crises in state finance

Cities and nation states may vie to promote their financial stability and prowess, but it is impossible for all territories to be stable at the same time. Volatility can be caused by declining trade or taxation, poor money management, civil unrest or natural disaster; and exacerbated through speculative investing by global hedge funds and arbitrageurs.[3] Modern state finance therefore abounds with trust 'booms and busts', triggering insolvencies when states are at their least creditworthy. The stigma of untrustworthiness spreads from the insolvent government to its domestic financial institutions. Consequently, PR campaigns to restore trust in a state's creditworthiness are especially challenging. After the shock of the Latin American debt crisis in 1982, the region's undercapitalised banks competed to raise their profile through roadshows and promotion in international financial media. In 1989, Mexico tried to blame Citicorp for its financial woes through an advertisement in the *International Herald Tribune*. The move backfired since investors read the advertisement as an admission of insolvency (Kunczik 2000). In 1994, Brazil's central bank 'refreshed' its financial brand by launching a new real to replace its old inflation-plagued currency. Brazil's central bank promoted its stable, modernised currency in leading European business papers above the central bank's strapline, *'A history of trust'* (Kunczik 2003). Peru similarly bolstered its floundering financial brand in 2007, promoting an 'atmosphere of trust', and reassuring international investors and policymakers that Peru played 'by the rules', had good fiscal discipline and had a solid economy (IIG 2007).

No matter how tirelessly countries work to restore trust in their creditworthiness, some countries have an easier time than others. Argentina defaulted on monumental debts in 2002, but was only temporarily excluded from global finance markets. Other defaulters have been excused for geopolitical reasons, or in return for diplomatic favours (Ross 2013). Meanwhile, trust symbols such as sovereign credit ratings matter less for industrialised nations with established reputations for stable monetary policy. Japan was rated AA for nearly a decade, but found it cheaper to raise funds than Australia, which was rated AAA during the same period. When Standard & Poor's downgraded the US from AAA in 2011, America's cost of borrowing became even cheaper. National efforts to restore trust through international PR activity are thus directly affected by a state's position in the global hierarchy of trust relations, as was painfully evident during the global financial crisis.

The global financial crisis, and the euro crisis which followed, required one of the largest state-backed crisis communications offensives of modern times. Iceland was the first country to be hit, its banking system having grown to five times the size of the economy before going 'bust'. The Icelandic government faced a complex trust dilemma – it needed rhetoric to reassure its citizens, and action to reassure both investors and the thousands of European consumers with Icelandic bank accounts. Iceland had borrowed £3 billion from the UK to repay victims of one failed Icelandic bank, but in late 2008, the country was forced to approach the IMF for US$6 billion (Mason 2009). In an attempt to placate citizens, the government called two referendums. The electorate voted to refuse payment to foreign creditors, invalidating an earlier parliamentary decision (Ross 2013). Trust between Iceland and its creditors dissolved instantly. Several governments launched legal action, while Britain froze Icelandic banking assets (Mason 2009). In 2009, Iceland launched a PR campaign to restore confidence in its domestic banking system. The campaign, handled by FD, the financial PR consultancy, targeted a vast range of stakeholders (Mattinson 2009B). Iceland also worked closely with the IMF to communicate with its citizens, trade unions, European account holders and creditors via traditional and social media. By 2012, Iceland announced its economic recovery via a joint press conference with the IMF, attracting 11,000 participants online (Shafik 2013). Other countries would not experience the same fortune.

IMF and crisis response

As lender-of-last-resort, the IMF found itself at the epicentre of the global crisis, mobilising its 'war chest' not just for Iceland but for scores of other states, from Pakistan to Ukraine (Mason 2009, Shafik 2013). Previously, the IMF's entire legitimacy had been in question, but the global financial crisis rescued it from obscurity. The Fund's post-crisis loan book bulged with vast new loans, ensuring its financial future for years to come (Swann 2011). The IMF's makeover was assisted by a new PR approach to state negotiations. In the past, it had publicly accepted the role of scapegoat when it made 'tough choices' for the public good (Shafik 2013). Its documents were kept confidential, and its board meetings were held in secret. The teams who regularly visited countries never spoke to the media (Shafik 2013). However, throughout the crisis, the IMF found that the more people knew about its operations, the more it was appreciated (Shafik 2013). Its communications team increased the number of languages used in IMF communication, and organised regular blogs, earning millions of IMF followers across Facebook, Twitter and Weibo (Shafik 2013). The Fund also learned to speak with 'one voice', spending more time internally agreeing a view on major global issues, then coordinating messages with key partners (Shafik 2013).

Yet, the IMF's new PR 'playbook' masked rampant inequality in its relations with states, and the Fund's alignment with creditors rather than debtor nations. For decades, the IMF's stance toward developing nations has been problematic. It has cast debtor countries as 'unruly' children, while deflecting attention away from the harmful policies of industrialised nations (Popke 1994, De Goede 2005). Developing countries had long complained of 'sweetheart' deals offered by the Fund to Western nations. By 2010, Europe accounted for nearly 60 per cent of outstanding IMF loans. Yet when poor or developing countries applied for IMF emergency funds, they found that rich countries voted against them (Swann 2011). The IMF's legitimacy was further implicated in the global financial crisis. A year before the credit crunch, the IMF's Global Financial Stability Report applauded banks for dispersing credit risk across the world, arguing that this had made the overall financial system more resilient (Dodd 2014). Meanwhile, IMF arrangements with developing countries emphasise inequality in state fiscal power. While industrialised nations have been able to use 'creative' monetary tools such as quantitative easing to shore up their economies post-crisis, developing countries are barred from any such monetary 'printing press'.

So where does the IMF figure in global trust relations? Should we be cheered by its improved PR efforts? The IMF has always owed more to disciplinary power than it is has to trust. It has never mattered whether debtor nations trust the IMF, only whether the IMF is trusted by its OECD partners with whom it is closely aligned. What may be more interesting from a PR perspective is the success of promotional efforts by new lending institutions launched by non-Western interests to redress the IMF's bias. The expanded BRICS nations (now including South Africa) launched the New Development Bank in 2015, while the China-led Asia Infrastructure Development Bank was launched that same year. It remains to be seen whether these new institutions can stem the industrialised world's tendency to deflect blame for monetary problems onto industrialised nations, a prevailing discourse of international lending (Popke 1994). Meanwhile, the eruption of the euro crisis in 2009 put the IMF in the spotlight once again. The primary blame for the euro crisis centred on Greece, which not only received the largest bailout in IMF history, but the Fund broke its own rules by lending to a country that could not repay.

The euro crisis

Western Europe had avoided much of the bad banking debt plaguing the US and the UK, adopting only mild economic stimulus in the wake of the global financial crisis. The euro crisis changed all that. In October 2009, Greece's newly elected social democratic party came to power only to discover that the country's misrepresented budget deficit had reached 12.7 per cent. The resulting fallout planted the seeds of distrust in the entire eurozone project, as the twin threat of sovereign debt default and currency devaluation loomed (Mason 2009). An unpleasant 'North vs South' battle played out in European negotiating rooms and across Western media, obscuring the real problem – that stress from the financial system had been transferred to the state, enabling a banking crisis to be re-labelled a sovereign debt crisis (Mason 2009). A struggle ensued between currencies, between trading blocks, between governments and taxpayers, and between social classes (Mason 2009, p. x).

The eurozone is the largest, most ambitious monetary union ever attempted. As a symbol of trust, the euro was supposed to bring stability, peace and prosperity to a region. However, the eurozone is a fiction on two levels: first, the eurozone suggests a homogenous financial state. For years, creditors treated the area accordingly, artificially lowering the cost of borrowing for newly joining member states (Dodd 2014). Second, unlike sovereign currencies, the euro has no sovereign government to act as guarantor when economies become volatile (Mason 2009, Dodd 2014). The euro crisis ended the illusion of homogeneity as Northern European eurozone governments with stronger financial reputations now enjoy cheaper borrowing than Southern Europe, effectively dividing the eurozone into core and periphery (Dodd 2014). The ultimate fiction behind the euro's launch, however, was the promise that a single currency would stimulate regional economic growth. It would be intriguing to measure PR's more recent contribution to propping up the euro, and supporting the inequality inherent in the core-periphery status of the eurozone's financial brand, post-crisis.

Credit ratings agencies implicated in both crises

Credit rating agencies were directly implicated in triggering both the global financial crisis and the euro crisis by over-inflating then dramatically plunging their globally recognised assessments of corporate and sovereign debts. The top three rating agencies – Moody's, Standard & Poor's and Fitch – were forced into crisis communications mode twice in one decade, as they became the subject of media headlines, government inquiries, litigation and probing exposés by journalists, market experts and academics. As voluntary trust mechanisms, rating agencies have unique status in financial markets. First, the 'big three' rating agencies are effectively a 'US government-mandated' cartel, further legitimised through ratings-dependent international regulation (Partnoy 2001, Mutti 2004, Yandle 2008). Yet rating agencies identify themselves as part of the business media, not financial organisations, defining their ratings as merely 'opinions' with no official authority (Standard & Poor's 1986). Second, while central banks and other governance mechanisms improved on clarity during the era of radical transparency, rating agencies' valuation models remained opaque and difficult to fathom. Third, rating agencies are not paid by lenders/investors but by borrowers/issuers, typically investment banks arranging debt issues. Rating agencies can therefore earn more fees by assigning higher ratings to as many debt issues as possible (Yandle 2008).

Rating agencies played a direct role in triggering the 2007 credit crunch. Having marketed high-risk instruments as trustworthy 'Triple-A' products, agencies discovered their models were flawed. They failed to revise them publicly until 2007, when their mass downgrades caused instant contagion across high-risk instruments. Similarly, rating agencies helped to trigger the eurozone crisis by downgrading the sovereign ratings of Greece, Ireland and Portugal too far and too fast, having previously failed to challenge country reports (House of Lords 2011). Rating agencies' approach to crisis communications remained stubbornly similar in each crisis. In the short term, rating agencies 'dialled down' their significance to financial markets. Standard & Poor's (S&P's), for example, had long promoted itself as an independent, objective arbiter of the quality and safety of debt, yet recanted when faced with litigation, describing these terms as mere 'puffery' (Tauberman 2013). Rating agencies also competed with each other to be the first to identify risks that might trigger the next crisis (House of Lords 2011). However, agencies' long-term PR strategy doggedly defended the status quo. Communications chiefs at Moody's and S&P's both lamented that rating agencies been made scapegoats, hated by everyone and blamed for everything (Moody's 2007, Pulsepoint 2009). When PR representatives defend the indefensible, casting blame everywhere else but within their client-organisations, they are not trust strategists but simply henchmen.

If credit rating agencies are staunch defenders of their financial territory, those representing international financial centres (IFCs) are more so. The two largest IFCs – London and New York – were geographic epicentres for the global financial crisis. Yet, when faced with growing resentment over taxpayer bailouts of parasitic financial institutions, both London and New York protected their IFC fortress. Not only did they lobby hard to avert tougher regulation, they also used softer techniques such as public education campaigns spreading the gospel of financial centres' contribution to the real economy (Wigley 2008, Bloomberg 2009, Darling and Bischoff 2009). London's reliance on system trust is particularly fragile. Whereas New York does much of its business within the US, some 80 per cent of London's financial centre transactions come from outside UK borders (Gumbel 2007). Moreover, London's complex relationship with UK and EU regulators, its voluminous shadow banking system and competitive threat from emerging financial centres forced it to campaign hardest to defend its position against New York. London already had an established ritual following successive trust breaches in financial markets. The ritual began by positioning lost trust as a 'jeremiad' (Seligman 1997), followed by media headlines 'naming and shaming' guilty financial institutions leading to public demands for accountability, then government remonstrations and public inquiries. In the case of the global financial crisis, the UK Treasury further exacted a levy on banks (later reduced) and disbanded the old financial regulator, forming two new ones, thus ending with a ritualistic 'image makeover'. Meanwhile, global PR consultancies profited from crisis communication mandates from emerging IFCs such as Dubai seeking image redress with Western investors (Mattinson 2009A). For IFCs, PR's role supports territorial tug of war, rarely leading to any reflection on moral conduct and behavioural change.[4]

Central banks: post-crisis and 'radical uncertainty'

The chapter's exploration of state finance ends with a fuller discussion of central banks as the chief 'trust communicators' of state finance. While a state's financial reputation does not begin with its central banking leadership, it almost certainly *ends* there. This is particularly true in a financial crisis, when a central bank's ultimate purpose is to prevent a banking sector collapse and ensuing panic (Irwin 2013). Central banks were also implicated in the global financial crisis, accused of stoking market excesses through weak governance, inconsistent inflation targeting and 'too easy' monetary policies. Central banks were further criticised for failing to heed the pundits who did predict the crisis, then collectively refusing to take action (Warner 2011, Kirsner 2012). The mythical 'Age of the Central Banker' was over. There was no 'Committee to Save the World' as there had been following the Asian Financial Crisis (Irwin 2013). The chief central bankers at the Federal Reserve, ECB and the Bank of England were quiet, cerebral types who maintained their distance from many political and financial elites (Tett 2009, Ewing and Erlanger 2010). Events caught central bank communication teams unawares. The three central bankers broke ranks, dealing separately with the press (Tett 2009, Irwin 2013). The radical transparency mandate to 'speak with one voice' flew out the window.

Behind the scenes, central banks acknowledged their communications failures, acknowledging that the post-1990s focus on communicating monetary policy came at the expense of financial stability. This soon changed. Governments had little fiscal room to stimulate economies, so central banks became 'activists' for economic recovery (Shafik 2013). In the post-crisis era, central bankers moved beyond open market operations to 'open mouth operations', using communications as their 'weapon' (Shafik 2013). PR officers within central banks bolstered their training on post-crisis themes and communication techniques (Central Banking Events 2013). Communication officers were tasked with making greater use of television, where messages were less likely to be botched by market commentators. Central banks increased direct dialogue via chat rooms, blogs, social media and data-related apps (Savage 2011, Meyersson and Karlberg 2012). Press conferences were organised more frequently (Vayid 2013). Communication teams commissioned more frequent surveys measuring awareness, favourability and reputation.

Initial post-crisis communication efforts yielded success in some jurisdictions, where surveys showed continued mistrust in banks, but rising trust in central banks (Skinner 2010, Meyersson and Karlberg 2012). But the 2010s proved increasingly challenging for central banks, as nuanced messages about systemic risks proved tricky to convey (Meyersson and Karlberg 2012). New communication tools such as 'Enhanced Forward Guidance' yielded mixed results (Vayid 2013). By 2015, global markets spluttered yet again. The world's largest central banks had run out of tools – and run out of productive ways to narrate their faltering economies. The biggest central banks ditched radical transparency for the element of surprise, cutting rates unexpectedly to create healthy two-way volatility. In the final analysis, sluggish economic growth had stymied trust restoration more than any communication missteps ever could.

Conclusion

So what are the concluding thoughts on trust, power and public relations at the apex of financial markets? Applying the trust practice framework, all five trust strategies – protecting, guaranteeing, aligning, opening up and simplifying – are indeed evident. Yet, PR cannot be said to play the lead role in state finance where power relations are intricate and constantly shifting. Since state finance represents the apex of financial markets, it is particularly useful to identify where the most powerful trust strategies are most evident. As pillars of state financial trust relations (Lapavitsas 2007), central banks play an integral role in *protecting*, the most power trust strategy in the framework. Central banks provide guarantees to national currencies and national banking systems. More importantly, they are tasked with *protecting* national economies, a precious asset to all citizens. If PR professionals are indeed trust strategists in financial markets, it is in central banks that they stand to wield greatest influence. However, the chapter has shown that central bank communications is so important and so nuanced that it belongs to no single group of experts. PR professionals in central banks belong to a community-of-practice, which they do not necessarily lead (Meyersson and Karlberg 2012).

If the most powerful financial trust strategy entails protecting and safeguarding assets or vulnerable parties, then rating agencies do neither. Their role is *guaranteeing*, the second trust strategy in the framework. Rating agencies guarantee the trustworthiness of corporate and state debt repayments. Yet the trust produced by rating agencies is entirely discursive; a Triple-A credit rating can dissolve with a single pronouncement. So why do markets and states trust credit ratings? Perhaps they don't trust them at all. Malsch and Gendron (2009) argue that, for investors, quantitative tools such as credit ratings act as a form of *trust-by-proxy* between market experts, who privately exhibit scepticism in these tools while publicly backing their necessity. Governments may be equally cynical. For governments, the voluntary governance provided by credit ratings reduces the public cost of policing markets, and allows states to offload the blame to third parties if things go wrong (Taylor & Burt 2005, p. 28). In all likelihood, many PR campaigns in financial markets promote trust-by-proxy mechanisms rather than actual trust.

The third trust strategy, *aligning*, opens up uncomfortable debates linked with the institutions featured in the chapter. The IMF, for example, primarily aligns with creditor countries, not debtor nations. What matters to the IMF is whether it is trusted by its creditors, not its debtors. Meanwhile, eurozone nations were able to maintain trustworthiness in their collective financial brand for years. This trustworthiness was based on the eurozone's transparent criteria for admission to the currency alliance. But Europe broke its own rules, admitting nations that did not meet the criteria and allowing existing members to bend those criteria. Today, nations at the 'core' of the eurozone are deemed more trustworthy than those at the periphery. Another uncomfortable debate concerns IFCs, which are integral nodes in financial discourses. The issue here concerns the forms of trust which underlie system trust formation. London, the world's largest IFC, has long been more closely aligned with global markets than it is with the citizens of the UK, compromising London's social pact with its own citizens and with the rest of the UK.

The fourth trust strategy, *making visible and transparent*, is equally controversial in state finance. The regime of 'radical transparency' has been largely illusory, since states are just as able to lie about their liabilities as companies are (Resche 2004, Mason 2009). It is also apparent that the international financial architecture finds it easier to 'speak with one voice' when the global economy is growing. During extended economic stagnation, states adopt a blinkered nationalist approach once again. This deters any chance of a 'fully trusting' relationship between monetary authorities and financial markets. In this construct, PR exists to represent competing interests, not to build overall trust in the financial system. The fifth strategy, *simplifying*, marginally excluded during the era of radical transparency. However, economics and state finance remain cryptic languages to the average citizen. There are also instances when financial markets over-simplify with destructive results – for example, when distilling an entire country's economic endeavour down to a single credit rating.

Ultimately, the greatest trust dilemma in state financial relations is that Western economies are slowing down and scrambling to retain trust in what they offer, while simultaneously trying to prevent developing economies from becoming trustworthy enough to rebalance the global power equation. When the most powerful PR influencers in the world are from the West, how likely is the PR profession to remedy this imbalance? The next chapter moves on to another layer of global and national governance in the form of trade associations, and the campaigning activity mounted by these organisations to protect their respective industries from tougher regulatory measures.

Notes

1 This government political forum coalesces around annual summits, first organised in 1975 for the Group of 6 (G6) nations, then G7, G8, and more recently the G20.
2 A common currency would be backed by a federated government. The single currency only shares a common central bank.
3 These investors aim to profit from price inefficiencies in markets by making simultaneous trades that offset each other, capturing risk-free profits. Currency markets are a popular place for arbitrage techniques.
4 I cite one possible exception to this in Chapter 4, in my discussion of UK-based industry body, TheCityUK.

References

ADB (African Development Bank). (2009). *African Development Bank: Communication and External Relations Medium Term Strategy*, External Relations and Communications Unit. Tunis, Tunisia: African Development Bank.

Blinder, A., Ehrmann, M., Fratzscher, M., De Hann, J. and Jansen, D. (2008). 'Central bank communication and monetary policy: A survey of theory and evidence', *NBER Working Paper*, No. 13932, April.

Blinder, A., Goodhart, C., Hildebrand, P., Lipton, D. and Wyplosz, C. (2001). *How Do Central Banks Talk?* Geneva: International Center for Monetary and Banking Studies.

Bloomberg, M. (2009). *Financial Services Revitalization Plan*, 18 February, New York: New York City Economic Development Corporation.

Boak, J. (2012). 'Ben Bernanke's frugal PR push', *POLITICO*. Retrieved from: http://www.politico.com/news/stories/0312/74210.html

Bourne, C. (2015). 'Thought Leadership as a trust strategy in global markets: Goldman Sachs' promotion of the 'BRICs' in the marketplace of ideas', *Journal of Public Relations Research*, 27 (4), 322–336.

Caufield, C. (1996). *Masters of Illusion: The World Bank and the Poverty of Nations*, New York: Henry Holt.

CEMLA (Center for Latin American Monetary Studies). (2004). 'Code of principles and best practices in central bank communication', *CEMLA Central Bank Communication Group*, March.

Central Banking Events. (2013). *Communications and External Relations for Central Banks*, 17–20 September, London: Incisive Media.

Cohen, B.J. (2000). 'Life at the top: International currencies in the 21st century', *Cuadernos de Economía*, 37 (110), pp. 9–34.

Darling, A. and Bischoff, W. (2009). *UK International Financial Services – The Future*, London: HM Treasury.

De Goede, M. (2005). *Virtue, Fortune and Faith: A Genealogy of Finance*, Minneapolis: University of Minnesota Press.

Dodd, N. (2014). *The Social Life of Money*, Princeton, NJ: Princeton University Press.

Dooner, M. and McAlister, D. (2013). 'Investor relations and communications: An overview of leading practices in the OECD area', *OECD Working Papers on Sovereign Borrowing and Public Debt Management*, No. 6, Paris: OECD Publishing.

Ewing, J. and Erlanger, S. (2010). 'Trichet faces growing criticism in Europe crisis', *New York Times*. Retrieved from: http://www.nytimes.com/2010/05/21/business/global/21trichet.html?pagewanted=all&_r=0

Giddens, A. (1990). *The Consequences of Modernity*, Oxford, UK: Polity Press/Blackwell.

Gumbel, P. (2007). 'London vs New York smack-down: Will the real financial capital of the World please stand up?', *Fortune*, 27 August (14), pp. 22–28.

Hiebert, R.E. (1966). *Courtier to the Crowd: The Story of Ivy Lee and the Development of Public Relations*, Ames: Iowa State University Press.

Holmes, D.R. (2014). *Economy of Words: Communicative Imperatives in Central Banks*, Chicago: University of Chicago Press.

Holmes, D.R. (2016). 'Public currency: Anthropological labor in central banks', *Journal of Cultural Economy*, 9 (1), pp. 5–26.

Hosking, G. (2010). *Trust: Money, Markets and Society*, Chicago: University of Chicago Press.

House of Lords. (2011). 'Sovereign credit ratings: Shooting the Messenger?' *European Union Committee 21st Report of Session 2010–12, HL Paper 189.*

IIG (International Investment Guide). (2007). 'Peru: Entering a new golden age: Investment series 2007'. *Fortune, Special Advertising section*, 27 August, (14), pp. S1–S6.

Irwin, N. (2013). *The Alchemists: Inside the Secret World of Central Bankers*, London: Headline Publishing.

Kirsner, D. (2012). 'Trust and the global financial crisis'. In Long, S. and Sievers, B. (eds) *Towards a Socioanalysis of Money, Finance and Capitalism*, Abingdon: Routledge, pp. 278–291.

Kunczik, M. (2000). 'Globalization: News media, images of nations and the flow of international capital with special reference to the role of rating agencies', *IAMCR Conference*, Singapore, 17–20 July.

Kunczik, M. (2003). 'Transnational public relations by foreign governments'. In Sriramesh, K. and Verčič, D. (eds) *The Global Public Relations Handbook*, Mahwah, NJ: Lawrence Erlbaum, pp. 399–424.

Lambert, R. (2005). 'Inside the MPC', *Bank of England Quarterly Bulletin*, Spring, pp. 56–65.

Lapavitsas, C. (2007). 'Information and trust as social aspects of credit', *Economy and Society*, 36, pp. 416–436.

Malsch, B., and Gendron, Y. (2009). 'Mythical representations of trust in auditors and the preservation of social order in the financial community', *Critical Perspectives on Accounting*, 20, pp. 735–750.

Martin, R. (2002). *Financialization of Daily Life*, Philadelphia, PA: Temple University Press.

Mason, P. (2009). *Meltdown: The End of the Age of Greed*, London: Verso.

Mattinson, A. (2009A). 'Poor comms fuelled Dubai crisis', *PR Week*, 4 December, p. 9.

Mattinson, A. (2009B). 'Iceland launches financial charm offensive with FD', *PR Week*, 24 July, p. 1.

Meyersson, P. and Karlberg, P.P. (2012). *A Journey in Communication: The Case of Sveriges Riks Bank*, Stockholm: SNS Förlag.

Moody's. (2007). *Moody's Investor Service: Managing Director's Town Hall Meeting, Final Transcript. September 10*, New York: Moody's/AT&T.

Mutti, A. (2004). 'The resiliency of systemic trust', *Economic Sociology*, 6, pp. 13–19.

Partnoy, F. (2001). 'The paradox of credit ratings'. *Law and Economics Research Paper No. 20*. San Diego, CA: University of San Diego.

Popke, E.J. (1994). 'Recasting geopolitics: The discursive scripting of the International Monetary Fund', *Political Geography*, 13 (3), pp. 255–269.

Porter, T.M. (1995). *Trust in Numbers*, Princeton: Princeton University Press.

Pulsepoint. (2009). 'Chris Atkins on being a credit agency during the economic crisis', *Pulsepoint Group*, 1 July. Retrieved from: http://www.pulsepointgroup.com/2009/07/chris-atkins-on-being-a-credit-agency-during-the-economic-crisis

Resche, C. (2004). 'Investigating 'Greenspanese': From hedging to 'fuzzy transparency'', *Discourse & Society*, 15 (6), 723–744.

Riles, A. (2006). 'Real time: Unwinding technocratic and anthropological knowledge'. In Fisher, M.S. and Downey, G. (eds) *Frontiers of Capital: Ethnographic Reflections on the New Economy*. Durham, NC: Duke University Press, pp. 86–107.

Ross, A. (2013). *Creditocracy and the Case for Debt Refusal*, New York: O/R books.

Savage, J. (2011). 'Central bank communications: A view from Cleveland (really!)', *International Public Relations Association*. Retrieved from: http://ipra.org/itl/03/2011/central-bank-communications-a-view-from-cleveland-really

Seabrooke, L. (2014). 'Epistemic arbitrage: Transnational professional knowledge in action', *Journal of Professions and Organization*, 1 (1), pp. 49–64.

Seligman, A.B. (1997). *The Problem of Trust*, Princeton, NJ: Princeton University Press.

Shafik, N. (2013). 'Communication, engagement and effective economic reform: The IMF experience', *CIPR Annual Maggie Nally Lecture*, Houses of Parliament, London, 30 July.

Skinner, C. (2010). 'Can banks be trusted?' *The Financial Services Club's Blog*. Retrieved from: http://thefinanser.co.uk/fsclub/2010/11/can-banks-be-trusted.html

Smart, G. (2006). *Writing the Economy: Activity, Genre and Technology in the World of Banking*, London: Equinox Publishing.

Standard & Poor. (1986). 'Debt rating criteria', *Industrial Overview*, p. 3.

Swann, C. (2011). 'Steering between the BRICs and a hard place', *Financial World*, September, pp. 16–19.

Sweeney, P. (2001). 'Covering the World Bank'. In Thompson, T. (ed) *Writing about Business*. New York: Columbia University Press, pp. 180–187.

Tauberman, R. (2013). 'Rating S&P's words', *MWW/Absolute Value, Financial Communications and Investor Relations Blog*, 24 April. Retrieved from: http://www.mwwabsolutevalue.com/tag/crisis-communications/

Taylor, J. and Burt, E. (2005). 'Managing trust, generating risk', *Information Policy*, 10, pp. 25–35.

Tett, G. (2009). *Fool's Gold*, London: Abacus.

van Ham, P. (2002). 'Branding territory', *Millennium-Journal of International Studies*, 31, pp. 249–269.

Vayid, I. (2013). 'Central bank communications before, during and after the crisis', *Working Paper 2013–41*, Ottawa: Bank of Canada.

Vestergaard, J. (2009). *Discipline in the Global Economy*, New York: Routledge.

Warner, J. (2011). 'The governor-ready to rule the economy?' *Sunday Telegraph*, 29 May, p. 6.

Wigley, R. (2008). *London: Winning a Changing World*, London: Mayor of London/Merrill Lynch Europe.

Woods, N. (2006). *The Globalizers: The IMF, the World Bank and Their Borrowers*, Ithaca, NY: Cornell University Press.

Yandle, B. (2008). 'Lost trust: The real cause of the financial meltdown'. In George Mason University (ed) *Mercatus Center Working Papers*. Working Paper No. 09-02, February. Fairfax, VA: Mercatus Center, pp. 1–21.

Zucker, L.G. (1986). 'Production of trust: Institutional sources of economic structure', *Research in Organizational Behavior*, 8, pp. 53–111.

4 Financial trade associations

Territorial battles for trust

Chapter 4 continues the exploration of international financial centres, moving now to another layer of structural trust relations – the voluntary governance offered by trade associations (TAs). Whereas the international financial architecture polices financial markets from above, trade associations within these markets fight tooth and nail for the right to police *themselves*. Financial TAs primarily exist to protect market interests; as such, they play a visible role in the exercise of power over global financial markets, consistently and extensively producing and deploying power through collective influence (McKeen-Edwards and Porter 2013). Collective power requires organisation to function – it cannot rely solely on tacit understandings or secret backroom deals (McKeen-Edwards and Porter 2013). Since organising processes are communication-driven (Conrad and Poole 2012), the most effective TAs are full-time communicative vehicles, using internal communication to build cohesion between member organisations, lobbying policymakers behind the scenes, and using promotional techniques to argue their positions in the public sphere.

The chapter focuses on financial trade associations in London, the largest international financial centre, where nearly 50 trade associations represented UK financial services at the start of the 2010s (Patel 2013). While financial services may be a leading sector in the UK economy, historically, financial TAs had weak links with TAs in other sectors, weak alignment with the 'real' economy, and with UK society as a whole. As a result, financial TAs' trust strategies often recede in favour of mistrust strategies targeting authorities or competing sectors. These isolationist and combative approaches have stymied the UK financial sector's ability to rebuild trust after successive crises. Financial TAs are also known for employing questionable PR techniques (Measell 1992), leading to problematic outcomes in recent years. The chapter will explore some of the PR strategies used to defend the status quo in UK financial markets, particularly through industry lobbying in London and Brussels. The chapter illustrates the extent to which financial TAs use PR to perform 'boundary work' to control space in financial markets (Preda 2009).

Trade associations' role in financial markets

Trade associations come in many shapes and sizes, with differing representation and activities depending on the market economy in which they are
based. The defining characteristic of trade associations (TAs) is that they bring
together members who are otherwise competitors (Measell 1992). There are
three main interrelated ways that financial trade associations help produce and
deploy financial power (McKeen-Edwards and Porter 2013). The first role is to
influence public authorities, the second is to produce new markets and extend
existing ones, while the third is to enhance the capacities of particular members
(McKeen-Edwards and Porter 2013,p. 4). In practical terms, these roles involve
regular tasks such as gathering, analysing and disseminating authoritative information about their sector through consultation papers, guides and manuals
about industry practices; setting business standards for their industry; educating
stakeholders and dispelling myths through increased media presence; coordinating industry responses to political and legislative developments; representing
members and arguing cases at regulatory hearings; or just plain 'jumping up and
down' in a threatening fashion (Lascelles and Boleat 2002).

Much of this work is long-term, designed to create a climate in which
the industry's interests are more favourably received (Bourne and Edwards
2012), however a TA's focus can shift over time. Traditionally, the UK's financial TAs enjoyed cosy relationships with government, focused primarily on
information-gathering, churning out and disseminating routine statistics. However, as financial innovation proliferated, markets grew and the threat of regulation increased, more pressure was placed on financial services to defend its
special interests. The 2000s saw the formation of many more financial TAs, with
representation, lobbying and standard-setting assuming greater importance
(Lascelles and Boleat 2002). The greatest contemporary threat to a financial sector remains increased regulation and increased competition, particularly from
outside national borders. Trade associations therefore play an important role in
preserving the status quo – this leads to direct conflict with political authorities
and aggressive competition with other TAs for dominion over political markets.

Public relations plays an integral role in the communicative nature of trade
associations. Measell (1992) defines TAs as rhetorical organisations which *exist*
to carry out public education and lobbying – so much so that TAs are 'indige-
nous, if not ubiquitous, to contemporary public relations practice' (p. 225). Some
TAs are small and focused on single-issues. Others are large, high profile and
engaged in protracted PR campaigns. These large TAs have in-house PR teams,
as well as periodic support from external PR consultants. Large or small, financial TAs often focus their PR efforts on reputational issues in different market
sectors through media engagement, educational work including conferences
and training sessions, lobbying regulators and politicians, and engaging experts
to speak on the industry's behalf, as well as mounting defensive campaigns and
crisis communications as required. The power of PR when employed by trade
associations lies in the fact that where company narratives tend to have short

lives, perhaps three to five years before being discarded, industry narratives have 'long but contested lives' of up to forty years, particularly because industry narratives serve as an economising device for journalists, analysts and other market storytellers (Froud et al. 2006, p. 128). While these narratives seem publicly-oriented in tone, trade association PR is mostly aimed at rival stakeholder groups, with the general public as ill-informed bystanders (Corcoran and Fahy 2009). Indeed, since TAs must constantly justify their existence, their PR often works cynically to boost a TA's credibility with its own membership by convincing members their trade association is doing something useful.

My aim here is to explore trust, power and public relations in two areas of trade association activity in UK financial services – retail/consumer markets and wholesale capital markets. Whereas the UK's retail TAs have mostly domestic members, TAs in the wholesale markets juggle the requirements of members operating in various financial centres across Europe and the world (Patel 2013). This difference reflects the regulatory environment affecting both markets, with wholesale markets structurally changed by the shift in power from national to international regulatory bodies in the twenty-first century (Patel 2013). While the market sectors featured in Chapter 4 will be discussed in the context of collective trade association campaigns, several of these sectors will be explored vertically in other chapters: Chapter 6 covers the insurance, savings and investment sectors, while Chapter 7 is dedicated to banking sector. Wholesale activity such as hedge funds and bond trading is featured in Chapter 9. The discussion here focuses on issues of trust between individual TAs, and between the trade association landscape and government and regulatory authorities.

Emergence of financial trade associations in London

The UK financial sector is distinctive in the way its trade associations developed. Special interests in the UK financial sector were traditionally reluctant to practise open and formal representation with authorities, preferring informally created networks and control of their own affairs. Existing associations were often small and haphazard, with no permanent staff (Moran 1983). By contrast, other sectors of the UK economy understood that formal, bureaucratic approaches were the best way to influence policymaking; manufacturers, retailers and other services developed close contact with civil servants and participated in official advisory committees and executive bodies (Moran 1983). Equally, the level of cooperation between TAs in the financial sector and other economic sectors was weak. The powerful Confederation of British Industry (CBI) which represents UK big businesses eventually agreed to include financial sector members, but relegated them to associate membership for several years (Moran 2008).

The real transformation occurred when London's financial markets were liberalised in the 1980s. Multinationals replaced the dominance of family-owned firms, and financial relationships became more complex. London's lobbying environment became much more competitive, particularly in the aftermath of the EU's Financial Services Action Plan of 1999. The move toward a single market for financial services, the pre-eminence of European rules over national ones, and the creation of new markets such as Eurobonds, derivatives and hedge funds all required separate lobbying efforts (Lascelles and Boleat 2002, Moran 2008). At the start of the 2000s, there were some 50 financial TAs representing credit unions, building societies, hedge funds, vehicle leasing, mortgage lenders, hire purchase, stockbrokers, life insurance, life settlements, high yield, payment clearing services, underwriters, pension funds, futures and options, private equity and venture capital, bullion, primary markets, swaps and derivatives, and payday lenders (see Table 4.1 for the list of TAs featured in this chapter). This 'cacophony of voices' competes to defend geographic territory, avert proliferating regulation and demarcate legitimacy and expertise (Patel 2013). The landscape of UK financial TAs can be divided in two, with some TAs representing retail markets and others representing wholesale market interests. In retail financial services, TAs battle to protect the status quo particularly in the UK's

Table 4.1 Featured Trade Associations

AIMA	Alternative Investment Management Association	Hedge funds
AFME	Association for Financial Markets in Europe	Debt capital markets
ABI	Association of British Insurers	Life and general insurance
	Association of Financial Mutuals	Insurance
AIFA	Association of Independent Financial Advisers	Intermediaries
BBA	British Bankers Association	Banking
BIBA	British Insurance Brokers Association	General insurance
BVCA	British Venture Capital Association	Private Equity
BSA	Building Societies Association	Lending/Banking
CBI	Confederation of British Industry	Commerce
	Council of Mortgage Lenders	Lending/Banking
EFAMA	European Fund and Asset Management Association	Institutional investors
ELSA	European Life Settlements Association	Structured products
	Finance and Leasing Association	Lending/Banking
	International Capital Markets Association	Debt capital markets
IA	Investment Association	Institutional investors
	Lloyds Market Association	Insurance
ISDA	International Swaps and Derivatives Association	Structured products
	International Underwriting Association	Insurance
MFA	Managed Funds Association	Asset management
NAPF	National Association of Pension Funds	Pension schemes
	Peer-to-Peer Finance Association	Alternative lending
	The Payments Council	Card payments
	TheCityUK	Umbrella trade body
	UK Business Angels Association	Venture capital
	UK Cards Association	Card payments

mature market, where most consumers who need a financial product or service already have one. Some sectors, such as banking, have *several* associations working on their behalf (Lascelles and Boleat 2002). In wholesale financial services, market activity is marked by periods of extreme innovation followed by extreme regulation, which in turn shapes the campaigning activity of wholesale market TAs.

Retail financial markets – UK mis-selling scandals

Trade associations in UK retail financial services tend to be public facing and relatively high profile. Retail financial products play an important role in everyday life, attracting reams of daily coverage from the personal finance press. Furthermore, financial TAs come under close government scrutiny since long-term savings products operate as an outsourced form of welfare provision. While the market is diverse, this portion of chapter will focus on three main areas of retail financial services provision – insurance, investment management and banking. Although more than 30 TAs represent retail financial markets, three broad associations tackle a spectrum of issues (Patel 2013, Trade Associations 2015). The first of these, the Association of British Insurers (ABI), was created from the merger of various sector associations in 1985. The ABI now represents the general insurance, investment and long-term savings industry, and accounts for 90 per cent of insurance premiums in the UK market (Patel 2013). The second umbrella organisation is the Investment Association (IA), representing UK asset managers. The IA is also the result of a merger of several TAs in 2002; it now speaks for the majority of the UK's £5.7 trillion investment management industry (IA 2016). Finally, there is the British Bankers Association (BBA), formed in 1919; it has some 250 member organisations representing both retail and wholesale banking. At the time of writing, the BBA is currently contemplating a merger with other TAs representing mortgage lending and electronic payments.

Insurance, pensions and investment

The market for insurance products has thrived in the UK since the Victorian era. But insurance has repeatedly been a site of struggle with authorities, and the sector has repeatedly breached the public trust during that span. The industry recovered from significant mishaps, gradually developing a reputation for safety and respectability through increased regulation rather than industry campaigns. However, life insurance remains one of the most contentious sites of struggle in UK financial services because of its influence over the investment and pensions market, and the long-term duration of its risks. Life insurance is trusted as a guaranteed form of investment, preparing families for retirement and premature death (Alborn 2002). It is particularly popular with Britons who are 'the world's most insured people', paying more than 12 per cent of GDP on premiums, roughly a third more than Americans and nearly twice what Germans spend (Ferguson 2008, p. 200). UK life insurers gained significant financial power in the twentieth century when government permitted them to start investing in the rapidly globalising stock markets. By the mid 1950s, insurers owned a third of major UK companies (Ferguson 2008). The trend continued after liberalisation in the 1980s, when the state retreated from social security provision to the middle classes, exhorting every adult to become a shareholder. This effectively shifted trust (and risk) to financial providers, with new investment-linked products being introduced to meet growing demand (O'Malley 2002). Today, life insurance remains one of the main sources of UK investment finance and a keystone of modern financial trust structures (Hosking 2010).

Both the life and general insurance sectors have specialist trade associations, such as the Association of Financial Mutuals (for mutual insurers) and the British Insurance Brokers' Association (for brokers) (Patel 2013). However, the ABI has the resources to span the spectrum of life and general insurance matters, supported by a large in-house PR and public affairs team. For the ABI, the contemporary site of struggle with government is sharing the cost of public risks. With *general insurance*, many of these insured risks are unforeseen and dramatic. The ABI continually engages in debate over the industry's application of risk factors to motorists based on age or gender, for example. In the general insurance category, the ABI's major preoccupation concerns the impact of urbanisation and climate change on rising flood claims. The ABI (in line with European and North American counterparts) continues to lobby for regulation that would compel government and high-risk policyholders to share this growing risk. Meanwhile, in *life insurance*, the two long-standing issues concern the mis-selling of investment-linked products, and continuous legislative tinkering with pensions provision. The inherent risks in many investment-linked products were not made adequately clear to consumers, and many were mis-sold through providers incentivised by commission arrangements, resulting in several trust crises involving personal pensions, with-profits funds and precipice bonds, among others.

Since the 1980s, the ABI has dedicated more of its time to publicly addressing the mis-selling of investment-linked life insurance than any other issue. However, even the ABI concedes that it cannot successfully restore trust in the industry, since it cannot atone for individual behaviour by its members. According to the ABI, genuine trust restoration requires individual industry leaders to 'step up' (ABI 2015). Instead, it would seem that the ABI has opted, where possible, to shift public attention to other issues. It has done this successfully by declaring a 'pensions crisis' which has become one of the life and pensions sector's most enduring long-term narratives. This narrative has been ably supported by the UK personal finance press, which has picked up on the imagery of the pensions crisis as a 'ticking time bomb'. In portraying the pensions crisis, one ABI director (Segars 2005) summoned up the spectre of 12 million Britons not saving enough for old age, as state pensions declined in value, while employers withdraw from pensions provision. According to the ABI, these combined factors created a savings gap of £27 billion (Segars 2005), which poses a greater threat than the collapse of any UK insurer. While an upheaval in the pensions market has been undeniable, it has been linked with entirely foreseeable circumstances, including increased longevity in the UK population, overlooked by the very industry which positions itself as risk experts. The crisis in pensions remains a long-standing narrative promoted by both the ABI and the National Association of Pension Funds, which represents employers. PR has supported both narratives through speeches and industry surveys claiming widespread distrust in government's intention to safeguard private pension arrangements (Edmans 2003). The ABI did not step away entirely from attempts to restore trust in the insurance sector. Near the end of the global financial crisis, it published a report entitled *Rebuilding Confidence in Europe*. The report's primary aim was to distance UK insurers from the beleaguered banking sector, positioning insurers as trustworthy 'risk managers of the UK economy and society' who had 'weathered the crisis well' (ABI 2009 pp. 1–4).

In the post-crisis era, the ABI has occupied itself with the UK government's long-term 'personal responsibility' narrative (ABI 2015), behind cumulative transfers of retirement planning from the state to the individual. The 'personal responsibility' narrative has entered a new phase, driven by the government's inability to continue funding state pension for an expanding population of retirees. The ABI identifies this narrative as a source of tension between government and the insurance industry (ABI 2015). However, the resulting ABI rhetoric has been preoccupied not with consumers, but with employers who must 'shoulder the burden' of complying with state auto-enrolment requirements for personal pensions schemes. Amazingly, some of the ABI's promotional material on personal responsibility appears to blame consumers for sacrificing good savings habits in favour of instant gratification from consumer goods such as entertainment gadgets (ABI 2015). In health insurance, the ABI also champions its members rather than consumers, assertively positioning the industry to benefit from the UK government's creeping privatisation of the National Health Service. ABI publications isolate private health insurance as an ideal way to solve the insurance industry's main trust gap with consumers, by providing daily touch points for consumer engagement on health issues. Through private health insurance provision, the ABI identifies data applications or 'apps' and the 'internet of things' as a crucial means of building these daily touch points (ABI 2015).

Asset management

Like the insurance industry, asset managers have had vicissitudes in their relationship with UK governments. Various trade associations represent investment companies and wealth managers, but the largest of these, the Investment Association (IA), occupies the spotlight. The IA has continually defended the industry against accusations of exorbitant fees, poorly designed products, weak investment returns, as well as 'churning' – the practice of persuading consumers to surrender an existing investment product then take out a similar or less suitable one. The IA has also had to account for the conduct of companies its members invest in. UK asset managers have large shareholdings according them a much greater voice than 'mom and pop' investors. Yet despite vocal consumer concerns over excessive executive pay, corporate tax-dodging, unethical supply chains or weak corporate social responsibility (CSR), asset managers typically prefer to influence companies quietly via 'clubby' decision-making behind the scenes. In the post-crisis era, public rancour ran high over global corporations' puny UK tax bills. Activist groups targeted the IMA for claiming to engage with companies regarding 'over-elaborate tax planning'. The IA struggles to appear trustworthy on this issue since IA members are themselves structured to avoid as much tax as possible, promoting this as a selling point to clients (Hilton 2013). There are instances where the IA has successfully promoted the industry's mutual interest with government. For instance, UK asset managers and authorities have collaborated to strengthen promotion of the UK as a fund domicile, following competitive ground lost due to unfavourable tax rules and poor international marketing (HM Treasury 2013, IMA 2014).

Financial advisers

The final TA considered in the insurance, pensions and investment context is the Association of Independent Financial Advisers (AIFA). This TA is unique to UK financial services where independent financial advisers (IFAs) expanded in number, supported by changing regulation in the 2000s, only to have the regulatory rug pulled out from under them in the 2010s. AIFA has spent a great deal of time defending the professionalism and qualification of the IFA sector primarily from attacks by insurers and asset managers, who constantly accuse IFAs of lacking expertise. AIFA's defensive battles perfectly illustrate discursive power struggles between TAs for market share. In 2009, AIFA mounted a campaign to bolster IFA's trustworthiness and protect the sector from additional regulation by surveying trust levels across retail financial markets. The report became AIFA's flagship PR tool, since the survey revealed that IFAs were the *only* part of UK financial services experiencing strong levels of consumer trust, refuting contrary claims by the IA and the ABI. While the big industry trade bodies might plant the seeds of mistrust in IFA competence, AIFA argued that repeated surveys showed consumers trusted IFAs precisely for their perceived ability and competence, as well as their face-to-face customer relationships (AIFA 2009). The AIFA report attempted to shift the debate away from questioning IFA ethics or qualifications, and away from dismissing financial services as a failing sector to one of improving consumers' financial capability (AIFA 2009). The travails of the IFA sector will be discussed in further detail in Chapter 7.

Banks

The final area of collective retail financial campaigning discussed here is TA representation for the banking sector. Day-to-day retail banking is often positioned as a hygiene factor (current accounts, cash points and electronic payments are akin to financial 'plumbing'), but retail banking also represents one of the UK's most important forms of investing – not just individual savings, but more importantly, mortgage loans for the UK's most beloved assets, houses. Several TAs have represented this end of the retail banking spectrum, including the Building Societies Association, the Council of Mortgage Lenders and the Finance and Leasing Association (Patel 2013). Meanwhile, the hidden part of banking – the technology, electronic and card payments side – is equally well represented, by the UK Cards Association and The Payments Council. This side of banking has also had trust issues, including its widely criticised decision in 2009 to phase out cheques, a decision eventually reversed (Patel 2013). The BBA, the largest trade association representing the banking sector, was also the most visible throughout the 2000s and 2010s. Much of the BBA's PR activity during this period was crisis communication, illustrating the difficulties of representing an umbrella trade association and, as it turned out, defending the indefensible. The BBA mounted a number of PR offensives during this period, changing tack periodically with relatively little success. In the end, the BBA's own reputation was as sullied as the individual banking interests it represented across retail, commercial and wholesale banking.

In *retail banking*, the fallout from the run on Northern Rock, the 2007 credit crunch and the ensuing banking crisis meant that the trust restoration challenge faced by the BBA were unequalled in UK financial services. The issues were many: a massive taxpayer bailout for UK banks was met with arrogant, unapologetic behaviour by bankers, and continued 'fat cat' excesses in bankers' bonuses. The bank-bashing marathon continued in the post-crisis era. Consumer organisations lambasted banks for exorbitant current account fees and opaque pricing across their savings and current accounts. The BBA went into full combat mode, which undoubtedly led to missteps in its crisis response. The BBA chief executive waged an aggressive media relations campaign. During her five years as chief spokesperson, she gave more than 800 broadcast interviews, a thousand speeches and made nine appearances before the House of Commons Treasury Select Committee (McGhie 2012). Her PR team appeared equally staunch, even willing to destroy the BBA's general rapport with the media in order to assert the BBA's 'rightness' on the issues. At one event, the BBA's PR chief accused the media of assigning journalists with little experience in covering finance (Mattinson 2009A). There was no respite for UK retail banks in the post-crisis era, as the sector faced the largest retail financial product scandal in UK history, with revelations over the mis-selling of Payment Protection Insurance (PPI). The scandal uncovered serious conflicts within the BBA when the TA mounted a judicial challenge on the principle of mis-selling. The challenge was brought to a sudden halt when Lloyds Bank broke ranks with the BBA and paid compensation. Several BBA members blamed the TA's management for poor representation. The PPI scandal cost the UK banking sector upwards of £21 billion in compensation (Treanor 2016).

In *commercial banking*, the BBA's main issue concerned relationships between small businesses and the banking sector. Not only had banks promoted high-risk loans associated with interest rate swaps, leading to another mis-selling scandal, relationships with business owners worsened as banks stopped lending to small businesses altogether. The BBA adopted a more constructive PR stance on this issue, launching a Business Taskforce in 2010 to improve small business relations (Mattinson 2011). By then, however, many small businesses had already turned to alternative finance, such as crowdfunding and peer-to-peer lending. The burgeoning alternative finance market now has its own trade associations, including the Peer-to-Peer Finance Association and the UK Business Angels Association, promoting alternative finance. Finally, there is the Libor scandal – unique among financial scandals, since it was directly caused by a trade association. The BBA Libor price-setting mechanism was widely used to calculate interest rates for retail and wholesale financial instruments around the world. Libor was managed daily by the BBA, earning millions in annual fee income. BBA members had steadfastly refused to interrogate Libor's little-understood calculative process, claiming ignorance of its manipulation by member banks. The BBA was forced to cede control of Libor, and with it the valuable accompanying fee income. Libor class action suits were filed against the BBA, which may yet spell its epitaph. Meanwhile, BBA members voiced displeasure with the cost of their many overlapping TA memberships, and launched plans to merge the BBA with other TAs. By 2012, the BBA had a new chief executive and was less aggressive in its public tone, dedicating its annual conference to 'Restoring Trust' in the banking sector (BBA 2012).

Wholesale markets – product innovation and European regulation

Trade associations in wholesale markets are less visible to the general public, but have equally demanding representational needs. During the early 1990s, the International Swaps and Derivatives Association (ISDA) based in Washington DC set the benchmark for what financial TAs could achieve in wholesale financial markets. ISDA became a formidable force, lobbying aggressively with US Congress to alter proposals for national legislation when serious problems emerged with the industry's use of derivatives[1] (McKeen-Edwards and Porter 2013). The campaign was so effective that four anti-derivatives bills were shelved (Tett 2009). ISDA remains the primary source of governance in the multi-trillion-dollar market for over-the-counter debt instruments.

In the UK, the regulatory backlash following recurring crises in wholesale financial markets led the industry to realise that its collective voice was weak (Moran 2008). A period of consolidation took place giving rise to TAs such as the International Capital Market Association (debt capital markets) and the Association for Financial Markets in Europe (AFME), the latter covering the spectrum of wholesale markets issues, bringing in subscription revenues of almost £17 million in 2011 (Patel 2013). Other specialist TAs include the Loan Market Association (syndicated loans), the Futures and Options Association (mostly exchange-traded derivatives) and two associations representing insurance underwriters – the International Underwriting Association and Lloyd's Market Association. Although many wholesale market TAs are based in London, they typically represent institutions internationally (Lascelles and Boleat 2002). They are also far more EU-focused than their retail counterparts due to greater regulatory integration over wholesale financial instruments. London's wholesale market TAs must increasingly make their impact felt in the EU, where the scale of lobbying now surpasses that found in Washington DC (Corcoran and Fahy 2009). Brussels is wary of London-centric special interests. Consequently, wholesale market TAs have become more proactive, adopting a 'permanent' campaigning approach, drawing on tactics once characteristic of Washington DC (du Marchie Sarvaas 2011).

Brussels now regularly hosts more than 15,000 lobbyists organised into some 1,000 lobby groups, including PR and public affairs companies, law firms offering lobbying services, and think tanks with an estimated €1 billion in turnover (Corcoran and Fahy 2009). The sheer quantity of detailed EU regulation requires more specialist technical knowledge, with a corresponding need for more well-argued, published technical responses, where once a speech might have sufficed (Patel 2013). For PR practitioners in wholesale financial markets, permanent EU campaigning has led to greater professionalisation and integration of communications within TAs. A new generation of public affairs professionals has begun to lead TAs, streamlining communications, forming coalitions for joint campaigns, and using new media and other techniques for stakeholder engagement (du Marchie Sarvaas 2011).

Wholesale market TAs play a vital role in maintaining 'light touch' regulation, thus enabling continued financial innovation. This has long been the focus of the Alternative Investment Management Association (AIMA), the London-based hedge fund body. For decades, hedge funds were generally unregulated, and did not seek out the formal mechanisms that generate trust in mainstream finance. As natural 'outliers', hedge funds occupied the margins of the financial system by choice (Ertürk et al. 2010). Largely invisible to the general public, they generated profit from a relatively small global community of wealthy private investors. Stiff competition inevitably drove them to seek new forms of profit from mainstream investors, who have stricter regulatory requirements. Consequently, hedge funds needed to inspire trust from these new mainstream customers. AIMA therefore launched investor education campaigns, speaking out in favour of 'better' regulation, transparency and 'sound practices', and published a 'Due Diligence Questionnaire' and best-practice guides for hedge fund managers (Bourne and Edwards 2012).

Wholesale market TAs also work to legitimise the latest financial innovations, thus making new products appear more trustworthy to mainstream clients. In the UK, TAs were often responsible for introducing European markets to innovations previously created in North America. For example, the European Life Settlements Association (ELSA) launched in London in 2009 to promote 'life settlements', life insurance policies sold on to third parties as underlying assets for sophisticated investment products designed to manage longevity risk. Sometimes, UK associations are tasked with differentiating the performance of European financial products from North American counterparts. For example, AFME is a 'post-crisis' TA, created in 2009 from a merger of eight pre-existing TAs in order to promote securitisation – the process of pooling and repackaging high-risk assets into sophisticated investment products – in European markets. Securitised instruments were heavily implicated in the global financial crisis. AFME has worked assiduously to legitimise securitisation as a good thing for European markets with 'direct relevance to the real economy, including European auto, residential mortgage, SME, consumer and credit loans' (AFME 2012). AFME argued that while some categories of asset backed securities or ABS had defaulted during the crisis, the majority of European ABS 'were performing just fine' (AFME 2015, p. 12). AFME also launched a trust mark to help investors differentiate best-practice securitisations (AFME 2012).

As with their peers in retail financial markets, TAs in wholesale market have been critiqued on their response to the global financial crisis. There was enormous public pressure on governments to take visible action, and similar pressure on financial institutions to acknowledge what went wrong, and be helpful and constructive in providing solutions. Many financial TAs alienated stakeholders by arguing that their respective areas of finance hadn't caused the crisis at all. AIMA, the hedge fund TA, did so in 2007 when regulators identified short-selling,[2] a common hedge fund practice, as a contributor to the 'credit crunch'. Regulators' proposed ban on short-selling threatened to put some hedge funds out of business (Griffiths 2011). AIMA fought back, issuing press releases depicting short-selling as a widely accepted hedging and risk management technique, thereby situating short-selling in more readily trusted areas of mainstream finance (Bourne and Edwards 2012). AIMA and other financial TAs have been accused of arrogance, and of adopting a self-serving approach rather than spelling out how financial industry proposals benefit the broader economy or society (Levitt 2010). TAs have been further criticised for adopting a patronising tone with policymakers, and for invoking a climate of fear about the risks of regulation to the competitive position of international financial centres (Levitt 2010) wherever TAs are based.

The most contentious aspect of contemporary financial TA activity has been the toxic atmosphere created between the UK financial sector and the European Union, best illustrated by the aggressive campaign to thwart an EU directive designed to curtail trading in high-risk financial instruments. Commonly known as the 'hedge fund directive', the proposed regulation was implemented in 2011, but not before AIMA had lobbied London policymakers intensively, with hedge funds mounting a letter-writing campaign to the *Financial Times*, for example. AIMA lobbied both UK and EU policymakers and regulators before pitting one jurisdiction against the other. AIMA cast doubt in the knowledge and expertise of European regulators, while promoting UK regulators' legitimacy, grounded in the continued success of London as the world's largest international financial centre.

While AIMA's success in watering down the first version of the hedge fund directive was hailed as an example of effective media and regulatory engagement (Mattinson 2010), it dented the broader reputation of UK financial services in Europe. Some accused the hedge fund industry of unethical tactics, and 'buying off' UK politicians (Stewart 2009). The hedge fund industry was nominated for the 2010 'Worst EU Lobbying' Awards (WorstLobby 2010). For EU policymakers, AIMA's heavy-handed approach was considered short-termist, devoid of vision, and dismissive toward EU ambitions and concerns (Levitt 2010). Some trade associations distanced themselves from AIMA's approach. The British Venture Capital Association (BVCA), representing the UK private equity sector, was keen to differentiate private equity from hedge fund investing, and did not want the two asset classes lumped together under the same legislation. The BVCA's PR chief argued that while both industries represented 'alternative' assets, they had little else in common. The BVCA's PR chief engaged in the trust practice of simplifying – bifurcating the 'alternative' investment sector into hedge funds as 'masters of the universe-type institutions' (Mattinson 2009B, p. 8) versus private equity as trustworthy champions of growing businesses. The BVCA described its communications approach as 'decades ahead' of AIMA's in its focus on relationship building with EU regulators (Mattinson 2009B).

Conclusion

The chapter has highlighted examples of questionable engagement by London's financial TAs with regional and national regulators. In particular, London TA's forays in Brussels contrasted unfavourably with the constructive engagement between Brussels and TAs from the US and Europe (Levitt 2010). UK's financial TAs were too reactive, choosing to liaise only with a select list of EU politicians, while avoiding participation in EU think-tank discussions where early warnings on new policy initiatives often emerged. London TAs also avoided building cross-national alliances with TA counterparts across Europe (Levitt 2010). PR was typically reactive to problems once they had erupted, with TAs suddenly 'parachuting in' to Brussels to condemn proposed legislation. As I argued at the start of this chapter, organising processes are communications-driven (Conrad and Poole 2012). A successful TA must therefore be exceptional at PR, hence the UK's financial TAs must raise their game. Their self-seeking and inconsistent communication with members, with regulators and with each other has had a detrimental effect on public trust.

This is not to say that UK financial interests have been blind to the problem. TheCityUK was formed in 2012 to become UK financial services' foremost promotional body, and to rehabilitate the industry's reputation domestically, while championing its competitive interests abroad (Patel 2013). Recognising the persistent silos in UK financial markets, TheCityUK launched a programme to bring young financial professionals from various parts of financial markets together, to take a holistic view of the sector and develop a vision for London as a better-behaved financial centre (TheCityUK 2014). The programme is well-intentioned, yet TheCityUK is funded by membership subscriptions from the very financial institutions that are intent on maintaining the status quo, so the organisation's laudable programmes are unlikely to achieve radical change. Both the financial sector and the UK government are highly motivated to protect the status quo, since this protects London's position as a major international financial centre. Small wonder then that a planned regulatory review of the UK's banking culture was scrapped in 2015.

Viewing financial market TAs as trust mechanisms is idealistic, since TAs develop certain subjectivities, knowledge and expertise as 'regimes of truth' to normalise industry practice. Furthermore, Financial TAs commit discursive 'violence' through Darwinian struggles with authorities and between competing industries over market boundaries and demarcations. When financial TAs successfully defeat state efforts to curtail questionable market practices, this happens at the expense of consumers, taxpayers and citizens, illustrating TAs' capacity to normalise *un*trustworthy practices. Why then do financial TAs repeatedly launch trust restoration campaigns following financial crises? And why do they persist in these campaigns when even TA insiders acknowledge that 'trust restoration' over-steps TAs' role for a number of reasons. First, TAs do not, themselves, have capital at stake since they are not repositories for client assets (Patel 2013). Second, TAs can organise in order to communicate effectively, but true industry leadership comes from powerful individuals at the helm of powerful financial institutions, not from TA managers and staff (ABI 2015). Finally, TAs can neither hold members to account nor recommend change unless *all* members agree to change (Patel 2013).

Applying the trust practice framework, there are instances when TA activity looks like trust production. TAs often take the lead on simplifying complex industry issues, for example. Periodically, financial TAs align with other 'trust guardians', including consumer organisations, in highlighting consumer issues such as the need for long-term planning on UK flood protection or retirement provision. Despite this, many TA-led trust restoration campaigns seem to be less about building trust in specific industries and more about sowing the seeds of mistrust in policymakers and regulators, and in competing industries (Bourne and Edwards 2012). While the UK's extensive and highly competitive TA landscape is unique, as is London's position as a major international financial centre, it is indisputable that TAs exist to protect member interests, *not* the public interest. As power relations in financial markets continue to shift, it is only infrequently that industry interests and the public interest ever align.

If TAs are not focused on the public interest, it is unfeasible to assign a trust restoration role to such organisations, or to their PR advisers. Instead, what merits deeper scrutiny is the role played by PR in performing boundary work (Preda 2009) and exerting control over space in financial markets through the successful promotion of narratives that support the status quo. Trade association PR constructs many of the long-term narratives that organise trust and mistrust in financial markets. The next chapter takes a contrasting approach, exploring short-term narratives that inject excitement, adventure, as well as trust, into global stock markets.

Notes

1 A derivative involves financial commitments based on the performance of another financial instrument, e.g. when a seller of a Credit Default Swap promises to pay the buyer if a third party defaults on its debt.
2 Short-selling involves selling a security you don't own (borrowed from someone else in the market). If the price drops, you can buy back the stock at a lower price and make a profit on the difference.

References

ABI (Association of British Insurers). (2009). *The Insurance Industry: Rebuilding Confidence in Europe*, London: Association of British Insurers.

ABI (Association of British Insurers). (2015). *A Brave New World: The Changing Landscape for Insurance and Long Term Savings*, London: Association of British Insurers.

AFME (Association for Financial Markets in Europe). (2012). 'Finance industry launches 'PCS' securitisation label to revitalise market', *Association for Financial Markets in Europe. Press Release*, 12 June. Retrieved from: http://www.afme.eu/Documents/Press-Releases,-Comment-Letters,-and-Open-Letters.aspx

AFME (Association for Financial Markets in Europe). (2015). 'From words to action: AFME's fight for ABS pragmatism', *ABS Daily*, 17 June, pp. 11–19.

AIFA (Association of Independent Financial Advisers). (2009). *Restoring Trust in Financial Services*, London: Association of Independent Financial Advisers.

Alborn, T. (2002). 'The first fund managers: Life insurance bonuses in Victorian Britain', *Victorian Studies*, 45, pp. 65–92.

BBA (British Bankers Association). (2012). 'Restoring trust', *British Bankers' Association – Annual International Banking Conference*, 8 Northumberland Avenue, London, 17 October.

Bourne, C. and Edwards, L. (2012). 'Producing trust, knowledge and expertise in financial markets: The global hedge fund industry 're-presents' itself', *Culture and Organization*, 18 (2), pp. 107–122.

Conrad, C. and Poole, M.S. (2012). *Strategic Organizational Communication in a Global Economy* (Seventh Edition), Chichester: Wiley-Blackwell.

Corcoran, F. and Fahy, D. (2009). 'Exploring the European elite sphere: The role of the Financial Times', *Journalism Studies*, 10 (1), pp. 100–113.

du Marchie Sarvaas, C. (2011). 'New trends in EU trade associations', *Public Affairs World*. Retrieved from: http://www.publicaffairsworld.com/?q=trade-associations

Edmans, L. (2003). 'A market fit for consumers', *The Actuarial Profession 2003 Life Convention*, Hilton Birmingham Metropole Hotel, UK, 9–11 November.

Ertürk, I., Leaver, A. and Williams, K. (2010). 'Hedge funds as 'war machine': Making the positions work, *New Political Economy*, 15 (1), pp. 9–28.

Ferguson, N. (2008). *The Ascent of Money: A Financial History of the World*, London: Penguin Books.

Froud, J., Johal, S., Leaver, A. and Williams, K. (2006). *Financialization and Strategy: Narrative and Numbers*, Abingdon: Routledge.

Griffiths, T. (2011). 'Finding the industry's voice', *HFM Week*, March 16.

Hilton, A. (2013). 'Tax avoidance and the Vodafone twist', *Evening Standard*, 12 June, p. 44.

HM Treasury. (2013). *The UK Investment Management Strategy*, March. London: HM Treasury.

Hosking, G. (2010). *Trust: Money, Markets and Society*, Chicago: University of Chicago Press.

Investment Association. (2016). 'About', *Investment Association*. Retrieved from: http://www.theinvestmentassociation.org/about-the-investment-association/

IMA (Investment Management Association). (2014). 'Representations for Budget Report', *Chief Executive's Letter to the Chancellor of the Exchequer*. Retrieved from: http://www.theinvestmentassociation.org/assets/files/consultations/2014/20140213-imarepresentationsforbudgetreport.pdf

Lascelles, D. and Boleat, M. (2002). 'Who speaks for the city? Trade associations galore', *Centre for the Study of Financial Innovation, No. 58*, November.

Levitt, M. (2010). *Getting Brussels Right: 'Best Practice' for City Firms in Handling EU Institutions*, London: Centre for the Study of Financial Innovation.

Mattinson, A. (2009A). 'Banking industry lashes out at negative media coverage', *PR Week*, 23 January, p. 1.

Mattinson, A. (2009B). 'Private funds fight EU restrictions', *PR Week*, 1 May, pp. 8–9.

Mattinson, A. (2010). 'Funds' rule change victory'. *PR Week*, October 29, p. 11.

Mattinson, A. (2011). 'Banks go solo on SME comms', *PR Week*, 2 December, p. 13.

McGhie, T. (2012). 'Angela Knight Interview: Former banks' defender-in-chief admits huge bonuses were not always justified', *Mail on Sunday*, 30 September. Retrieved from: http://www.thisismoney.co.uk/money/news/article-2210564/INTERVIEW-Former-BBA-boss-Angela-Knight-admits-shocked-greed.html

McKeen-Edwards, H. and Porter, T. (2013). *Transnational Financial Associations and the Governance of Global Finance*, Abingdon: Routledge.

Measell, J.S. (1992). 'Trade associations: Whose voice? Whose vice?' In Toth, E.L. and Heath, R.L. (eds) *Rhetorical and critical approaches to public relations*, Mahwah, NJ: Lawrence Erlbaum, pp. 225–239.

Moran, M. (1983). 'Power policy and the City of London'. In King, R. (ed) *Capital and Politics*, Abingdon: Routledge Library Editions, pp. 49–68.

Moran, M. (2008). 'Representing the corporate elite in Britain: Capitalist solidarity and capitalist legitimacy', *The Sociological Review, Special Issue*, 56, pp. 64–79.

O'Malley, P. (2002). 'Imagining insurance: Risk, thrift, and life insurance in Britain'. In Baker, T. (ed) *Embracing Risk: The Changing Culture of Insurance and Responsibility*. Chicago: Chicago University Press, pp. 96–115.

Patel, K. (2013). *Batting for the City: Do the Trade Associations Get It Right?* London: Centre for the Study of Financial Innovation.

Preda, A. (2009). *Framing Finance*, Chicago: University of Chicago Press.

Segars, J. (2005). 'Pensions crisis: Will anyone fix it?' *BBC Online*, 4 January. Retrieved from: http://news.bbc.co.uk/1/hi/business/4119215.stm

Stewart, H. (2009). 'Boris Johnson accused over hedge funds' election donations'. *Guardian.co.uk*, October 11. Retrieved from: http://www.theguardian.com/politics/2009/oct/11/boris-johnson-hedge-funds-accusations

Tett, G. (2009). *Fool's Gold*, London: Abacus.

TheCityUK. (2014). *Next Generation Vision: A Positive Future for Financial Services*, London: TheCityUK.

Trade Associations Review. (2015). *Rethinking the UK Financial Services Trade Association Landscape*, London: Financial Services Trade Association Review.

Treanor, J. (2016). 'Government tax adviser 'sorry' for banking role during Libor crisis', *The Guardian*, 12 January. Retrieved from: http://www.theguardian.com/business/2016/jan/12/government-tax-adviser-angela-knight-apologises-mps-libor-rigging-crisis-role

WorstLobby, T. (2010). *Worst EU lobbying awards 2010*, Brussels: Corporate Europe.

5   Stock market storytelling

Dalliances with trust

Chapter Five focuses on investment in stock markets, one of the most visible areas of finance. While bonds and derivatives trading make up the bulk of global capital market activity, traditional stock exchanges are still perceived as the most direct connection between capital markets and the 'real' economy, enabling ordinary citizens to own shares in familiar and exotic companies. Professional investors regard stock markets as a paradigm of the good society, and the best source of long-term investment returns (Aldridge 1997). Ordinary investors and professional investors are all motivated to 'beat the market' (McGoun et al. 2003). While stock markets are a declining portion of global capital, stock exchanges are on the rise – there are now hundreds around the globe. The largest, most active stock exchanges are located in international financial centres, including the two largest, London and New York; as well as centres such as Hong Kong, Tokyo, Chicago, Frankfurt, Paris, Toronto and Zurich, Sydney and Johannesburg. These financial centres have expanded rapidly in size, complexity and distribution channels as more companies turn to the capital markets for finance, issuing bonds and shares, and merging with or acquiring other companies.

Unlike industry narratives promoted by trade associations in Chapter 4, stock market narratives have short lives and are constantly changing (Westbrook 2014). Rather than conjuring up notions of staid, trustworthy activity, stock markets are an incitement to adventure and exploration, a place of myths and legends, excitement, fashion and trends, even the 'visual abundance of corruption' (Ståheli 2008, p. 248). Such drama and excitement is achieved through storytelling. Capital markets are a discursive domain, where numbers – specifically price, value and capital – are bound together through storytelling and narrative (de Goede 2005, Westbrook 2014). Stock markets, in particular, are a 'marketplace of stories', crafted with the media in mind, engaging with investors' imaginations to stimulate excitement about future opportunities, enhancing investor acceptance of associated risks (Clark et al. 2004, Westbrook 2014). The value of stock market investments is bound up in the media image created by stories associated with public companies and their traded shares (Harrington 2008, Westbrook 2014). Hence, stock market storytelling is a crucial expertise, in which PR plays an integral role, positioning stock market investing as the discovery of hidden financial opportunities, and supporting overall market growth. The need for storytelling expertise has grown with the expansion of stock markets, and the complex network of global investors from ordinary shareholders to institutional asset managers, pension schemes and charities, to sovereign wealth funds and hedge funds. PR also supports the many consultants and specialists who provide services to stock markets – from global investment bankers, lawyers and accountants to financial technology firms, as well as the stock exchanges themselves.

Stock markets as opportunity and discovery

Why do stock markets draw so heavily on storytelling, dramatic staging and visual narrative? The promotion of stock exchanges helps transform their locations into themed, 'Disneylike' environments (McGoun et al. 2003, p. 648), where investors can adopt the figure of the adventurer (Stäheli 2008). Markets offer the promise of romance, thrilling movement and freedom, with the seductive appeal of the 'crash' that ends it all (McGoun et al. 2007). In this respect, investors also experience the 'emotional surges of gambling' without the unsavoury associations with organised crime (McGoun et al. 2003, p. 650). This theatrical approach to promoting investments is linked with the invisible nature of the 'products' created by stock markets. In the language of economic production, the investor produces 'prices' and nothing else – such an immaterial, 'lacking' product is phenomenally difficult to represent (Stäheli 2008, p. 244). Consequently, market actors adopt various means of representation to help investors to 'see' inside the stock market (Stäheli 2008). Seventeenth-century stock exchange buildings were designed along classical lines, borrowing from Greek temples and amphitheatres (Stäheli 2008). London-based broker John Castaing collated and published stock, commodity prices and exchange rates in *The Course of the Exchange*, an important forerunner to the nineteenth-century stock ticker (Crosthwaite 2014). 'Ticker tape' expanded stock market boundaries so that the market existed everywhere (Stäheli 2008). Stock exchanges still have a geographic location, but the real activity takes place outside the physical buildings, with virtual locations extended by twentieth-century inventions such as electronic display boards, computer screens and, eventually, broadcasts of daily trading on financial television.

Now that many stock exchanges have replaced the visual theatre of open-outcry trading with silent electronic trading, exchanges rely even more heavily on PR and other promotional techniques to create stock market spectacles. At the London Stock Exchange, companies and dignitaries invited to open the day's trading undergo a PR ritual that is 'part symbolism, part theatre' (Stafford 2016, p. 15). They stand on the first floor of the new London Stock Exchange (LSE) building's atrium and drop a Perspex block into a slot, at which point, screens and a globe below light up, carrying the first share prices and indicating that the day's trading has begun (Stafford 2016). Similarly, at the New York Stock Exchange (NYSE), companies stage promotional freebies at the NYSE's iconic Wall Street location on the day of stock market flotation. Some companies hire live bands to entertain passers-by, while one pesticide company even handed out insect-flavoured biscuits to drum up attention for its flotation (Green 2014). Nasdaq, New York's other major exchange, is fully automated, yet it too takes part in theatrical spectacle by maintaining premises in the centre of Times Square. Nasdaq rebranded in 2014 with the strap line 'Ignite Your Ambition'. Its Times Square storefront now features a two-storey-high interactive digital wall featuring images and social media inviting passers-by to interact with the markets (Maddox 2014).

Many investment companies draw on advertising, marketing and PR to construct brands with strong associations of romance and exploration. Some UK investment companies are named after constellations – Jupiter Fund Management, Neptune Investment Management, Taurus, and New Star Asset management. Others draw their names from mythology, such as Hermes Investment Managers, Artemis Fund Managers and Janus Capital. Still others draw on the exotic landscapes – Sierra, Parnassus, Polar Capital and Ignis Asset Management. Then there are funds themselves, e.g. Fidelity's Magellan or Spartan International or Primecap's Odyssey Funds. Vanguard, the world's largest index fund, is named for Horatio Nelson's ship. Investing also promotes fashionable investment styles and destinations – absolute return funds and exchange-traded funds, emerging markets funds or BRICs funds.

Investment companies can also 'breathe life' into less-than-compelling propositions through sporting events, which account for as much 52 per cent of the financial industry's sponsorship budgets (Miller 2013, Hampson 2014). South African investment firm Investec is associated with Britain's derby festival, women's hockey, test cricket, rugby and golf. BNY Mellon is the latest in a line of investment firms to sponsor the annual Oxford-Cambridge boat race. Artemis closely associates its brand with sailing, sponsoring a race at the annual Cowes Week festival around the Isle of Wight. In the US, Lincoln Financial Group sponsors the NFL football team, the Philadelphia Eagles, and owns the naming rights to Lincoln Financial Field, the team's stadium (Lincoln Financial 2016). TD Ameritrade partnered with the 2014 Winter Olympics to promote a crowdfunding campaign for up-and-coming US athletes (Hampson 2014). While sponsorships can breathe remarkable, if sporadic, excitement into investing, the most theatrical stock market storytelling medium is 24/7 news television (Clark et al. 2004). Of course, television has been effective in engendering desire in all sorts of products, hence television viewers are particularly valuable to most brands (Tkacik 2011). Financial television, however, has special clout because mainstream media does not typically employ financial journalists, and avoids forensic coverage that might bore audiences, opting instead for financial stories focused on personalities, events, intrigue and public controversy (Doyle 2006). Twenty-four-hour financial television can offer forensic rigour, while simultaneously injecting excitement by 'visualising the market' through techniques such as rapidly circulating stories that provide the daily fuel for programming, representing financial stories through personality and celebrity, promoting fashionable products and investing styles, producing and catalysing emotion – all backed by a constant moving display of multiple stock market tickers, global clocks and ever 'breaking' news (Clark et al. 2004, Stäheli 2008).

Among the best-known financial TV brands are Bloomberg and Reuters, the global news agencies which also operate cable TV channels. Other channels include CNBC, Fox Business Network, Sky News Business, BFM Business (France), DAF TV (Germany), Intereconomia Business (Spain), and ET Now and CNBC TV-18 (India). CNBC's programming format quite deliberately resembles ESPN's 'Sports Center', with its colourful array of constantly shifting real-time charts, graphs and indices, supported by 'futuristic' sound effects (Tkacik 2011). Thus, financial television 'ramps up' the excitement of storytelling to investors, focusing on those company earnings offering the element of surprise while ignoring those which do not (Westbrook 2014, p. 190). Financial TV channels have created new avenues for promotional activity. PR consultants target TV producers and anchors who may have worked in investment markets themselves, putting forward investment experts as spokespeople. Understanding television as medium is an integral skill; on financial TV, the best 'talking heads' excel at quips and sound bites. PR support often includes specialist media training to prepare spokespeople for the bewildering programme format, and liaising with producers to find out what makes for 'great TV'.

Rise of trust-based investing

While the visual aspects of stock market storytelling might instil a degree of trust by *opening up* stock markets, this is largely a by-product of visualising investment as adventure. By contrast, concerted efforts to build *trust-based* investing began in the early twentieth century, with a drive to include mass citizenry in stock market activity. In the US, this drive stemmed from the need to overcome mistrust between various groups within the market and outside it. Within stock market enclaves, the 'old guard' of sophisticated, professional investors disagreed with new, reformist retail brokers over the need to embrace the 'smaller' investor. Outside the markets, workers' groups attacked large corporations for their 'soulless' behaviour, leading many companies to set up PR departments to demonstrate that their organisations had a conscience (Marchand 1998, Traflet 2013). It was hoped that cultivating an image of popular share ownership would counter criticisms of the stock market as a 'private club' for wealthy elites. The NYSE already relied on PR by the early 1900s, establishing its first PR department, known as the 'Library Committee', which eventually became the 'Committee on Public Relations' in 1935 (Traflet 2013). While less reputable brokers unabashedly used advertising to attract smaller investors, the NYSE favoured PR, deeming advertising too undignified and unethical for esteemed financial professionals (Traflet 2013).

The Great Stock Market Crash of 1929 drove a wider chasm of mistrust between small and large investors. Immediately after the Crash, many bankers blamed little investors for turning a market decline into a full-fledged crash through their lack of financial knowledge or strength, and allegedly panicky behaviour (Traflet 2013). Average Americans were equally disillusioned with professional investors, following the US government's well-publicised market investigation into the crash (Traflet 2013). Those Americans who had doubted the morality of stock market investing, only felt deeper distrust. In the post World War II period, the NYSE still laboured under the 'Shadow of 1929'. Despite rising disposable personal income levels, Americans overwhelmingly chose to place their savings elsewhere – bonds, life insurance, real estate or savings accounts. In 1952, only 4 per cent of Americans owned any common stock, below the 1920s level of 15 to 20 per cent (Traflet 2013, p. 4). Retail brokerage firms desperately needed more business. The NYSE 'craved legitimacy' so that more Americans would invest, and launched a promotional campaign in the early 1950s to bring more small investors into the stock market.

The campaign 'Own Your Share of American Business' ran from 1954 to 1969. It drew on US concerns with communism and the Cold War, positioning the NYSE as a 'citadel of capitalism' (Traflet 2013, p. 10). Here, trust strategies were definitely employed: the NYSE established trust by aligning share ownership with principles of US democracy, positioning the investor as 'patriot' (Harrington 2008, Stäheli 2008, Traflet 2013). The campaign's PR elements included speeches, promotional films, books, educational seminars and promotion in schools – all designed to assure different stakeholders that small investors were 'average' investors (Traflet 2013). The successful campaign led to a surge in personal finance magazines offering advice on money-related issues (Davidson 2012). British efforts to 'democratise' stock market investing began rather later, triggered by extensive market liberalisation in the 1980s. UK promotional efforts included the eponymous 'Sid', the 'average bloke', promoting the flotation of state-run British Gas (Aldridge 1997). The success of campaigns in the US, UK and elsewhere drove stock market growth, rapidly increasing the number of investors, and an influx of professionals marketing advice on the bewildering array of investment opportunities and complex forecasting techniques (Olsen 2004). These increased connections across time and space, together with the need to position investment as part of a rational market democracy increased the need for system trust.

Trust-based narratives

Trust-based investment narratives are shaped by a 'priestly caste' who interpret the mysteries of the market from their various positions of technical competence (Olsen 2004), whether CEOs of publicly listed companies, research analysts, investment bankers, fund managers, stock brokers or the media. What matters first and foremost is who decides what investments are trustworthy by endorsing, modifying and challenging investment narratives regarding a stock's investment value and profit potential (Harrington 2008, Westbrook 2014). No one source controls market narratives, so the various storytellers act as checks and balances in the flows of trust and mistrust.

Public relations represents the range of investment storytellers, shaping attitudes toward financial markets in ways that unlock value – whether by promoting a new company share issue or company results, or building credibility in the experts who opine on companies, or on new investing styles and market trends (Westbrook 2014).

Research analysts are ever-present investment storytellers who want to be trusted for producing the best ideas to 'beat the market'. These prominent 'sell-side' storytellers' create charts, graphs and interpretations of company information, 'hyping' up companies and 'puffing up investment fashions' in order to earn commissions from the buying and selling of shares (Davis 2007, pp. 216–217). Analyst reports need to communicate trust with clients through attentiveness and added-value offered through daily stock tips and special insights into the market. Asset managers also need to communicate trust to their clients, as well as to global investment consulting firms who rate fund manager performance. Both research analysts (sell-side) and asset managers (buy-side) have repeatedly compromised their status as trust intermediaries due to conflicts of interest in the way they operate. Sell-side analysts were once the 'rock stars' of stock market storytelling, while markets also hung on every opinion issued by 'star' fund managers. But analysts are conflicted by their firms' desires to underwrite and sell securities, starkly revealed after the dot.com crash in 2000. Fund managers are conflicted by mediocre performance and the rise of passive funds (of which more later). Yet these expert perspectives are still regularly reported on by the financial media, particularly the 24/7 financial channels in need of 'content' to fill the airwaves. Analysts and fund managers willingly provide 'rent-a-quotes' to fill this airtime. PR professionals work hand-in-hand with the media to promote these 'rent-a-quotes'. In so doing, PR props up stock market activity in a way that is largely untrustworthy, yet undeniably colourful and compelling.

CEOs as chief corporate storytellers

For public companies, building trustworthy relationships with investors increases the likelihood that investors will become long-term shareholders (Chandler 2014). Some public companies focus on meeting minimum disclosure requirements, while others use hyperbole to boost future expectations. But the more value-laden route to attracting long-term investors entails compelling stories based on a company's *present* strategy, position and performance, thus stimulating excitement and enthusiasm for the future (Westbrook 2014). PR techniques help develop corporate stories, perhaps tracing a company's history of venturing into new markets or successful crisis recovery (Westbrook 2014). Communications tools used to develop these narratives and promote trustworthiness include annual reports, results presentations and regular company updates. PR practitioners also promote specific plot developments such as raising further investment through share issues, building support for mergers and acquisitions, or offering strategic and crisis communications support.

During a market upturn, PR focuses most on 'sell-side' activity, raising the company's profile with research analysts, brokers and the media. In a market downturn, it becomes crucial for companies to build long-term relationships with core investors, conveying an impression of good management, seeking a fair share price and building trust with key stakeholders (Westbrook 2014, p. 91). 'Buy-side' communications is the specialism of investor relations (IR) practitioners, responsible for rapport with active and activist shareholders, corporate legal counsel, compliance and risk. In both markets, PR is required to maintain good shareholder relations by garnering investor perceptions of company and market activity.

PR plays an integral role in building trust with long-term investors by presenting the CEO as 'chief storyteller' (Westbrook 2014). A good CEO embodies several trust strategies, while balancing competing concerns and keeping promises to multiple stakeholders. CEOs are trusted to provide *transparency* through timely, reliable information to investors, including financial problems or changes in strategy. A CEO's interests are supposedly tightly aligned with investor interests through ownership of stock options tied to the market value of their firms. If CEOs can fulfil their promises, they embody trust in the form of *guarantees*. CEOs must demonstrate alignment with market regulation, by walking the 'tightrope' of rules concerning market disclosure (Chandler 2014, p. 169). The most effective 'chief storytellers' can strengthen trust relations even further by personalising the company through the cult of the CEO (Davis 2013, Becker et al. 2014). However, trust discourses are neither linear nor straightforward. In Anglo-American markets, system trust in stock markets is now heavily intertwined with the late-twentieth-century ideology of shareholder value. Shareholder value's main tenet is a higher share price, which vastly simplifies the challenge of 'beating the market'. CEOs' generous salaries are typically linked to share price, through stock options. This can lead to particular problems, even operating as a mistrust strategy (Pixley 2004). First, linking CEO pay to share price has encouraged CEOs to take a short-term approach to the role, even as CEOs encourage investors to take a long-term approach to the company – a misalignment of trust. CEOs increasingly move on to new roles after three to five years, and are conflicted by the temptation to cash in stock options after very short holding periods. At the same time, market regulation and risk-averse legal teams constrain what CEOs can say in public.

Consequently, a common feature of stock markets is CEOs manipulating company narratives (via PR advisers) in order to boost the company's share price, glibly explaining away a company's performance issues only months before they announce their resignation. Company directors may abuse their insider information, selling out in the 'nick of time' (Pixley 2004). Working in tandem with their PR advisers, these chief storytellers can be skilful at subterfuge, waxing lyrical in the media about the success of the business in boosting sales in some specific area, when one bright spot might mask an otherwise negative set of numbers. CEOs may also trade information as a commodity by leaking information about future earnings to analysts, in order to forewarn the market of what is to come. These effectively withhold information from select investors such as uncooperative analysts (Swedberg 2005), while forging stronger links with favoured journalists and analysts. Furthermore, CEOs are able to employ mistrust techniques to spread rumours about other companies or run market interference. PR practitioners representing CEO interests are known to have brokered share tips with financial editors, particularly during market upturns (Pitcher 2003). Equally, PR is involved in defending CEO and company interests against mistrust campaigns, going directly to key stakeholders 'behind the scenes' and sharing information off the record with the media.

Corporate accounting can also pose a damaging clash between trust-based investing and shareholder value. As trust guardians (Shapiro 1987), accounting and audit professionals are supposed to safeguard system trust by setting standards, then scrutinising companies against those standards (Turner 2009). However, company accounts are often used to drive shareholder value through 'impression' management (Brennan and Merkl-Davies 2013). Impression management often constructs a facade of trust, as was the case with Tesco, a major UK supermarket chain, caught misrepresenting its accounts to the stock market. Tesco deferred payments to suppliers for as much as two years in order to boost its own operating margins, resulting in a £326 million fraud reportedly hidden from external auditors (Simpson 2016). For years, Tesco suppliers had campaigned over unfair treatment, but the powerful supermarket always defended itself vigorously in the media. Yet the shareholder still reigns supreme – Tesco suppliers may never be fully compensated, but Tesco shareholders have been free to launch a class action suit against the company (Chesters 2016).

Tesco was highly respected before manipulating its operating margins. Other companies choose to go 'rogue' altogether, setting aside staid messages linked with long-term investing, concentrating on drama and excitement instead. US energy company Enron remains one of the most spectacular examples of rogue behaviour of its era, using theatrics to entice both sophisticated and ordinary investors. Enron once made its money from gas pipelines, but by 2000, Enron had reinvented itself in energy trading and related services, and had become the seventh-largest company in the Fortune 500 (McLean 2001). Yet no one could explain how Enron actually made money. Its asset valuations were suspect, many of its transactions were opaque and hidden off balance sheet, but its theatrics fooled investors for years. The name 'Enron' was a last-minute revision of the Greek word 'Enteron' proposed then quickly amended by Enron's PR firm when it emerged that 'Enteron' meant 'intestines' rather than 'pipeline' (Boje et al. 2004). CEO Jeffrey Skilling enjoyed promoting theatrics; he cultivated the image of Darth Vader, the infamous villain of the *Star Wars* franchise. He referred to his energy traders as 'Storm Troopers', while naming various Enron offshore vehicles after *Star Wars* imagery – JEDI LP, Chewco, KenobeInc and Obi-1 Holdings. One of the company's divisional chiefs added to market spectacle by riding in on elephant to promote one of Enron's Indian ventures (Boje et al. 2004).

Back at headquarters, Enron performed transparency through trading days using simulated trades to educate analysts about how the Enron trading process worked (Westbrook 2014). The company trumpeted its risk management skills and 'magical' numbers (Pitcher 2003, Westbrook 2014), while investing substantially in a PR approach intended to keep its publics unaware (Boje et al. 2004). Enron had a large internal PR, investor relations and lobbying operation, as well as external PR agencies across the US, UK, Europe, Japan and Australia (Williams 2001). Enron was a large political campaign contributor, and had a cosy relationship with the Bush administration. Enron spent extensively on advertising, bragged about corporate values on its website, and paid large sums to prominent pundits and economists to advise the company chairman (Holmes 2002). As the truth about its poor cash flow and unprofitability began to emerge, experts began to question Enron's credibility and offload company shares. Enron's share price fell, its chief executive resigned and the firm was forced to report an initial US$618 million loss (McLean 2001). Since Enron's collapse marked the 'rise' of corporate America's trust restoration industry, how did Enron's own PR officers make sense of their role in constructing Enron's facade? PR directors reported hearing rumbles that Enron was not doing well. The rumbles intensified when Enron's CEO refused to field simple questions about company operations from financial journalists. If many analysts and journalists had neither the time nor expertise to dissect Enron's complex facade, then neither apparently did Enron's PR advisers. Eventually, these supposed Enron 'trust strategists' found their access to company management cut off altogether, as the lawyers took over (Boekelheide 2011). The Enron PR advisers' claims of ignorance may be credible, yet it positions PR experts as mere pawns rather than trust strategists.

'Rogue' corporate activity of the scale of Enron may not be a regular stock market occurrence, but corporate battles are. Mergers and acquisitions (M&A) often pit companies and stakeholders against each other via narratives of mistrust (Buenza and Stark 2005). In 'friendly' M&A transactions, PR's role is to make sure both sides 'sing from the same hymn sheet'. By contrast, in contested battles, PR often boosts one side's credibility as a bidder or attacks the trustworthiness of the opposition. A company's debut onto the stock market through a flotations or initial public offering (IPO) can also be contentious as companies strive to 'debut' on the stock market with a 'high' share price. Flotation objectives therefore require compelling narratives to bring new company listings to life (Westbrook 2014). PR activity prior to flotation takes place openly – through carefully placed news stories drumming up interest in the company, and through road shows staged by company management, essentially closed-door meetings giving large investors a privileged window into the company (Rusli et al. 2012). Closed-door promotional activity can present trust issues, particularly as smaller investors are left out of the loop. Facebook's infamous IPO caused an uproar over unfair access to information. When Facebook floated on the stock market in May 2012, its investment bankers shared a negative outlook about the company, but only with select analysts who adjusted their Facebook growth estimates accordingly. Unsurprisingly, ordinary investors felt that Facebook's IPO had been rigged against them (Rusli et al. 2012).

Why trust the experts? DIY investors resist

Enron's showman-like illusions and Facebook's allegedly rigged IPO are just two of many stock market scandals that have led some ordinary investors to fight back. Grass-roots investors now target the 'profit-hungry sharks' who provide investment advice, the powerful and corrupt companies that abuse smaller investors, and even the 'egg-headed intellectuals' whose theories about beating the market are now discredited (McGoun et al. 2003, p. 657). Empowered by relaxed regulation across many jurisdictions, these DIY investors now generate an 'effloresence' of market stories (Harrington 2008, p. 49). For these grassroots investors, the digital era has been both a blessing and a curse. On the one hand, the internet bombards small investors with thousands of confused and distorted financial messages (Hermann 2007, Harrington 2008). On the other hand, the internet has been a great equaliser for DIY investors, because 'ownership rights' to investment narratives are no longer the exclusive domain of insiders. Real-time financial information is now regularly generated by internet media channels, financial bloggers, chat rooms and other social media, empowering entrepreneurial 'day' traders and ordinary investors.

The digital era has also levelled the playing field for smaller companies suffering from reduced analyst and media coverage. They can now provide information to markets globally and quickly, communicating via electronic newsletters, websites and social media. The digital era has also opened up a discursive space for DIY financial experts. Websites such as Motley Fool contain robust contrarian narratives woven into their advice (McGoun et al. 2003). Other sites such as Seeking Alpha essentially 'crowd source' advice through more than 4,000 professional and nonprofessional author-analysts (Saxton and Anker 2013). High-quality bloggers can earn a living through clients and advertising revenue based on the frequency and quality of their financial posts. With thousands of new financial 'experts' engaged in their own self-promotion and PR activity, market 'high priests' and their PR advisers have lost some power over investment storytelling amidst the 'narrative cacophony' of contemporary stock markets (Harrington 2008, p. 51). Nevertheless, many PR practitioners have fought back, embracing the blogosphere as a means of fire-fighting lies spread about clients or spreading rumours about competitors, with a corresponding impact on share price (Westbrook 2014).

Shareholder resistance and market warfare

While DIY investors may resist the stock market status quo, they lack the collective power to disrupt it altogether, since the vast majority of shares are held by institutions. It is left to these institutions to resist in a more organised way. Since the 1990s, many fund management houses have switched part or all of their product range to passive or 'tracker' funds, which track and replicate relevant stock market indices directed by algorithms. Passive fund managers do not need to generate or promote their own ideas, and they pay little attention to the corporate image that public companies attempt to project. With passive funds, if a company is part of an index, it will be tracked. Another form of resistance is pension fund socialism, which seeks control of investment in order to serve other stakeholders, not just shareholders, concentrating for example on community investment in infrastructural projects (Langley 2008). Other pension funds and charities apply ethical or environmental 'screens' to the companies they invest in – avoiding 'sin' stocks such as alcohol, tobacco or gambling, or selecting stocks in companies promoting human rights or renewable energy. Ethical investment funds are also actively promoted to investors through roadshows, investor education and brochures – so much so that ethical investing is now seen as emotive marketing rather than a means of resistance. Nor are 'ethical' funds a straightforward product. Many use outdated screens that no longer reflect investor concerns (Hyde 2013). Others are opaque, failing to fully disclose their shareholdings. Langley (2008) argues that invoking the 'ethical investor' as a subject of dissent, then packaging and promoting that category as a product contained genuine attempts to politicise everyday investment, but is today little more than promotional misdirection.

The most powerful form of stock market resistance is 'shareholder activism', which uses voting power from substantial share ownership to push for shareholder rights and company reforms, resisting company share buy-backs or even ousting recalcitrant management. Through giant public sector pension schemes, charities and NGOs, shareholder activism became a key site for contestation between capital and labour (Langley 2008). But these institutional investors no longer dominate global shareholdings; that power has passed to hedge funds. Unlike other 'dissident' shareholders, hedge funds have little interest in discovering intrinsic value in long-term shareholdings. Instead, hedge funds exploit discrepancies, unearthing a company's untapped potential or exposing its faults – a lagging stock price or relative underperformance (Buenza and Stark 2005, Westbrook 2014). Once hedge funds acquire enough company stock, they commonly demand seats on the board, asset sales, sale of the entire company or return of capital through stock repurchases or special dividends (Westbrook 2014). Thus, what is referred to as 'hedge fund activism' amounts to stock market warfare in which hedge funds attempt to plant seeds of mistrust in companies' long-term value stories to achieve market volatility in order to 'beat the market'.

Hedge fund activism has boosted opportunities for financial PR advisers on both sides of the stock market 'battlefield', particularly since hedge funds create drama and seek out media 'oxygen' wherever they stand to make profit off resulting market volatility or corporate disputes. Hedge fund managers pose as journalists, calling company press offices hoping to extract sensitive information, or to stir up stories of their own. Hedge funds use PR advisers to support their activist campaigns, although not all hedge fund-led shareholder revolts receive wide support (Mattinson 2009). Equally, public companies use PR to defend hedge fund disruption of company narratives, even initiating *secret* dialogue with hedge funds to avoid media scrutiny (Westbrook 2014). Companies may also hire proxy advisers to help 'bring out the vote' when hedge fund activists air their issues. When market relations become warfare, PR practitioners become military strategists rather than trust strategists. Unlike long-term investors, hedge funds have low personal risk; they typically do not use their own money to speculate, borrowing cash or securities instead. Hedge funds operate more as traders than investors, using hedging techniques so that if one trading position doesn't work out, theoretically the other position should. While they are not trust-neutral, hedge funds have a lower dependency on market trust relations (Leonidou et al. 2008).

Stock market adventures in the risk management era

The relentless pressure of shareholder value, the growth of algorithmic tracker funds and the expansion of hedge fund influence have all transformed stock markets beyond their original purpose and potentially ended trust-based investing. Fibre-optic technology catalysed high frequency traders who exploit volatility which creates new prices they can see before the rest of the market, then trade in microseconds, leaving traditional professional investors unaware. High-frequency trading has diluted stock market democracy, creating a class system based on speed 'haves' and 'have-nots' (Lewis 2014, p. 34). Private exchange mechanisms, second-hand markets and small, start-up exchanges now trade voluminous levels of global capital, dwarfing the world's most iconic stock exchanges. When two of these iconic exchanges, the London Stock Exchange (LSE) and Deutsche Börse merged in 2016, neither mentioned their traditional stock exchange business. Instead, their press announcements focused on synergies from their newer business areas – clearing houses, global indices, market data and analytics (LSE 2016).

In more than a century of formal PR support in stock markets, the fluid nature of PR as an occupation has allowed it to adapt to every major new market development, re-inventing itself in response to periods of boom or bust, thus transporting PR work into new areas of market growth (Pitcher 2003). The one constant for PR has been the stock market's inexorable need for stories of drama, adventure and exploration. Fibre-optic cabling has triggered not only high frequency trading but also high frequency newsgathering and rumour-mongering as thousands of stock market storytellers transmit company news around the world in minutes. PR consultants certainly participate in this new information game. But PR is far less able to 'stage-manage' and control market news through established mechanisms such as investor road shows, general meetings or conference calls (Pitcher 2003). The speed of information and rumour now exacerbates the risks of managing reputation, thus increasing demand for PR counsel. Companies are under greater pressure than ever from long-term institutional investors who want their shareholdings to deliver stability, reduced costs and risk-free approaches (Westbrook 2014). This increased pressure has led many public companies to back away from stock market financing, opting instead to hoard company capital or spend it on dividends, share buy-backs and executive options – all designed to enhance share price without the risks associated with innovation, product and people development (Clark 2013). In Western markets, which remain governed by low interest rates that have even dipped below zero per cent, companies have many cheaper capital-raising options, which impose less public scrutiny.

Olsen (2004) argues this risk management era is the backlash to repeated 'trust-driven bubbles' where market booms are followed by financial crises. While stock market malfeasance did not cause the global financial crisis, long-term investors – the market's trust-based investors – continue to spread caution throughout their investment portfolios. Since short-term traders (hedge funds and arbitrageurs) depend little on trust and control ever-larger portions of the market, stock market PR is busily reinventing itself as management consultancy (PR Week 2012). Elsewhere in financial markets, PR is tasked with presenting an image makeover for the banking sector, while behind-the-scenes, banks re-engineer their business models. The banks' trust restoration campaign is the subject of the next chapter.

References

Aldridge, A. (1997). 'Engaging with promotional culture: Organised consumerism and the personal financial services industry', *Sociology*, 31 (3), pp. 389–408.

Becker, J., Einwiller, S.A. and Medjedovic, J. (2014). 'The effect of incongruence between CEO and corporate brand personality on financial analysts' attitudes and assessment of a company's performance', *International Journal of Strategic Communication*, 8 (3), pp. 146–159.

Boekelheide, A. (2011). '10 years later: Behind the scenes of the Enron scandal', *USC Annenberg News*, 10 November. Retrieved from: http://annenberg.usc.edu/news/around-usc-annenberg/10-years-later-behind-scenes-enron-scandal

Boje, D., Rosile, G., Durant, R.A. and Luhman, J.T. (2004). 'Enron spectacles: A critical dramaturgical analysis', *Organization Studies*, 25 (5), pp. 751–774.

Brennan, N. and Merkl-Davies, D.M. (2013). 'Accounting narratives and impression management'. In Jack, L., Davison, J. and Craig, R. (eds) *The Routledge Companion to Communication in Accounting*, London: Routledge, pp. 109–132.

Buenza, D. and Stark, D. (2005). 'How to recognise opportunities: Heterarchical search in a trading room'. In Knorr-Cetina, K. and Preda, A. (eds) *The Sociology of Financial Markets*. Oxford: Oxford University Press, pp. 84–101.

Chandler, C.S. (2014). 'Investor relations from the perspective of CEOs', *International Journal of Strategic Communication*, 8 (3), pp. 160–176.

Chesters, L. (2016). 'Another day of shame for Tesco', *Daily Mail*, 26 January, p. 61.

Clark, G.L., Thrift, N. and Tickell, A. (2004). 'Performing finance: The industry, the media and its image', *Review of International Political Economy*, 11 (2), pp. 289–310.

Clarke, N. (2013). 'Deconstructing the mythology of shareholder value: A comment on Lynn Stout's 'The shareholder value myth'', *Accounting, Economics and Law – A Convivium*, 3 (1), pp. 15–32.

Crosthwaite, P. (2014). 'Framing finance'. In Crosthwaite, P., Knight, P. and Marsh, N. (eds) *Show Me the Money: The Image of Finance, 1700 to the Present*. Manchester: Manchester University Press, pp. 35–59.

Davidson, R. (2012). 'The emergence of popular personal finance magazines and the risk shift in American society', *Media, Culture and Society*, 34 (1), pp. 3–20.

Davis, A. (2007). 'The economic inefficiencies of market liberalisation: The case of financial information in the London Stock Exchange', *Global Media and Communication*, 3(2), pp. 157–178.

Davis, A. (2013). *Promotional Culture*, London: Polity Press.

De Goede, M. (2005). *Virtue, Fortune & Faith*, Minneapolis: University of Minnesota Press.

Doyle, G. (2006). 'Financial news journalism: A post-Enron analysis of approaches towards economic and financial news production in the UK', *Journalism*, 7(4), pp. 433–452.

Green, T. (2014). 'Big Board's still the place to be for a slice of the real share action', *Evening Standard*, 3 July, p. 61.

Hampson, M. (2014). 'TD Ameritrade grabs gold in 'PR Campaigns' during Sochi games', *McGrath Power Public Relations and Communications*, 13 March. Retrieved from: http://www.mcgrathpower.com/2014/03/13/td-ameritrade-grabs-gold-pr-campaigns-sochi-games/

Harrington, B. (2008). *Pop Finance: Investment Clubs and the New Investor Populism*, Princeton, NJ: Princeton University Press.

Herrmann, A.F. (2007). 'Stockholders in cyberspace: Weick's sensemaking online', *Journal of Business Communication*, 44 (1), pp. 13–35.

Holmes, P. (2002). 'The Enron scandal impacts every aspect of PR – Part 2', *The Holmes Report*, 28 May. Retrieved from: http://www.holmesreport.com/latest/article/the-enron-scandal-impacts-every-aspect-of-pr-part-2

Hyde, D. (2013). 'Ethical funds: good investments or emotive marketing?', *Daily Telegraph*, 20 October. Retrieved from: http://www.telegraph.co.uk/finance/personalfinance/investing/10389799/Ethical-funds-good-investments-or-emotive-marketing.html

Langley, P. (2008). *The Everyday Life of Global Finance*, Oxford: Oxford University Press.

Leonidou, L.C., Talias, M.A. and Leonidou, C.N. (2008). 'Exercised power as a driver of trust and commitment in cross-border industrial buyer-seller relationships', *Industrial Marketing Management*, 37, pp. 92–103.

Lewis, M. (2014). *Flash Boys: A Wall Street Revolt*, New York: WW Norton & Co.

Lincoln Financial. (2016). 'A winning investment: About the sponsorship', *Lincoln Financial Group*. Retrieved from: https://www.lfg.com/LincolnPageServer?LFGPage=/lfg/lfgclient/abt/lff/win/index.html

LSE (London Stock Exchange). (2016). 'Potential merger of equals between London Stock Exchange Group plc ('LSE') and Deutsche Boerse AG ('Deutsche Boerse')', *Press Release: Regulatory News Service. RNS Number 9016P*, 23 February.

Maddox, K. (2014). 'Nasdaq launches rebranding campaign, 'Ignite your ambition'', *Advertising Age*, 8 October. Retrieved from: http://adage.com/article/btob/nasdaq-launches-rebranding-campaign-ignite-ambition/295326/

Marchand, R. (1998). *Creating the Corporate Soul*, Berkeley: University of California Press.

Mattinson, A. (2009). 'Shareholders stand up to boards and turn to financial PR to make their case', *PR Week*, 27 May, p. 8.

McLean, B. (2001). 'Is Enron Overpriced?', *Fortune*, 5 March. Retrieved from: http://archive.fortune.com/magazines/fortune/fortune_archive/2001/03/05/297833/index.htm

McGoun, E.G., Bettner, M.S. and Coyne, M.P. (2007). 'Money n' motion – born to be wild', *Critical Perspectives on Accounting*, 18, pp. 343–361.

McGoun, E.G., Dunkak, W.H., Bettner, M.S. and Allen, D.E. (2003). 'Walt's Street and Wall Street: Theming, theatre, and experience in finance', *Critical Perspectives on Accounting*, 14, pp. 647–661.

Miller, M.J. (2013). 'Financial brands continue love affair with sports sponsorships', *Brand-Channel*, 11 November. Retrieved from: http://brandchannel.com/2013/11/11/financial-brands-continue-love-affair-with-sports-sponsorships/

Olsen, R. (2004). 'Trust, complexity and the 1990s market bubble', *The Journal of Behavioral Finance*, 5 (4), pp. 186–191.

Pitcher, G. (2003). *The Death of Spin*, Chichester: Wiley & Sons.

Pixley, J. (2004). *Emotions in Finance: Distrust and Uncertainty in Global Markets*, Cambridge: Cambridge University Press.

PR Week. (2012). 'FTI launches London-based research arm', *PR Week*, 20 January, p. 13.

Rusli, E.M., Protess, B. and De La Merced, M.J. (2012). 'Questions of fair play arise in Facebook's IPO process', *New York Times Dealbook*, 24 May. Retrieved from: http://dealbook.nytimes.com/2012/05/23/regulators-ask-if-all-facebook-investors-were-treated-equally/

Saxton, G.D. and Anker, A.E. (2013). 'Financial blogs and information asymmetry', *Journal of Communication*, 63, 1054–1069.

Shapiro, S.P. (1987) 'The social control of impersonal trust', *American Journal of Sociology*, 93 (3), pp. 623–658.

Simpson, E. (2016). 'Tesco knowingly delayed payments to suppliers', *BBC News*, 26 January. Retrieved from: http://www.bbc.co.uk/news/business-35408064

Stafford, P. (2016). 'Bourse tie-ups put clearing risk in spotlight', *FT Weekend*, 5/6 March, p. 15.

Stäheli, U. (2008). 'Watching the market': Visual representations of financial economy in advertisements'. In Ruccio, D.F. (ed) *Economic Representations: Academic and Everyday*. Abingdon: Routledge, pp. 242–256.

Swedberg, R. (2005). 'Conflicts of interest in the US brokerage industry'. In Knorr-Cetina, K. and Preda, A. (eds) *The Sociology of Financial Markets*. Oxford: Oxford University Press, pp. 187–206.

Tkacik, M. (2011). 'The real housing crisis of Orange County'. In Schifrin, A. (ed) *Bad News: How America's Business Press Missed the Story of the Century*, New York: The New Press, pp. 122–147.

Traflet, Janet M. (2013). *A Nation of Small Shareholders: Marketing Wall Street after World War II*, Baltimore, MD: The Johns Hopkins University Press.

Turner, A. (2009). *The Turner Review: A Regulatory Response to the Global Banking Crisis*, London: Financial Services Authority.

Westbrook, I. (2014). *Strategic Financial and Investor Communication: The Stock Price Story*, Abingdon: Routledge.

Williams, H. (2001). 'Enron axes PR firms and staff outside US', *PR Week*, 7 December. Retrieved from: http://www.prweek.com/article/117086/enron-axes-pr-firms-staff-outside-us#LAHcGfoGJMFtajcB.99

6   Changing banking models, shifting trust relations

Chapter 6 explores trust communications *across* the banking system, and the intersection between everyday banking and wholesale banking. No single area of financial markets has faced a larger trust conundrum than the banking sector. Structurally, the banking system sits high on the hierarchy of trust relations within nation states. The banking system underpins trust, allowing strangers to reduce risks by pooling their resources for more reliable returns. Applying the trust practice framework, banks employ the most powerful trust practice of all – protecting assets of millions of individual customers, small and large businesses, charities and governments. However, while we might be attracted to a particular bank for its special product offers or services, it is actually the wider banking system we trust. Since we have little choice in having to deal with banks, we give little thought to the illusory nature of that trust – it is an illusion that suggests our funds are readily accessible, when most are tied up in long-term loans of securitised instruments. We unconsciously trust the system to work on the basis that everyone will not need to withdraw their cash at the same time. Even more unconscious is the notion of who 'everyone' is – not only are banks highly interconnected, many large banks are further interwoven into the global banking system – so our bank may be dependent on faceless customers millions of miles away.

From the 1980s to 2000s, banks enjoyed a market-driven era, during which they promoted their scope, scalability and geographic reach (Sotelino and Gonzalez 2012). Many large banks are publicly listed, thus pressured to deliver shareholder value. This they did through acquisitions, increased 'efficiencies', shedding unprofitable business lines and creating new product lines through financial innovation. The success of these market-driven strategies drove unprecedented growth; the UK banking sector became four times larger than the UK economy. Banking success also created and spread risky, opaque financial instruments around the globe, helping to trigger the global financial crisis. Customer and shareholder trust in banks reached an all-time low. Above all, banks did not trust each other, as no one could be sure which banks were harbouring what toxic instruments. The sheer size and importance of banking to national economies meant that bailing out the banking system became a precondition for rescuing national economies. It was the banking system rather than individual banks that was deemed too big to fail (*Economist* 2008), but the most interconnected banks received secret government support long before 'official' bailouts (Mason 2009).

At first glance, the image of banking would seem to be the opposite of stock market investing featured in Chapter 5. There is little about everyday banking that conjures up excitement, romance and adventure. Everyday banking is perceived as necessary, but dull. Regulatory restrictions constrain how everyday banks promote financial products, and the products are largely the same – one bank's current account, savings account, and mortgage looks very like another's, making it difficult for consumers to compare benefits, structure and pricing. Differentiation is an integral tactic in PR campaigns for everyday banking, and is further complicated by the many financial providers selling banking products in large, mature markets – from retail banks, building societies, cooperatives, mortgage brokers, and even 'white-labelled' products sold through department stores or mobile phone providers. PR for everyday banking has long focused on the three 'e's' – choice editing, third party endorsement and financial education – designed to underscore several trust practices, including guaranteeing, aligning, opening up and simplifying (Bourne 2013). 'Choice editors' include family, friends and like-minded people who can help consumers make purchase decisions (FSA 2005). PR supports choice editing by sourcing case studies, targeting personal finance media and featuring 'like-minded' people sharing hints, tips and personal experiences that humanise banking products (Dye 2007). Third party endorsement goes further than choice editing, lending credibility and trust to financial products through 'seals of approval' from authoritative sources, league tables and industry surveys (Ehrlich and Fanelli 2004). Third party endorsement can notably produce *mis*trust, by naming and shaming providers who rip off customers (Dye 2007). The third 'e', financial education, explains how financial products and services work, clarifying associated risks and simplifying complex terms. Financial education is often carried out by government departments, regulators and consumer organisations (Bourne 2013).

PR techniques are very different in wholesale banking, which is less regulated since customers are presumed to be more sophisticated in financial matters. Wholesale banking encompasses corporate and investment banking. Corporate banking targets businesses with corporate loans, treasury and cash management, equipment lending, trade finance and commercial real estate. However, modern wholesale banking is best defined by investment banking, which creates capital for companies, governments and other entities by financing company flotations, mergers and acquisitions, arranging bond issues and structuring a range of complex instruments. Many investment banks also promote and trade shares, bonds and structured products. Global investment banks, such as Goldman Sachs and Morgan Stanley, are able to provide all these services across multiple jurisdictions, tapping on powerful positions held by banking alumni in governments, global stock exchanges, central banks and development banks. Global investment banks therefore wield significant influence in global market trust relations, disciplining markets through rules and mechanisms of inclusion and/or exclusion to determine which investments are trustworthy and which are not (Hardt and Negri 2000, Bourne 2015). For investment banking to work, people must implicitly trust the ability of its experts to demonstrably reduce risk by delivering anticipated returns on managed investments (Giddens 1990, Bourne 2015). Investment banks leverage this expertise to produce an impressive track record in market transactions, cementing an investment bank's trustworthiness (Turnbull and Moustakatos 1996). To this end, the key criterion for investment banks is their 'culture of smartness' and ability to 'wow' clients by assembling colonies of the brightest people in the world under one roof (Ho 2009, p. 40).

PR for wholesale banking often uses influential financial media to mobilise support for banks from elite stakeholder groups in companies, governments and international institutions (De Cock et al. 2011). One effective communications tool for mobilising support and trust in wholesale banking is thought leadership – a firm's 'intellectual firepower' assembled and published in communications material designed to transform the way we think (McCrimmon 2005, Brocklebank-Fowler 2008). Thought leadership builds trustworthiness in wholesale banking activity in a number of ways. First, it helps banks establish authority when entering new markets or when introducing untested, risky product innovations (Shaughnessy 2011). Second, thought leadership can demonstrate a firm's commitment to a specific field (e.g. clean energy technologies or infrastructure), so that even the largest firm can appear specialist. Third, thought leadership is scalable, so a firm can issue research to thousands of prospects whom it would take years to visit (Czerniawska 2012). Sustained thought leadership programmes require significant resources which global investment banks possess. Once their 'big ideas' are generated, banks have an army of analysts, technical writers, communication specialists, sales people and business heads to develop and distribute ideas, then monitor and curate content (Hayes 2013, Noble 2014, Bourne 2015).

Because wholesale banking is less regulated than retail banking, risk is viewed attractively since greater risks can generate greater profits. Risk in wholesale banking is often couched in terms of exploration and bold initiatives taken at the 'frontiers of finance' (Giddens 1999). Wholesale bankers take on *other* people's risks on a large scale, pricing these risks and packaging them up to be sold via financial products and services, thus distributing risk away from wholesale clients who are best able to purchase safety and freedom from risk (Beck 1992, Giddens 1999). Derivatives, collateralised debt obligations and other structured products are promoted to elite stakeholders as a means of *reducing* risk throughout the banking system. Risk-reducing instruments were promoted so successfully in the 2000s, that even central bankers and finance ministers waxed lyrical about the wonders of financial engineering. The appetite for risky products exceeded the banks' PR and marketing efforts. But risk has its winners and losers. When there are enough losers, borrowing and lending becomes constrained, and markets become risk-averse and 'freeze up'. Wholesale banking became the 'crucible' of the global financial crisis – an inappropriate appetite for high-risk products, including murky structured investment vehicles, exposed many banks to large unsecured debts, while inconsistent accounting practices and inappropriate credit analysis improperly evaluated product risks. Corporate banking also contributed to the crisis, particularly through over-concentration on property. In Ireland, where land value tripled from the 1990s to 2000s, property developers became such a powerful customer base they were all but running the banks before the property bubble burst, taking the Irish economy with it (Carswell 2011). Since banks such as Barclays, Citigroup, Credit Suisse, HSBC and ING had become 'universal banks', combining the full range of retail and wholesale services, the toxic wholesale activities affected the banks' overall performance and reputation. Some banks were able to absorb other faltering banks before needing support themselves. The initial regulatory response was that banks needed to split their retail and wholesale operations, severing 'good' banks from 'bad'. The banks' response was to launch a trust restoration offensive.

Trust restoration offensive and banking PR

Addressing the negative public perception of banks was the most prominent communication challenge in the aftermath of the global financial crisis (Makovsky & Company 2012). Onlookers might have expected the first phase of the trust restoration offensive to follow established crisis communications protocol – complete disclosure of errors or wrongdoing in order to prevent later retractions and further destruction of trust, a 'full and heartfelt apology', acceptance of responsibility, restitution to victims and a description of steps taken to repeat any recurrence (Conrad and Poole 2012, p. 456). In the early phases of the banks' trust restoration offensive, the opposite happened; senior bankers behaved defensively, arrogantly and unapologetically, with full or partial support from PR advisers. How could PR strategists have allowed the banking sector to commit such an extensive faux pas? Several answers present themselves. At least one large bank had lost experienced members of its PR team to personnel changes and retirement; in this instance, PR counsel to senior management may have been weak. Many large banks are publicly listed, and directors might have sacrificed short-term reputation in order to minimise litigation risks and plummeting share prices if they admitted culpability.

Equally, in an industry where bank PR teams are often organised like palace troops, ready to do battle for their assigned product lines, many seasoned communicators had become inured to repeated uproars over scandals in the banking sector. PR, IR and public affairs teams were accustomed to waging endless skirmishes with journalists, activists, politicians and institutional shareholders. Powerful banking PR machines had spent years 'leaning' on journalists regarding coverage, while lobbyists had spent hundreds of millions pressuring politicians and regulators (Amos 2009, TBIJ 2012). When bankers appeared at public hearings to account for their role in the crisis, their 'insincere', 'over-rehearsed' PR performances and lack of contrition (Mattinson 2009A) reflected their battle-hardened advisers. Some PR advisers felt that politicians deserved more blame than the bankers but had successfully deflected it with populist rhetoric (PR Week 2010). A sense of injustice pervaded commentary by financial PR advisers in the PR trade press. Financial PR experts lamented public vitriol toward PR's attempts to promote even 'mildly positive' articles either human-ising bankers or defending the banking sector's contribution to the economy (Gray 2007, Miles 2009). There was a feeling that the bankers had lost the rhetorical battle with government, with each side trying to scapegoat the other (PR Week 2010). Governments' successful populist rhetoric also hinted at more clever, nuanced PR counsel in government circles, while the banking sector continued to communicate in a more heavy-handed manner through its trade associations (see Chapter 4). Some global banks even threatened to relocate to other jurisdictions (Pixley 2012). The most heedless PR 'own goal' by a banker may have former Barclays CEO Bob Diamond's decision to call for an end to banker apologies and remorse while at a UK parliamentary hearing in 2011 (Wilson and Armitstead 2011). As he soon discovered, the public disagreed.

Can the public's continued hostility toward the banking sector years after the financial crisis be blamed on weak PR counsel? Even the sagest PR counsel would have encountered giant obstacles in the effort to rebuild trust in banks. First, despite hefty taxpayer bailouts in several countries, bankers refused to mend their ways, adding insult to injury by rewarding themselves with excessive bonuses. Wholesale banks were discovered rigging crucial Libor interest rate benchmarks and foreign exchange rates. In the UK, several investment banks were found to be avoiding corporate tax. Investigations into banking prac-tices yielded everything from rogue traders, questionable regional hiring prac-tices, dealings with international terrorists, cocaine barons and 'rogue nations' (Atherton 2012, Metro 2012, English 2013). Despite record fines, legal set-tlements, resignations, suspensions and the occasional incarceration, wholesale banking culture remained unchanged. Meanwhile, malfeasance was prevalent on the retail side of banking too – public scandals erupted over the mis-selling of income protection insurance to consumers, and inappropriate interest rate swaps to small businesses (*Evening Standard* 2013, *Economist* 2014). Retail banks translated increased regulatory requirements into more stringent terms for mortgage lending and other forms of borrowing, particularly for younger cus-tomers and the over-50s. Little was done to improve the dismal array of bank-ing products, with their bewildering interest rates and terms, excessive charges and overdraft fees. Consumers continued to be annoyed by unsolicited cross-selling of personal loans, general insurance and credit card offers. Customers were strong-armed into 'free-if-in-credit' current accounts, which cost the cus-tomer over the long-term yet are difficult to compare when shopping around. More irritating still were continuous computer meltdowns as banks struggled with legacy computer systems in a digital age.

There was arguably little that PR could do to redeem the banking sector in the public's eyes, since bankers were doing little to redeem themselves. The communications response was to reflect the regulatory mood by separating perceptions of 'good' dull, everyday retail banking from 'bad' high-octane, risky wholesale banking, thus engaging in the trust practice of simplifying. Retail banks spoke repeatedly about the need to restore trust, while conceding that it might take a generation for banks to be trusted again (Shaw 2014). Wholesale banks largely gave up on mainstream PR activity in the post-crisis period (Hilton 2010). This second phase of the trust restoration offensive was heavily intertwined with the same marketing discourse that had long governed retail banking – a twentieth-century marketing discourse bent on 'valorising' the consumer (Knights et al. 2001, p. 439). This valorisation of the consumer intensified in the twenty-first century through relationship marketing, which invokes the need to 'engage' with the consumer in an ongoing relationship regardless of whether the organisation has anything immediate to 'sell'. Underpinning this marketing discourse is a relentless need for information about the customer: one bank regularly surveyed its own brand's trust levels by talking to 300 customers and 150 non-customers every month (Delin 2013). Other banks launched surveys benchmarking their reputation against competitors (Mattinson 2009B). What these retail banks learned came as no surprise. Several years after the crisis, people continued to distrust banks. But while they might not like banks and feel underserved by them, consumers felt they had nowhere else to go. So retail banks took the approach that time would heal all wounds, and focused instead on promoting more emotional connections with consumers, complete with friendlier products and services (Barda 2008, Hargreaves 2011).

During this emotional 'reconnection', UK bank NatWest explained why it was trustworthy by promoting its customer charter. NatWest also promoted its friendly, intrepid mobile service for rural customers. Lloyds Bank celebrated its 250th anniversary by promoting itself as a reliable source to turn to in a domestic crisis (Hargreaves 2011). The new CEO of Santander's UK operation, Ana Botin, announced that she would put customers at the heart of the bank (Cartmell 2011), without explaining where customers had previously been positioned. Barclays's Bob Diamond attempted to erase memories of his 'time to move on' speech by delivering the BBC's inaugural business lecture exploring ways for banks to restore trust through good citizenship (Diamond 2011). In the US, several banks began replacing branch bank tellers with a 'cafe' format for customers to get gourmet coffee and free Wi-Fi. What customers could not do in the new cafe format was drop off a loan application or sit with a banker to open an account (Rexrode and Sidel 2015).

Across various markets, banks introduced new customer incentives such as free magazine subscriptions, cinema vouchers and competitions for small businesses to win prize money. Bank marketing and PR teams slowly abandoned cynicism toward social media. Banks overcame regulatory and compliance constraints governing marketing communication, revamping clunky websites, increasing interactive communication and optimising mobile phone use (PR Week 2008, Fidelzeid 2013). There are now 'kitemarks' acting as trust guarantees in digital banking 'apps', even though there is still little external guidance on how much a current account really charges. Coutts, the private bank, followed European competitors in launching video banking, enabling customers to see and talk to advisers over mobile devices round-the-clock (Arnold 2014). Online bank First Direct encouraged crowdsourcing techniques including social media feedback on product and site designs for QR (Quick Response) codes (Barber 2011). Some banks encouraged online discussion forums to tackle customer problems or clarify product issues, but others proved half-hearted in responding to social media comments.

In view of Barclays's repeated transgressions in fixing foreign exchange and interest rates, the bank provided an interesting example of efforts to reconnect with customers on an emotional level. When the Libor crisis 'erupted', Barclays published an apology and pulled much of its advertising. However, it remained on the UK social media forum, Mumsnet, where its ongoing relationships with users suggested that trust levels remained unaffected (Dunne 2014). A Barclays 'Life Skills' campaign taught young people how to manage money, write CVs and handle job interviews, among other skills (Hargreaves 2011). Barclays's 'Digital Eagles' campaign targeted older customers, but this relationship marketing effort provoked controversy. What began as a campaign to train staff in new technologies was extended to help older customers who supposedly trusted Barclays over IT experts (Bennison 2014). The campaign undoubtedly distracted from Barclays's legal issues, although it backfired when customers complained bitterly about Barclays's inappropriate focus on teaching people IT skills instead of improving customer service, reducing queues or even responding to comments on its own Digital Eagles-sponsored posts (Nueta Ventures 2014).

Sceptical pundits regarded several of the banking sector's 'friendly' engagement measures – video banking and branch cafes – as little more than cost-cutting measures. Banks' digital engagement was mocked as 'the Emperor's New Clothes' (PR Week 2011, p. 18), a thinly veiled attempt to gather ever *more data* on customers (Tiessen 2015). The criticisms were well-founded, since retail banking's marketing discourse contains a fatal internal contradiction (Knights et al. 2001). Retail banking pretends to be customer-led when it is actually production-led. Hence, the only customer 'needs' retail banks provide for are those of *new* customers, and those existing consumers deemed *profitable* (Carswell 2011). So in the very period that banks were supposedly restoring trust, they were also 'sacking' certain customers for their 'foreign connections', questionable credit histories, data errors or general unprofitability (Palmer 2015). Equally, banks extended flawed mobile technologies to customers with one hand, then blamed customers when their accounts were hacked (Russon 2016). Disgruntled customers were regularly flagged up through customer relationship systems, but complaints resonated faintly at board level since customers were not leaving in hordes (Skinner 2015).

Trust restoration campaigns masked genuine trust issues

The question therefore is not whether banks' trust restoration campaigns have worked, but whether they were actually trust restoration campaigns at all. The campaigns successfully disguise the foundational trust issue in retail banking, namely that retail banks do not trust their customers (Knights and Odih 1999, Burton 2008). Retail banks must exert control over money so bank lending is determined on customer trustworthiness, that is, our ability to pay off debts[1] (Burton 2008). In order to determine this trustworthiness, retail banks must extract information about their customers to prove they are suitable and appropriate people to do business with (Leyshon and Thrift 1999, Dodd 2014). Where banks once extracted this information via face-to-face interviews in branches, banks now reduce risks by gathering customer information at-a-distance through surveillance technologies such as credit scoring (Leyshon and Thrift 1999, Burton 2008). Banks place more trust in the 'super-included' – low-risk individuals with good credit histories, who pay their bills on time and fulfil their credit commitments (Burton 2008). These are the customers identified for 'cross-selling' additional services. By contrast, rising personal debt has made less trustworthy customers even more so. Such customers have either moved from 'applicant to supplicant' (Johnson 2005, p. 11) or been discarded altogether to join the castaways among the 'unbanked'[2].

Contemporary banking is modelled along new lines

Retail banks may be the storefront of the banking system, but in mature Western markets, retail banks are a declining profit-centre, with too many retail banks and not enough mass affluent customers to keep banks happy. Profits have been further disrupted by the march of regulation and new technologies. Regulators, seeking to increase competition and transparency, are limiting product bundling and ancillary sales, dictating fees and commission structures and requiring data about customers' history be made available to competitors (Allchin et al. 2016). Banking profits from payment processing for credit- and debit-card payments have been disrupted by new regulations reducing revenues. Powerful interlopers such as Amazon, Google and PayPal saw their opportunity to lure merchants to cloud-based platforms with discounted fees for participating in customer promotions (*Economist* 2014). Self-service tills at Home Depot, the US home-improvement store, lets customers use PayPal. Google offers a virtual wallet. Amazon allows customers to transfer money. Facebook and Apple are also interested in financial technology or 'fintech' (*Economist* 2014); like Google, they are amassing vast quantities of data on how users behave.

But banks were transforming their business models long before these latest pressures emerged. The traditional image of a bank is a place that makes old-fashioned loans to individuals and small and large companies. This is no longer the true image of banking in Western markets where low interest rates continue to dominate. Capital markets perform many of the services once performed by banks; free from heavy regulation, capital markets can apply innovations, greater risks and aggressive hedging activities (Dodd 2014). Twenty-first-century banking shifted its focus from lending to securitisation, advising companies on how to 'tap' capital markets for finance and converting financial assets into tradable securities, thus putting less of the banks' own capital at risk (Ben-Ami 2001). Now that banks no longer depend on assets on their own balance sheet, there is no limit to their capacity to create credit. Banks have effectively taken over the role of money-creation in national economies (Dodd 2014). What now defines the banking system's position on the hierarchy of financial trust relations is their role as the main repositories of risk (not as main issuers of debt); this is what makes the banking system too big to fail.

Large businesses have the option of turning to capital markets and 'shadow banking' if their traditional banks withdraw lines of credit (McBride 2014). But what of small businesses? And what of traditional retail consumers who have been 'sacked' by their banks (Palmer 2015), or those who cannot get a bank loan? Where are they being served? Small businesses have long complained about accessing finance from the banking system. After the global financial crisis, many small businesses were locked out altogether and have since turned to alternative finance, including equity-based crowdfunding to peer-to-peer lending, which supplies credit to small business owners, start-ups and consumers looking for easier ways to borrow money. The alternative finance market is thriving. Controversial payday lenders such as Wonga achieved success by applying technology to lending decisions, employing 'hordes of PhDs' to refine its algorithms (Rooney 2012). In Europe, alternative finance grew by 144 per cent in 2014. Google led a US$125 million investment in Lending Club, the biggest US platform in 2013 (*Economist* 2014). Traditional banks and asset managers are now investing in these lenders (Wardrop et al. 2015, Robinson and Muñoz 2016).

For consumers, banks continue to serve the 'super-included', increasingly through their wealth management operations which have eaten into the market once quietly dominated by boutique private banks. Meanwhile, 'middle of the road' customers are vast in number but not highly attractive to their current banks. For these customers, there are several options. Many choose to remain with their own banks, quietly accepting increased charges. Other consumers have been drawn to successful PR campaigns waged by the cooperative sector (credit unions, mutual societies and building societies). Cooperatives promote ethical values and 'folksy' regional management structures (Ashton 2013), and have firmly positioned themselves as the trustworthy savings and lending institutions, run by members not shareholders. Governments have bought into this positioning, offering cooperatives as part of a vision for a 'largely repaired' banking system (Ashton 2013). Yet cooperatives only offer the perception of consumer power through annual voting rights – members have no real say in day-to-day operations. Like traditional banks, some cooperatives have also fallen prey to financial malfeasance in their quest for growth (Willoughby 2013). Nor is it clear how cooperatives will survive in a world of unprecedented capital requirements.

Meanwhile, some 'middle-of-the road' customers have been attracted to challenger banks offering attractive joining terms or specialising in less-served groups such as younger customers or expatriates. Supermarket-owned

Sainsbury's Bank regularly battles it out with traditional banks to offer the lowest personal loan rate (Which? 2013). Giffgaff, the UK mobile phone network, launched Giffgaff Money, offering loans of up to £7,500 to customers aged over 21 (Ghosh 2015). Traditional retail banking, with its expensive branch networks and outdated technology, may be living on borrowed time. Central banks are pushing for international regulation to relax capital rules so that cooperatives and start-up banks have a fairer playing field (Titcomb 2014). The entire financial services industry in Western markets is shifting toward a modular business model in which products will be distributed by digital 'platforms' that steer demand to any supplier, allowing new product providers to proliferate, just as comparison websites disrupted general insurance by massively reducing the cost of searching for appropriate, cheaper products (Allchin et al. 2016). Another development likely to hasten the modular banking business model is blockchain. Once this technology has been perfected to work on a large scale, blockchain databases can operate a collective 'distributed ledger' across several financial institutions, keeping track of assets in separate databases. Regulators like the idea, as trades can be settled almost instantly, without the need for many different intermediaries, while improving compliance by automatically recording past transactions (*Economist* 2016).

Conclusion – what are we trusting banks for?

For the time being, durable trust in banking remains intact. People hold banking deposits and have faith in money. Banks also remain a powerful source of cash flow which reassures investors (Mills 2008). As long as this continues, banks' central role in the economy remains largely unchallenged. Undoubtedly, more of banks' traditional business lines are flowing to fast-growing exchanges, trading platforms and clearing houses. Eight of these providers have become so big that US regulators now label them 'systemically important' – in other words, 'too big to fail' (*Economist* 2014). Yet it is unclear whether new technologies threaten banks with extinction. Banks have proved successful in adapting to financial innovation in the past, and are doing so once again. Banco Santander, the Spanish bank, which became a global power player through acquisitions, has appointed a technology advisory board to underscore the importance of information technology to Santander's growth plans. The bank's venture fund has acquired stakes in several fintech firms, including online lenders and blockchain technology (Robinson and Muñoz 2016).

Having described the fast-paced change in the banking system, a number of disconcerting questions arise regarding trust, power and public relations in this sector. I began the chapter by asserting that the rock-solid reason for trusting banks is their role in protecting the assets of millions of customers. We retain our trust in banking so long as the system appears stable, with no signs of a collective stampede to withdraw those assets. Retail banks may be designed to mistrust their customers, yet those of us with student loans, credit cards and mortgages feel a moderate sense of alignment between our needs for funds and the bank's interest in seeing us repay. But the changes I have described in this chapter demonstrate that this everyday activity largely obscures the real business of modern banking, which is not lending money to everyday consumers and businesses, but arranging and spreading risks. If so, then what is the real basis of our trust relationship with the banking sector? And why is it that most of the messages in banks' trust restoration PR focus on trust in *traditional* banking services such as lending, when banks no longer make their biggest profits from these services? Why would retail banks invest in restoring consumer trust at all, when they long ago made it clear they would cede the consumer space to more interested providers? Furthermore, if the modular business model does cement itself, then retail banks will have even weaker trust relationships with their customers than ever (Allchin et al. 2016).

Meanwhile, wholesale banks may have been separated from retail operations in certain jurisdictions, but in the UK aggressive lobbying ensured that investment banking operations were only 'ringfenced'. Any banking profits made since the global financial crisis are partially attributable to the public subsidy implicitly offered by governments, which demonstrated a willingness to bail out troubled banks. Global banks are feeling the squeeze from unprecedented capital requirements and the cost of doing business across jurisdictions. By 2014, it was clear that wholesale banking was in trouble yet again over dodgy loans, risky assets and problems across business lines. Eastern Europe presented an early hotspot in 2014 when central bank inspectors flagged 51 per cent of loans in Slovenian banks as problematic (Dey 2014). Similar problems have since arisen in India and China. Credit Suisse, Deutsche Bank and Royal Bank of Scotland (RBS) all racked up billions of dollars in losses in 2015. RBS has lost money every year since the global financial crisis. The lowering of interest rates in Europe and Japan during 2015 to 2016 meant that banks were effectively paying to deposit funds with central banks.

Yet banks are still talking about 'trust' in their advertising and PR material, and claiming that trust and service remain more important to everyday customers than price (Titcomb 2014). The decade-long trust restoration campaign waged by banks since the global financial crisis has been a vital smokescreen – a survival strategy that has left banks 'alive' to fight another day (Wolfrom 2009). Speaking repeatedly about the need to restore trust in business areas that are on the decline has effectively given banks the necessary breathing room to look around and decide where future long-term profits will accrue – whether in challenger banks, peer-to-peer lending, a Google-type wallet or a PayPal platform. A decade on from the global financial crisis, the new winners of the future banking system are emerging, enabling traditional banks to invest in these winners or acquire them outright. Public relations may have contributed to the sector's survival, but just as with stock market PR (see Chapter 5), this kind of campaigning does little to position PR professionals as trust strategists. Instead, PR seems focused on 'whatever means necessary' to ensure the survival of banks as a financial 'species'. The next chapter moves on to advised financial services – insurance, pensions and asset management. It is to this area of financial markets that regulators would shift their scrutiny, after their urgent post-crisis concerns with banks.

Notes

1 Just as a state's trustworthiness is equated with creditworthiness in global markets (see Chapter 3).
2 See Chapter 8 for an in-depth discussion of PR activity on behalf of the financially excluded.

References

Allchin, C., Austen, M., Fine, A. and Moynihan, T. (2016). *Modular Financial Services: The New Shape of the Industry*, London: Oliver Wyman.

Amos, O. (2009). 'Journalists attack city 'PR machine' over banking crisis', *Press Gazette*, 24 February. Retrieved from: http://www.pressgazette.co.uk/node/43161

Arnold, M. (2014). 'Barclays and Coutts make a statement with plans for mobile video banking', *Financial Times*, 1 December, p. 18.

Ashton, J. (2013). 'The first banking crisis was the root of co-op's troubles', *Evening Standard*, 21 November, p. 65.

Atherton, J. (2012). 'Three arrested by Libor detectives', *Metro*, 12 December, p. 71.

Barber, L. (2011). 'Client view: Amanda Brown, First Direct – beyond the phone', *PR Week Advertising Supplement*, 4 November 2011. Retrieved from http://www.prweek.com/article/1100802/client-view-amanda-brown-first-direct---beyond-phone

Barda, T. (2008). 'Credit house of cards', *The Marketer*, November, pp. 28–31.

Beck, U. (1992). *Risk Society*, London: Sage Publications.

Ben-Ami, D. (2001). *Cowardly Capitalism: The Myth of the Global Financial Casino*, Chichester: John Wiley & Sons.

Bennison, S. (2014). 'Barclays marketer Sara Bennison: 'I'm proud of what we're trying to achieve'', *Marketing*, 2 June. Retrieved from: http://www.marketingmagazine.co.uk/article/1296659/barclays-marketer-sara-bennison-im-proud-were-trying-achieve

Bourne, C. (2013). 'Public relations in the World of Finance'. In Tench, R. and Yeomans, L. (eds) *Exploring Public Relations* (Third Edition), London: Pearson Publications, pp. 381–394.

Bourne, C. (2015). 'Thought Leadership as a trust strategy in global markets: Goldman Sachs' promotion of the 'BRICs' in the marketplace of ideas', *Journal of Public Relations Research*, 27, (4), pp. 322–336.

Brocklebank-Fowler, S. (2008). 'Differentiation wins the day', *PR Week Thought Leadership Series*, London, UK: Haymarket.

Burton, D. (2008). *Credit and Consumer Society*, Abingdon: Routledge.

Carswell, S. (2011). 'Built to crash', *Financial World*, pp. 24–25.

Cartmell, M. (2011). 'Santander in bid to grow British corporate brand', *PR Week*, 25 November, p. 1.

Conrad, C. and Poole, M.S. (2012). *Strategic Organizational Communication* (Seventh Edition), Chichester: Wiley-Blackwell.

Czerniawska, F. (2012). 'Thought leadership: too important to be left to consultants?' *SourceforConsulting*, 9 August. Retrieved from: http://www.sourceforconsulting.com/blog/2012/08/09/thought-leadership-too-important-to-be-left-to-consultants/

De Cock, C., Baker, M., and Volkmann, C. (2011). 'Financial phantasmagoria', *Organization Studies*, 18, pp. 153–172.

Delin, J. (2013). 'Trusting the high street bank'. In Candlin, C.N. and Crichton, J. (eds) *Discourses of Trust*. Basingstoke: Palgrave Macmillan, pp. 183–199.

Dey, I. (2014). 'Eastern Europe on alert amid fears of new banking crisis', *Sunday Times*, 15 June, p. P2.

Diamond, B. (2011). 'Today Business Lecture', *BBC 4*, 3 November, London: BBC Broadcasting House.

Dodd, N. (2014). *The Social Life of Money*, Princeton, NJ: Princeton University Press.

Dunne, H. (2014). 'Profile: Mum's the word', *CorpComms Magazine*, p. 87 (June).

Dye, P. (2007). 'Mortgage advice: Cheap at the price', *PR Week*, 3 August, p. 14.

Economist. (2008). 'The faith that moves Mammon', *The Economist*, 18 October, p. 108.

Economist. (2014). 'Shadow and substance: Special report – international banking', *The Economist Special Report*, 10 May, pp. 1–16.

Economist. (2016). 'The blockchain in finance: hype springs eternal', *The Economist*, 19 May. Retrieved from: http://www.economist.com/news/finance-and-economics/21695068-distributed-ledgers-are-future-their-advent-will-be-slow-hype-springs

Ehrlich, E. and Fanelli, D. (2004). *The Financial Services Marketing Handbook: Tactics and Techniques That Produce Results*, Princeton: Bloomberg Press.

English, S. (2013). 'Terrorists and drug lords targeted HSBC, bosses admit', *Evening Standard*, 6 February, p. 37.

Evening Standard. (2013). 'Letters to the Editor: The best way to fix the banks', *Evening Standard*, 11 April, p. 61.

Fidelzeid, G. (2013). 'Financial services roundtable: Digital investment', *PR Week*, 30 September. Retrieved from: http://www.prweek.com/article/1274508/financial-services-roundtable-digital-investment#FH0oRrpAcBMQrqIF.99

FSA (Financial Services Authority). (2005). *Consumer Paper 35: Towards Understanding Consumers' Needs*, London: Financial Services Authority and the Henley Centre.

Ghosh, S. (2015). 'Giffgaff moves into personal finance to disrupt banks', *Marketing*, 14 May, Retrieved from: http://www.campaignlive.co.uk/article/1347118/giffgaff-moves-personal-finance-disrupt-banks

Giddens, A. (1990). *The Consequences of Modernity*, Oxford, UK: Polity Press: Blackwell.

Giddens, A. (1999). 'Risk and responsibility', *The Modern Law Review*, 62 (1), pp. 1–10.

Gray, R. (2007). 'Barclays fights to save reputation', *PR Week*, 14 September, p. 17.

Hardt, M., and Negri, A. (2000). *Empire*, Cambridge, MA: Harvard University Press.

Hargreaves, D. (2011). 'Friendly banks – on a TV near you', *Financial World*, June, p. 21.

Hayes, J.W. (2013). *Becoming the Expert*, Petersfield, UK: Harriman House.

Hilton, A. (2010). 'Investment banks left out in the cold', *PR Week*, 26 March, p. 12.

Ho, K. (2009). *Liquidated: An Ethnography of Wall Street*, Durham, NC: Duke University Press.

Johnson, M. (2005). 'The future of finance', *Rebuilding Reputations in Financial Services, PR Week White Paper*, May, 12 pages.

Knights, D. and Odih, P. (1999). 'What's in a name? The dynamics of branding personal financial services', *Financial Services Marketing*, 4 (3), pp. 42–45.

Knights, D., Noble, F., Vurdubakis, T. and Wilmott, H. (2001). 'Chasing shadows: Control, virtuality and the production of trust', *Organization Studies*, 22 (2), pp. 311–336.

Leyshon, A. and Thrift, N. (1999). 'Lists come alive: Electronic systems of knowledge and the rise of credit-scoring in retail banking', *Economy and Society*, 28 (3), pp. 434–466.

Makovsky & Company. (2012). 'The 2012 Makovsky Wall St Reputation Study'. Retrieved from: http://www.makovsky.com/insights/presentations/24-insights/presentations/presentation/259-2012-wall-street-reputation-study

Mason, P. (2009). *Meltdown: The End of the Age of Greed*, London: Verso.

Mattinson, A. (2009A). 'Bankers' apologies are 'pathetic''', *PR Week*, 13 February, p. 3.

Mattinson, A. (2009B). 'Barclays calls review of reputation', *PR Week*, 7 August, p. 6–7.

McBride, E. (2014). 'Shadow and substance: Special report – international banking', *The Economist*, 10 May, pp. 3–5.

McCrimmon, M. (2005). 'Thought leadership: A radical departure from traditional, positional leadership', *Management Decision*, 43, pp. 1064–1070.

Metro. (2012). 'Laundering lands HSBC £1.2bn fine', *Metro*, 12 December, p. 71.

Miles, N. (2009). 'Don't pander to reader prejudice', *PR Week*, 31 July, p. 9.

Mills, A. (2008). 'Short on vision', *Financial World*, September, pp. 30–31.

Noble, S.P. (2014). 'The care and feeding of the thought leadership professional', *Bloom Group Newsletter*, 28 March. Retrieved from: http://bloomgroup.com/content/care-and-feeding-thought-leadership-professional-discussion-talentconsultant-sara-p-noble

Nueta Ventures. (2014). 'Barclays digital eagles – social media campaign gone bad', *Nueta Ventures*, 26 July. Retrieved from: http://nuetaventures.com/2014/07/26/barclays-digital-eagles-social-media-campaign-gone-bad/

Palmer, K. (2015). 'Why are banks giving customers the boot?', *Sunday Telegraph*, 8 November, p. 1.

Pixley, J. (2012). *Emotions in Finance: Booms, Busts and Uncertainty* (Second Edition), Cambridge: Cambridge University Press.

PR Week. (2008). 'Banks have bad websites', *PR Week*, 17 October. Retrieved from: http://www.prweek.com/article/854601/city–corporate-banks-bad-websites#Oowv Q4P3q3Dlsdos.99

PR Week. (2010). 'Reputation survey: "We blame bankers"', *PR Week*, 12 February, pp. 24–25.

PR Week. (2011). 'Is HSBC's social media plan likely to work', *PR Week*, 18 November, p. 18.

Rexrode, C. and Sidel, R. (2015). 'Is this a coffee shop or a bank?' *Wall Street Journal*, 6 July. Retrieved from: http://www.wsj.com/articles/is-this-a-coffee-shop-or-a-bank-14362 25586

Robinson, E. and Muñoz, M. (2016). 'Santander taps Summers, D'Souza as technology reshapes banks', *Bloomberg Technology*, 18 March. Retrieved from: http://www.bloomberg.com/news/articles/2016–03–18/santander-taps-summers-whitehurst-as-technology-reshapes-banks

Rooney, B. (2012). 'Bank start-ups seize on ire with older players', *Wall Street Journal*, 22 August. Retrieved from: http://blogs.wsj.com/peer-europe/2012/08/23/bank-start-ups-seize-on-ire-with-older-players/

Russon, M. (2016). 'Natwest online banking flaw enables hackers to drain bank accounts by stealing your smartphone', *International Business Times*, 7 March. Retrieved from: http://www.ibtimes.co.uk/natwest-online-banking-flaw-enables-hackers-drain-bank-accounts-by-stealing-your-smartphone-1548002

Shaughnessy, H. (2011). 'The growth of thought leadership as a marketing strategy', *NGE Think Tank*, 9 July. Retrieved from: http://ngethinktank.com/2011/07/09/the-growth-of-thought-leadership-as-a-marketing-strategy/

Shaw, G. (2014). 'The editor's letter', *Which? Money*, February, p. 3.

Skinner, C.M. (2015). 'Are customers so important for banks?' *The Finanser*, 18 January. Retrieved from: http://thefinanser.com/2016/01/are-customers-so-important-for-banks.html/

Sotelino, F. and Gonzalez, R. (2012). 'Universal banking post crisis', *Working Paper*. Retrieved from: http://dx.doi.org/10.2139/ssrn.2102863

TBIJ (The Bureau of Investigative Journalism). (2012). 'Revealed: The £93 m City lobby machine', *The Bureau of Investigative Journalism*, 9 July.

Tiessen, M. (2015). 'The appetites of app-based finance', *Cultural Studies*, 29 (5–6), pp. 869–886.

Titcomb, J. (2014). 'The future of banks is in the balance', *Sunday Telegraph*, 13 July, p. B5.

Turnbull, P., and Moustakatos, T. (1996). 'Marketing and investment banking II', *International Journal of Bank Marketing*, 14, pp. 38–49.

Wardrop, R., Zhang, B., Rau, R. and Gray, M. (2015). *Moving Mainstream: The European Alternative Finance Benchmarking Report*, London: University of Cambridge/EY.

Which? (2013). 'Supermarkets and banks in loans battle', *Which? Money*, October, p. 5.

Willoughby, L. (2013). 'Letter to the editor: clean up banking after the Co-op,' *Evening Standard*, 25 November, p. 57.

Wilson, H. and Armitstead, L. (2011). 'Bob Diamond: "Time for banker remorse is over"', *Daily Telegraph*, 12 January. Retrieved from: http://www.telegraph.co.uk/finance/news bysector/banksandfinance/8253523/Bob-Diamond-Time-for-banker-remorse-is-over.html

Wolfrom, M. (2009). 'The playbook for restoring trust', *Cohn & Wolfe White Paper*, January. Retrieved from: http://www.cohnwolfe.com/en/ideas-insights/white-papers/playbook-restoring-trust

7 Insurance, investment, pensions

Rise of the robo-experts

This chapter will focus on the complex distribution system of financial providers and intermediaries in large, competitive markets for investment, insurance and pensions. In these markets, governments have largely retreated from welfare provision, and consumers are increasingly expected to become more enterprising by using financial markets and financial services providers to meet core needs such as providing a decent income in retirement or protecting against financial risks of losing health, home and income. Financial self-management involves tasks such as planning ahead, managing money, choosing the right financial products, then staying informed about events influencing how those products perform (Nayak and Beckett 2008). Enterprising financial consumers are not alone in embracing uncertainties of the future, since they pool risks with other entrepreneurial financial subjects (French and Kneale 2009).

PR represents many sides of this complex financial distribution system, promoting the tools of financial self-management on behalf of government departments, as well as financial services providers, intermediaries or 'middlemen' in wholesale and retail markets Consumer organisations also use PR to promote advice on personal finance. Relationship building is important to any PR programme – financial providers build rapport with intermediaries who in turn build rapport with consumers, while both build relationships with the press through seminars, workshops and social events such wine-tasting or art exhibitions, together with competitions and giveaways. But investment, insurance and pensions products pose different communications challenges. While the prospect of investment products may instil excitement and adventure (as discussed in Chapter 5), insurance and pension products are more prosaic. Advertisers and marketers therefore opt to enliven these mundane products through lifestyle (Langley 2008, French and Kneale 2009). Insurance advertising often uses emotional messages to suggest pleasure and satisfaction in managing one's household security. Insurance advertising messages can be subtle and nuanced, suggesting expressions of love toward family without making direct references to money (Lehtonen 2014). By contrast, insurance and pensions PR is more direct, highlighting the tension between valued possessions or relationships and dreams of the future (Lehtonen 2014). These direct references to money are important, particularly when targeting the media, since money yields headlines.

Insurance and pensions PR narratives must also represent the personal finance media's bias toward middle-class worries over pensions, high taxes, lack of job security, and 'holding on by a thread' (Kendall 2005). PR reaches this middle-class audience by building trust in the expertise of financial providers and intermediaries by drawing on the three 'e's' – choice editing, third party endorsement and financial education. These three PR tactics underscore several trust strategies, including guaranteeing, aligning, opening up and simplifying (see Chapter 6). PR professionals are also aware that what counts as news to an insurance company or pensions adviser – new products, new hires etc. – may be of little interest to the mainstream media. Consequently, media relations work often promotes financial experts who can supply 'views as news'. Insurance, investment and pensions experts who supply interesting soundbites on major government announcements or market movements are useful media spokespeople. Expert spokespeople build trust by simplifying complex financial issues, becoming straight-taking champions, and translating complex jargon about insurance, pensions and savings into easily understood messages for the general public. The most trusted personal finance experts are often the most available to the media: some experts install their own audiovisual facilities to increase accessibility for TV and radio interviews. Most personal finance experts contribute newspaper and magazine columns, as well as blogging on social media.

No matter how 'lively' the expert, insurance and pensions remain a 'fusty' topic, so PR must generate additional ways to tell compelling stories. In the largest markets, where countless financial brands compete for attention with 'me too' stories about 'me too' products, PR caters to the media agenda by offering 'newness'. The survey-as-story is a popular communications tool used by personal finance providers in the UK, France, Switzerland, the US and Canada. Some financial companies commission a mammoth 'annual' survey on investment, pensions or insurance topics. Other companies spread their budget over a series of surveys linked to seasonal stories. The most-cited surveys provide 'news hooks' appealing to various audience segments by lifestyle or demographics. PR surveys publish statistics bemoaning the financial hardships facing key demographics – whether it be millennials forced to tap the 'bank of mum-and-dad', or middle-aged homeowners who don't know their mortgage rate, or pensioners facing rising funeral costs. Journalists may scoff at their proliferation, but PR surveys continue to provide fodder for traditional and digital media alike.

Misconduct – the rogue gene of financial services

No matter how compelling the PR narrative, promoting financial self-management is plagued with difficulties. Despite determined use of the three e's – choice editing, financial endorsement and financial education – many consumers remain uncertain about insurance, investment and pension products, and frequently make mistakes by deviating from normative advice (Bhattacharya et al. 2011). Less sophisticated investors often gravitate toward investment funds with more opaque pricing structures, despite strong evidence that opacity is negatively related to fund performance (Finke 2012, p. 18). Buying car insurance and home and contents insurance may be compulsory, but policy terms may not be clearly understood. Life insurance and pension products pose the greatest issues. Simpson (2001, p. 27) argues these products are so over-complicated they create a state of radical ignorance among consumers who 'do not know what it is they do not know'. Despite information and guidance provided by consumer groups, the financial media and government departments, radical ignorance has not abated.

The regulatory response to uncertainty, confusion and radical ignorance has been to create a buffer between enterprising consumers and complex finance through an array of intermediaries or 'middle-men'. When regulators stipulate that certain products can only be bought after seeking financial advice, this opens up the market to financial intermediaries comprised of varied professional groups, some acting independently, while others are attached to specific financial providers. Brokers and dealers are middlemen who execute only on the customer's instructions. Financial advisers go a step forward; they are qualified to advise on a range of financial products. Adjacent to financial advisers are professionals such as lawyers, accountants, tax advisers and wealth managers who can advise on financial products as part of business, tax and legal affairs. Where middlemen dominate the market for financial advice, the financial providers – the investment managers and insurers who 'manufacture' financial products in the first place – are forced to take a step back from the customer so as not to bias the process. Consequently, while system trust may be attached to financial brands and products, intermediaries who are closer to the customer are on the frontline of trust in financial services.

Despite government intervention (and sometimes because of it), the effort to provide consumers with unbiased financial advice is scuppered both by supply and demand. On the demand side, consumers who need financial advice are least likely to obtain it (Bhattacharya et al. 2011). On the supply side, the very existence of intermediaries is sometimes detrimental to consumers. First, when middlemen are paid by commission they can be motivated to recommend inappropriate products. When the customer has the option of buying a provider's products directly or via an intermediary, sometimes the advised products are of lower quality. Some mutual funds, for example, assign their best fund managers to look after funds sold directly to consumers, because customers investing via brokers are often more focused on the broker's add-on services (Finke 2012). Sometimes intermediaries are third parties recommended by the financial provider, yet that can go badly too. UK motorists have been left with huge legal bills when insurers recommended accident management firms to provide courtesy cars after car accidents, but the cars supplied were far more expensive models than stipulated by insurance policies (Coney 2010).

In addition, with long-term savings and insurance products, the risk of cheating is particularly great because of the long period between purchase and delivery. Mis-selling scandals in financial services are the industry's 'rogue gene' that neither regulation nor industry reorganisation has been able to eradicate (Prestridge 2005, p. 4). Worse still, while consumers are compelled to trust the very intermediaries who edit, endorse and advise on complex financial products (Simpson 2001), these same advisers consistently rank among the least trustworthy financial professionals. In the US, one in thirteen financial advisers have a misconduct-related disclosure on their record rising to one in five in districts with more wealthy and/or educated consumers (Egan et al. 2016). In the UK, financial advisers have been involved with a spate of mis-selling scandals spanning 30 years, involving endowment mortgages, pensions products, precipice bonds, split capital investment trusts, equity release and more.

Public inquiries rarely implicate PR professionals in mis-selling scandals. However, considering that much of the PR activity in highly competitive markets is driven by intermediaries, it is difficult to ignore PR's role in building advisers' legitimacy, and in propagating 'me too' products and messages. PR is also implicated in watered-down government responses following mis-selling scandals, as relentless industry lobbying ensures that new regulation never clearly defines remedies, and never clearly defines the right degree of consumer protection, thus contributing to a culture of mistrust in financial institutions. This is no doubt exacerbated by politicians' and regulators' shared mission to maximise bad press for the financial services industry in order to highlight their own disciplining role. Above all, PR eagerly positions itself to lead trust restoration exercises for financial providers and intermediaries after mis-selling scandals, even when the financial industry shows no clear signs of improvement.

Trust surveys, professional anxiety and robo-advisers

Financial intermediaries feature prominently in trust restoration exercises. UK financial advisers repeatedly commission trust surveys to prove they are the most trusted financial service operators – the ones who really care about customers, the ones whom consumers are happy to use and to recommend to others (Young 2009). PR efforts to promote trust surveys can convey a self-congratulatory tone, announcing, for example, that financial advisers truly are the 'winners' in the battle for trust. The spate of trust surveys commissioned by various professional groups hints at an unsettling level of anxiety among advisers and brokers in larger markets. This professional anxiety is directly connected with intermediaries' low status on the hierarchy of financial trust relations (Kincaid 2006). While intermediaries are responsible for protecting assets, and guaranteeing return – powerful trust practices – their structural power in markets is weak. After all, advisers initially thrived because regulation gave them an essential role in providing consumer advice (House of Commons 2004). Brokers and dealers have thrived wherever they help consumers find the cheapest, most appropriate products most quickly. Intermediaries' tenuous status in the financial trust hierarchy is under threat as both regulatory and market structures change. On the regulatory side, the UK, Switzerland, Germany, Italy and South Africa have abolished commission payments, requiring advisers to offer transparent fee-only structures (*Economist* 2014).

On the market side, intermediaries are threatened by obsolescence due to four major digital trends which have seen the rise of the 'robo-adviser'. The first digital trend has reshaped customer interaction with financial providers and intermediaries. Customers are increasingly using multiple channels:

face-to-face, phone and internet, as well as mobile phones and tablets. Second, the lack of product innovation in areas like insurance finally ended with the advent of digital technologies such as telematics and apps. Third, advanced analytics is helping financial services to make better use of 'big data' from many different sources. Finally, digital technologies have increased automation, speeding up customer service through self-learning algorithms and empowering the customer to add, edit or delete financial products and services from the customer end (Johansson and Vogelgesang 2016). Increased customer automation, in particular, is transforming the way many financial intermediaries work. More intelligent computing enables customers to be more enterprising; they can bypass human interaction altogether, assembling investment portfolios or comprehensive insurance coverage, avoiding conversations they may not necessarily want to have. While increasingly intelligent computing is positioned as an 'aide' to financial intermediaries, it has had far-reaching repercussions, because robo-advisers are now the competition. The fund supermarkets and other platforms, once touted as 'the future' and aggressively marketed throughout the 2000s, had become dated and clunky. Larger intermediaries invested in 'replatforming'. Smaller intermediaries merged or retreated altogether. All have had to reshape teams to cater for the skill-sets now required. Financial companies are downsizing support roles such as client data processing. The growth areas are customer problem-solving, quantitative skills and ICT skills, together with digital marketing and PR (Johansson and Vogelgesang 2016).

This technological disruption has created professional anxiety for all financial intermediaries, who face the prospect of becoming quantitative or computer gurus or being replaced by robots altogether. Online financial advisers or robo-advisers are some of the newest financial brands. UK brands include Nutmeg, Money on Toast and Wealth Advisor; they are able to undercut traditional adviser fees by using algorithms to perform many of the functions a human investment adviser could do. Machines automate customer searches, by responding to a series of online questions to determine the customer's risk appetite. The responses direct the customer toward suitable asset allocation, although the adviser ultimately dispenses advice. Nutmeg became one of the most recognisable new financial brands thanks to successful marketing, PR and fundraising. PR professionals carefully positioned Nutmeg as both an exciting, innovative start-up and a credible, stable business (PR Week 2013). The PR campaign built Nutmeg's profile as a fintech firm, targeting multichannel news sites such as *TechCrunch*, while piggybacking on events such as London Tech Week. Nutmeg was also positioned as a new model 'wealth manager' through interviews with the *FT*, *BBC Radio 4's Today* show, *CNBC* and profiles in the *Mail on Sunday* and the *Evening Standard*. The 'buzz' created around the new brand even helped it overcome a major customer data breach shortly after start-up. Technological disruption has also affected financial providers of investment, insurance and pension products, with varied PR responses and implications for trust. The rest of the chapter will focus on the impact of shifting trusting relations on financial providers.

Fund management and the cult of celebrity

The fund management sector[1] is the first group of providers to be considered in the context of shifting trust relations in financial services distribution. While institutional fund managers were able to target 'low hanging fruit' such as pension schemes, retail fund managers had to be much more aggressive in promotion, particularly as fund management brands played second fiddle to funds associated with well-known banks and insurers (PwC 2014). For years, retail fund managers' promotional machinery was fuelled by 'star fund managers', active fund managers able to deliver superior returns over the rest of the market for a year or two. Star fund managers were crucial to sales and mitigated hefty management fees (Langley 2008). A leading PR firm was even implicated in a 'dirty tricks' campaign, circulating misleading information about a competing star manager's performance (Hume 2001). PR has a tougher job defending mediocre fund managers. Journalists are underwhelmed by interviews in which mediocre managers describe their funds as 'consistent second-quartile performers' that aren't meant to 'shoot-the-lights-out'(Collinson 2005, p. 21).

Mediocre performance belied the PR and marketing campaigns promising customer wealth that never materialised. PR and marketing also contributed to pervasive issues of hidden costs and poor transparency. Marketing teams supervised the production of fund 'fact sheets' that contained general information on fund aims, but little detail on where the fund actually invested (Shaw 2014). By the 2008 global financial crisis, the fund management industry had already spent more than a decade grappling with how to regain investor trust. After the financial crisis, many high-net-worth customers voted with their feet (Mitchell 2010). Institutional customers were vocal about fund managers' lack of vision, the need for more client communication, better enunciation of risk and less inarticulate musing from fund managers (KPMG 2009).

During the crisis, many fund managers backed away from the media altogether, preferring to keep a low profile (Hilton 2008). However, they could not remain hidden forever. Investors were spooked after funds run by Bernie Madoff and Allen Stanford were exposed as Ponzi schemes, after the arrest of a Schroders equity trader for insider-dealing, and after revelations that Barclays Wealth America executives had covered up mismanagement. Trust became an 'overused word' at industry events (Newlands 2013). Fund managers emphasised trust through their marketing campaigns: 'Complex investment decisions are easier to make with people you trust' ran the strapline for Cazenove Capital Management; while Pictet Asset Management's campaign said 'Expertise, stability and trust. In asset management, they provide the calm required to think'. Meanwhile, trust 'remedies' prescribed by PR advisers included resurrecting the 'personal responsibility' message, which encouraged investors to become better educated about investment risks (Payne 2009). Investors were having none of the 'better education' message. The blame lay with fund managers who needed to be more vigilant and transparent about their own operational risks (KPMG 2009).

Post-crisis, fund manager performance continued to be elusive, while transparency did not improve. It was hard to see how trust could be restored, so investors sought other options. Some turned to private equity and hedge funds in the hope of greater investment returns. Many retail customers and pension schemes alike opted for the greater reliability of tracker funds, which do not try to beat the market, but replicate components of an asset class, typically charging lower fees. However, private equity and hedge funds have had patchy performance, while tracker funds have trust issues of their own. Many white-labelled[2] tracker funds charge more than actively managed funds (Eley 2014). And tracker funds can be optical illusions; some tracker funds are actually 'closet' stock-pickers, while some active managers are 'closet' trackers (Pitcher 2003, Oakley 2014). But tracker funds are here to stay, enabling the fund management industry to cut costs dramatically. The category has expanded to include popular exchange-traded funds and next-generation tracker funds known as 'smart beta'.

Regulators turned their attention to fund managers, post-crisis, scrutinising relationships with customers, as well as suppliers such as sell-side analysts (PwC 2014). Fund managers have also been subjected to more oversight in the post-crisis period. Regulators have scrutinised fund managers' relationships with customers, suppliers and analysts (PwC 2014), while probing the industry's high-pressured internal culture and its toll on fund management staff. Fidelity, one of the world's largest mutual funds, has attempted to enhance its reputation by becoming one of the first US financial employers to offer student debt relief to staff. The move was also heavily promoted by corporate PR to differentiate Fidelity's brand (Ryan 2016). The battle to increase fund management sales and profits has never been tighter, leading large fund managers such as Fidelity to launch its own 'robo' service, based heavily on tracker funds. The fund management industry's next step may be to harness artificial intelligence or AI, developing investment algorithms that can autonomously learn, adapt and scour vast data sets for tradable patterns (Wigglesworth 2016). As with banks, the future of fund management business models could lie with social media corporations like Facebook, with its network reach and alliances, or PayPal, with its back-office servicing specialism (PwC 2014). Until then, the fund management industry seems less troubled by the need to improve trust relations. UK-based fund managers even rebelled against a new code of conduct that promised to 'always put clients' interests first' (Bow 2015). In this environment, PR's role in supporting traditional fund management operations remains largely unchanged. PR professionals still promote fund managers' market opinions on the 'outlook for Asian economies', issue surveys about how millennial investors differ from their parents, and announce fund manager 'wins' through increased sales. PR experts seem more focused on pinning their colours to winning financial brands than in addressing the trust issues that fund managers are not prepared to address themselves.

General Insurance – the original risk experts

The insurance industry is centuries-old, and has been tackling trust issues far longer than fund managers. Insurance is the world's first 'risk' industry, designed to forecast and 'manage' risk by getting people to pool of money together in order to pay out on the probability of individual losses. Twenty-first-century insurance touches on social and economic life on an epic scale, from prosaic eventualities to the unforeseen. Insurance markets include giant wholesale markets such as Lloyd's of London, where massive projects such as satellites and shipping canals are underwritten; corporate insurance of trade, sales, mergers and acquisitions; and everyday insurance for motor vehicles, home and contents. Finally, there are reinsurance companies which provide cover to other insurers for very large risks such as natural disasters or political warfare. As with all aspects of financial markets, the wholesale side of the insurance market is far bigger than the retail side, yet it is far less visible to the general public and rarely seeks the limelight. This distance encourages perceptions of insurance as dull and dusty, while insurance jargon seems designed to scare off its own PR experts, with terms such as 'cedants' and 'retrocedants', 'commutations' and 'declinatures', 'sunset clauses' and 'run-off'. The industry's inward-looking nature always governed its approach to PR: 'to communicate or not to communicate, either was fine' (Eccles and Vollbracht 2006, p. 395).

Much of the global insurance sector emerged from the global financial crisis relatively unscathed. Insurers even received a flood of investment capital after the crisis. But the insurance industry has experienced more than its fair share of trust crises in the past, and like the fund management industry, soon found itself under regulatory scrutiny. New regulatory directives such as Solvency II are utopian in their desire to build trust by regulating away every last drop of risk from insurers' balance sheets (Power 2015). Only the largest insurers with the most diversified balance sheets can survive such scrutiny; this is driving insurers to merge and consolidate, particularly where governments have increased taxes on insurance cover. As with other parts of finance, new technologies have caused equal anxiety to insurers, sparking a spate of industry conferences such as the annual 'Innovation and Disruption' staged in London. However, insurers have traditionally been slow in adapting to new technologies. Efforts to move from paper to electronic trading in the 1990s happened in fits and starts (Knights et al. 1993). The move toward distributing insurance online was led by intermediaries. For example, insurance comparison websites offering a 'one-stop shop', converting previously slow and arduous financial insurance purchases into a speedy, efficient way to find the best deals on home, car and travel insurance (as well as savings accounts, mortgages, annuities and other products). Comparison sites promote trustworthiness by simplifying the insurance market, bifurcating 'good' products from 'bad'. They are so influential that some insurers have acquired or launched comparison sites of their own.

Meanwhile, technology has also created 'new, improved' insurance products, using data mining and monitoring to modify the behaviour of the riskiest customers (McFall 2015). The main source of anxiety for insurers is the threat of competing products from outside of the insurance industry. Investment banks, hedge funds and pension funds have invaded insurers' turf with financial products designed to diversify and manage risk using investment markets more cheaply (Ben-Ami 2001). External competition has finally motivated insurers to move with the times and to reclaim their trust credentials.

PR for insurers had a long-held imperative to present insurance companies as safe, stable and trustworthy (more so than other financial institutions). With competitive anxieties now gripping the sector, PR's new mandate was to demystify insurance markets so they remain central to national economies, by simplifying products and language while highlighting the clear benefits of insurance (Mattinson 2009). PR professionals set about finding opportunities to discuss the insurance risks presented by new trends, using communication tools such as the trade press, websites, conferences, webinars and white papers. For example, Zurich Insurance Group (2014) published white papers about new insurance policies designed to cover the risk of data hacking and cyber-crime. General Re targets corporate customers through its website, with company professionals blogging about everything from the business risks posed by 3D printers (toxic fumes and fire hazards) to storing unused oil rigs (General Re 2016).

Different PR approaches are required in retail insurance markets where products such as home and contents insurance are often compulsory, and the industry is frequently perceived as a haven for heartless gouging head offices, misleading agents and nickel-and-diming claims adjusters (Treaster 2001). Even insurance comparison sites are tarnished by the brush of unfairness. Years of analysis show that 'cheap' is not necessarily the best value on insurance comparison sites, which do not cover the whole of the market and are opaque about their behind-closed-door deals with insurers (West 2014). Unlike traditional insurance brands, comparison sites are not shrinking violets, aggressively targeting new customers. ComparetheMarket.com, represented by its animated meerkats, entered the Netherlands market under the brand Hoyhoy, and as LesFurets (the ferrets) in France. The brand now engages in relationship building, offering cinema tickets to customers, supported by online PR campaigns featuring Arnold Schwarzenegger. Meanwhile, insurers are sorting out their own digital presence, so that customers can combine all their health, general insurance and life insurance policies on their mobiles or tablets (Rangar 2016). Insurers have also stepped up product innovation, from digital apps to telematics, machine-to-machine communication that can monitor homes and motor vehicles remotely, lowering premiums for prudent homeowners and better drivers. PR's messages here are more concerned enlivening insurance through newness rather than trustworthiness.

Health, well-being and retirement

The final part of the chapter looks at long-term financial provision – health insurance, life insurance and pensions – where governments have made the largest retreat from welfare provision, invoking a personal responsibility crusade.

I begin first with health insurance, an area of financial provision that varies dramatically from country to country. My discussion centres on the US market, where PR has played a role in the growing power of private health care. This matters because despite health insurers' booming success throughout the financial crisis, the industry has embarked on steep cost-cutting, resulting in falling standards of provision. New technologies are now transforming health insurance just as they are other financial services. Remote doctor-patient consultations cut the cost of medical care, and downloadable health records speed administration, while new products such as fitness apps promise policyholders financial rewards for achieving fitness goals (McFall 2015). While the industry's increased control over sensitive patient data is troubling, the biggest trust issue in health insurance is the industry's lack of transparency and its flouting of the very regulations designed to protect consumers (Potter 2010). Former insurance PR executive Wendell Potter exposes a range of mistrust strategies used in US health insurers' corporate communications. These range from 'rapid response' media relations used to manage down patient 'horror stories', e.g. the rising incidence of 'drive-through mastectomies' in which health insurers require hospitals to discharge breast cancer patients on the same day they undergo surgery (2010, p. 25).

More unsettling is Potter's description of PR's role in driving insurers' retreat from comprehensive healthcare provision by promoting so-called consumer-driven plans. These high-deductible, limited-benefit policies have dramatically reshaped trust/mistrust discourses in US healthcare. Consumer-driven plans were hyped as the response to growing 'consumerism', whereby Americans demanded greater control over their health care dollars (Potter 2010). Once customers were attracted (or forced) into the new consumer-driven plans, insurers increased deductibles[3] to levels far exceeding customers' annual incomes. When insurers were blamed for driving people into the ranks of the uninsured, insurance PR experts responded by cherry-picking US national statistics to suggest that most uninsured people were either illegal immigrants or 'simply shirking their personal responsibility to buy coverage' (Potter 2010, p. 71). Potter also details PR's manipulation of US healthcare policy, successfully scuppering President Clinton's 1990s health care reforms, and subsequently watering down the 2010 Affordable Care Act, known colloquially as 'Obamacare'.

Life and pensions

Trust issues in the life and pensions market are perhaps the most disturbing, because this is where consumers are required to be most enterprising with least certainty, and where there has been the greatest retreat in welfare provision. For those in workplace pension schemes, changes to accounting rules position employee pension schemes as a risk to corporate balance sheets, particularly in societies where people are living longer, requiring more years of pension payouts. Employers are closing final salary schemes, which are riskier to companies, and switching employees to defined contribution schemes where employees bear all the risks. Governments have reduced pension provision by changing taxation, increasing state pension age (as people are living longer) and nudging people toward individual pension provision, typically through life insurance.

Life insurance has not been an ideal solution to individual pensions. Most life products are investment-linked; they work well enough when stock markets are buoyant but fall apart in a downturn. Customers pay large amounts upfront for taking out a policy, and hefty penalties for withdrawal. Surrendering a life insurance policy can take days to 'action'. As with many industries, life insurers are more focused on finding new customers rather than improving the experience for existing customers. For example, large global insurers have attempted to develop sharia-compliant insurance products to market to Muslim customers who are restricted from buying investment-linked policies. One indictment on PR in the life and pensions markets has been its failure to build trust by simplifying the industry's jargon. Life and pension products may be among the worst communicated areas of financial services. 'Endowment' life policies are complex to understand, yet they are a crucial form of individual pension provision. Most consumers refer to a 'pension' as the money they are paid in retirement, but financial professionals refer to a pension as the pot of money built up while in employment. The pension then converts to a second financial product with another name *after* retirement. There have been half-hearted PR-led competitions to re-brand pensions, but the confusion remains. More importantly, terms like 'protected' and 'guaranteed' often used by insurers to build trust in long-term savings products are a pretence – it remains impossible to guarantee a rate of investment return, except perhaps a very low one (Simpson 2001).

The inability to provide guarantees on stock market earnings for retirement has been exacerbated by a lengthy period of low interest rates in many markets, affecting yields on fixed-income instruments such as government bonds. Elected governments know this threatens a key constituency, baby boomers, as they move into retirement facing lower pension payouts. In response, the UK government announced 'pension freedoms' from 2015 allowing the over-50s greater flexibility to withdraw from their individual pension pots. In 2016, the government also announced the creation of a new lifetime tax-free savings account, the oblique introduction of a US-style 401k individual pension plan. All these changes were announced as UK employers raced to comply with the deadline for 2008 reforms requiring UK workers to auto-enrol in some form of workplace pension scheme. The combined reforms had several consequences, all with PR implications.

First, the UK government launched PR and advertising campaigns to promote no fewer than three government services – the Money Advisory Service, the Pensions Advisory Service and Pension Wise. All three were able to provide *guidance* on pension freedoms, but not *advice*. Then it emerged that the three highly publicised services not only misled consumers on pension choices, but the guidance from each was different and sometimes technically incorrect (North 2016). Meanwhile, the life and pensions industry's PR and marketing response to pension freedom took various routes. Consumers' greater freedom to withdraw tax-free lump sums from pension savings directly threatened insurers with large annuities businesses. Pension freedom may dismantle the UK's annuities business altogether, as happened in New Zealand. As consumers withdrew pensions savings, life insurers scrambled to introduce replacement services to fill the gap. Insurance PR teams were forced to defend customer service operations as they struggled to cope with the volume of customers withdrawing savings.

At the industry level, trade and professional associations launched defensive campaigns and lobbying efforts on a range of pension-related issues. Life insurers were concerned they would be blamed for yet another mis-selling scandal once consumers withdrew pension savings and ended up with smaller pension pots in retirement. The Association of Consulting Actuaries lobbied the UK government to halt further pension reforms, and establish an independent pension commission to assess the challenges. The Institute and Faculty of Actuaries commissioned a survey claiming that a significant minority of over-55s thought pension freedom was a negative step. Barnett Waddingham, an actuarial consultancy firm, issued a survey highlighting UK employees' poor levels of pensions knowledge (Barnett Waddingham 2016). One NGO, the Financial Inclusion Centre, branded pension freedom a 'scorched earth policy' that would help 'destroy' the UK pensions system (Brodbeck 2015). However, one corner of the financial world positively relished the advent of pension freedom: financial intermediaries – from stockbrokers to financial advisers, accountants, tax experts, wealth managers and, of course, robo-advisers. After years of being chastised from various quarters, pension freedom presented a welcome new market of over 55s needing tailored advice on what to do with their newfound finnancial freedom (*Business Reporter* 2015). UK pension freedom aptly demonstrates the range of industry voices represented by public relations in the battle for trust in financial services.

Conclusion: industry anxiety over consumer anxiety?

This chapter on insurance, investment and pensions, and the preceding two chapters on the stock markets and banking, together illustrate the dramatic transformation underway in financial markets and services. The changes – regulatory, technological and societal – all have implications for what people trust in finance since the 'what' is shifting dramatically. While fund managers, insurers and pension providers may not wield the same power as banks, their role in financial trust relations is crucial because, in the long run, the trust breaches that cause a loss of savings, investments, healthcare and pensions are the most damaging to families and to society. Yet there seems to be no cohesive role for public relations in improving the quality of financial services, and the quality of consumers' relationships with financial providers and intermediaries. Instead, what the chapter demonstrates is the opportunistic nature of PR activity: in other words, PR does not follow genuine trust issues, PR follows the money. Opportunistic PR serves its purpose, for example, when PR jumps on the bandwagon of fintech start-ups and other innovators to help them build market presence, tout new products and services, and be 'heard above the noise'. However, opportunism also shapes PR's more troubling contribution behind the scenes, helping large, powerful financial providers – the status quo – protect their status through lobbying. PR also contrives two-faced 'charm offensives' in which financial providers offer public support for government reforms, while battling savagely to prevent or reverse change behind the scenes (Potter 2010).

This chapter has examined financial services' anxiety over growth and competition, and governmental anxiety over electoral legitimacy. Unfortunately, as I have suggested, very little transformation in financial services seems designed to assuage consumer anxiety or rebuild trust. Products can now now be accessed more quickly, easily and efficiently, but there is little evidence that consumers' financial decision-making is any better. For fund managers, insurers, pension providers and intermediaries alike, trust relations seem focused on promoting financial products and services that offer safety and protection from risk, while avoiding issues of fairness, soundness or quality. Governments exacerbate trust relations in financial services by flip-flopping on policies concerning so-called personal responsibility and financial self-management. At one end of the election cycle, governments curry favour with voters by declaring that 'people aren't stupid' and must be encouraged to be enterprising and self-sufficient. At the other end of the cycle, governments reverse this stance by denying consumers' financial choice, even when choice had been governments' mantra (Cumbo 2015). No aspect of government flip-flopping has been worse than its attitude to financial intermediaries. Whatever 'mood' a government adopts – pro-financial advisers or against them – nothing seems to shift the stubborn fact that the vast majority of consumers do not use a financial adviser, and have increasingly limited places to turn to for genuine financial advice. The resulting rise in financial exclusion, and PR's role in associated battles over trust/mistrust, is the subject of the next chapter.

Notes

1 I previously mentioned PR activity in fund management in Chapters 4 and 5.
2 A white-labelled fund is produced by one company, then re-branded by other companies to appear as their own product.
3 Deductibles refer to the amount customers must pay out of pocket before an insurer will step in to cover costs.

References

Barnett Waddingham. (2016). 'Major generational differences exist in financial knowledge', *Barnett Waddingham Press Release*, 23 March. Retrieved from: https://www.barnett-wadd

ingham.co.uk/comment-insight/press/2016/03/24/major-generational-differ
ences-exist-financial-kno/

Ben-Ami, D. (2001). *Cowardly Capitalism: The Myth of the Global Financial Casino*, Chichester: Wiley & Sons.

Bhattacharya, U., Hackethal, A., Kaesler, S., Loos, B. and Meyer, S. (2011). *Is Unbiased Financial Advice to Retail Investors Sufficient?* Retrieved from: http://papers.ssrn.com/sol3/papers.cfm?abstract_id=1669015

Bow, M. (2015). 'Fund managers: Don't ask us to be transparent over fees', *The Independent*, 8 October. Retrieved from: http://www.independent.co.uk/news/business/analysis-and-features/fund-managers-don-t-ask-us-to-be-transparent-over-fees-a6685531.html

Brodbeck, S. (2015). 'Cash for access: Chancellor's 'scorched earth' reforms open annuities minefield', *Money Marketing*, 19 March. Retrieved from: https://www.moneymarketing.co.uk/cash-for-access-chancellors-scorched-earth-reforms-open-annuities-minefield/

Business Reporter. (2015). 'New pensions advice service launched', *Business Reporter*, 23 June. Retrieved from: http://business-reporter.co.uk/2015/06/23/new-pensions-advice-service-launched/

Collinson, P. (2005). 'The low-down on fund managers', *Fund Strategy*, October, p. 21.

Coney, J. (2010). 'Beware the car insurance courtesy car trap', *This is Money*, 28 July. Retrieved from: http://www.thisismoney.co.uk/money/cars/article-1692116/Beware-the-car-insurance-courtesy-car-trap.html

Cumbo, J. (2015). 'Annuities cash-in idea has 'potential', say insurers', *Financial Times*, 17 January, p. 4.

Eccles, R.G. and Vollbracht, M. (2006). 'Media reputation of the insurance industry', *The Geneva Papers*, 31, pp. 395–408.

Economist. (2014). 'Will invest for food', *The Economist*, 3 May, pp. 19–22.

Egan, M., Matvos, G. and Seru, A. (2016). 'The market for financial adviser misconduct'. Retrieved from: http://papers.ssrn.com/sol3/papers.cfm?abstract_id=2739170

Eley, J. (2014). 'So, you think you need a fund manager?' *FT Money*, 11 October, p. 3.

Finke, M. (2012). *Financial Advice: Does It Make a Difference.* Retrieved from http://papers.ssrn.com/sol3/papers.cfm?abstract_id=2051382

French, S. and Kneale, J. (2009). 'Excessive financialisation: Insuring lifestyles, enlivening subjects, and everyday spaces of biosocial excess', *Environment and Planning D: Society and Space*, 27, pp. 1030–1053.

General Re. (2016). 'Our perspective', *General Re Blogs*. Retrieved from: http://www.genre.com/knowledge/blog/?categorySearch=1104021

Hilton, A. (2008). 'Maintain a high profile in a crisis', *PR Week*, 7 November, p. 9.

House of Commons. (2004). *Restoring confidence in long-term savings*, House of Commons Treasury Committee Report, HC 71–1, 28 July, 79 pages.

Hume, N. (2001). 'Fund fury over 'dirty tricks'', *The Guardian*, 5 November. Retrieved from: http://www.theguardian.com/business/2001/nov/05/2

Johansson, S. and Vogelgesang, U. (2016). *Insurance on the Threshold of Digitization: Implications for the Life and P&C Workforce*, Geneva and Hamburg: McKinsey & Company.

Kendall, D. (2005). *Framing Class: Media Representations of Wealth and Poverty in America*, Plymouth: Rowman & Littlefield.

Kincaid, J. (2006). 'Finance, trust and the power of capital', *Historical Materialism*, 14, pp. 31–48.

Knights, D., Murray, F. and Willmott, H. (1993). 'Networking as knowledge work: A study of strategic interorganisational development in the financial services industry', *Journal of Management Studies*, 30, pp. 975–993.

KPMG. (2009). *Renewing the Promise*, London: KPMG International.

Langley, P. (2008). *The Everyday Life of Global Finance*, Oxford: Oxford University Press.

Lehtonen, T. (2014). 'Picturing how life insurance matters', *Journal of Cultural Economy*, 7 (3), pp. 308–333.

Mattinson, A. (2009). 'Insurers seek help to ditch jargon', *PR Week*, 31 July, p. 8–9.

McFall, L. (2015). 'Is digital disruption the end of health insurance? Some thoughts on the devising of risk', *Economic Sociology*, 17 (1), pp. 32–43.

Mitchell, R. (2010). 'Investing: The trust crisis, the new world of wealth', *Economist Intelligence Unit*, April.

Nayak, A. and Beckett, A. (2008). 'Infantilised adults or confident consumers? Enterprise discourse in the UK retail banking industry', *Organization*, 15 (3), pp. 407–425.

Newlands, C. (2013). 'Arrests and resignations – a bad week for fund industry', *Financial Times FTfm*, 28 January, p. 6.

North, K. (2016). 'Ditching guidance in favour of advice', *Money Marketing*, 30 March. Retrieved from: https://www.moneymarketing.co.uk/kim-north-ditching-guidance-in-favour-of-advice/

Oakley, D. (2014). 'Closet huggers of the index drag the City down', *Financial Times FTfm*, 1 December, p. 4.

Payne, A. (2009). 'Investment funds need to educate', *PR Week*, 21 August, p. 7.

Pitcher, G. (2003). *The Death of Spin*, Chichester: John Wiley & Sons.

Potter, W. (2010). *Deadly Spin: An Insurance Company Insider Speaks Out on How Corporate PR Is Killing Health Care and Deceiving Americans*, New York: Bloomsbury Press.

Power, M. (2015). 'Building the behavioural balance sheet: An essay on Solvency II', *Economic Sociology*, 17 (1), pp. 45–53.

PR Week. (2013). 'A flavour of Lansons' work', *PR Week*, 7 July. Retrieved from: http://www.prweek.com/article/1302254/flavour-lansons-work

Prestridge, J. (2005). 'Time for a sea change, Rebuilding reputations in financial services', *PR Week White paper*, May, p. 4.

PwC (PricewaterhouseCoopers). (2014). *Asset Management 2020: A Brave New World*, London: Pricewaterhouse Coopers.

Rangar, B.S. (2016). 'When the going gets digital, the digitals get going', *Insurance Times*, 17 March. Retrieved from: http://www.insurancetimes.co.uk/innovation-blog-when-the-going-gets-digital-the-digitals-get-going/1417679.article

Ryan, G. (2016). 'Fidelity paying down student debt for over 10% of employees', *Boston Business Journal*, 15 March. Retrieved from: http://www.bizjournals.com/boston/news/2016/03/15/fidelity-paying-down-student-debt-for-over-10-of.html

Shaw, G. (2014). 'The editor's letter', *Which? Magazine*, p. 3.

Simpson, D. (2001). 'Trust in life assurance', *Economic Affairs*, 21 (1), pp. 23–28.

Treaster, J.B. (2001). 'The insurance industry'. In Thompson, T. (ed) *Writing about Business*, New York: Columbia University Press, pp. 272–279.

West, C. (2014). 'Cleaning up price comparison sites', *Which? Money*, January, p. 7.

Wigglesworth, R. (2016). 'AI tools prove a hard sell with fund managers', *FT Weekend*, 26–27 March, p. 17.

Young, S. (2009). 'Industry voice: Building on trust', *Investment Adviser*. Retrieved from: http://www.ftadviser.com/2011/10/26/ifa-industry/your-business/industry-voice-building-on-trust-2g5ay04CwZ7A2LAKDyzXhO/article.html

Zurich Insurance Group. (2014). *Tackling the Growing Risk of Cyber Crime: Discussion Points for Financial Institutions*, Zurich: Author.

8 Financial exclusion

PR as activism and resistance

Throughout the book, I have highlighted the public's changing relationship with financial services, influenced not just by the state's retreat from welfare provision, but by financial institutions' retreat from less profitable customers. This retreat from broad financial provision contributes to shifting trust relations in financial markets by creating a widening inequality gap. On one side of the gap are 'trustworthy' citizen-consumers: those in full-time, permanent employment, preferably married, homeowners, with good credit histories, paying bills on time and fulfilling credit commitments (Leyshon and Thrift 1999, Burton 2008). These fortunate citizen-consumers are the *super-included*, who have more financial products at their disposal and more access to financial information, hence more opportunities to make money (Leyshon and Thrift 1999, Burton 2008). Scattered across the gap itself are middle-class citizen-consumers who no longer meet all the criteria for financial trustworthiness and have become *marginalised* from certain aspects of finance. These middle-class consumers may have rising personal debt or questionable credit histories. Some occupy 'functionally poor' households, with above-average incomes but little or no assets and high debt (Karger 2005). Some no longer meet narrowing criteria for mortgage lending because they cannot raise large deposits or are deemed 'too old' to borrow. In some countries, middle-class consumers cannot afford escalating bank fees, driving them toward alternative finance (James 2015).

On the other side of the gap are the citizen-consumers who fail to meet all standard criteria for financial trustworthiness, becoming *persistently excluded* from formal finance, either because they are not in paid work, living on income support or on very low incomes (Burton 2008, Marron 2013). Even though the financially excluded may periodically move into paid work, other realities contribute to their persistent marginalisation. Financial exclusion disproportionately affects groups such as young adults and ethnic minorities (Marron 2013, Pardoe et al. 2015). The financially excluded are most likely to live in disadvantaged communities, poorly served by bank branch networks (Marron 2013). Exclusion from banking is particularly serious, as the 'unbanked' have no current account or debit/credit card. No current account restricts access to 'free' digital wage deposits, bill payments, rental agreements and ATM use. No bank card restricts users to cardless transactions – increasingly difficult to do when dealing with many companies, especially dot coms. In terms of long-term financial provision, the financially excluded are least likely to have life insurance, particularly where affordable insurance sold door-to-door is now defunct (Burton et al. 2005). They are also least likely to have interpersonal connections with finance professionals or access to financial advisers, who do not serve the poor.

Marginalised and excluded consumers still engage with financial services, primarily through alternative finance such as microfinance organisations, credit unions, cooperatives, friendly societies, burial societies, community savings clubs and lending clubs. Unfortunately, penalised by poor access, the marginalised frequently resort to predatory lenders in the 'fringe economy', which includes licensed moneylenders, payday lenders, pawnbrokers, loan sharks, home credit, catalogue credit, hire purchase, cheque cashers, tax refund lenders, auto title pawns, 'buy-here, pay-here' used-car lots; as well as pre-paid phone cards and other businesses charging excessive interest rates or fees, or exorbitant prices for goods or services (Karger 2005).

This chapter will focus on the precarious trust relations between marginalised consumers and alternative finance, particularly the fringe economy. While many forms of alternative finance have existed for centuries, often playing a role in community cohesion, the fringe economy is the 'darker' side of alternative finance where there has been phenomenal growth, fuelled by a growing customer base of marginalised consumers and the phenomenal profits to be made. Wherever there are new markets, new providers and new profits, there is PR. Whole portions of the fringe economy use PR and marketing techniques aggressively. I argue in this chapter that financial exclusion represents a breach of *societal* trust relations with growing segments of citizens. While system trust may drive financial markets, societal trust is even more vital to welfare and society. For this reason, it is important not just to examine PR's role in creating and/or solidifying financial marginalisation, but to consider PR's contribution to financial dissent in its many forms. The next section explores the relationship between public relations and financial dissent. Thereafter, I look at various aspects of alternative finance – from the cooperative movement and consumer organisations, to financial inclusion programmes and microfinance. The third section of the chapter looks at PR's role in predatory lending and the fringe economy. In the final section, I look at 'prosocial PR' and 'protest PR' and active resistance to marginalisation through grassroots financial activism.

Resisting exclusion: public relations and financial dissent

Financial dissent takes many forms, from within financial markets and externally. Since financial dissent comes from the top, bottom and all around, adopting multiple and contradictory subject positions and interests, its relationship with system trust is complex, as is the relationship between financial dissent and power. Within financial markets, the marginalised have been able to resist the financial status quo through 'constructive' financial dissent, joining small, community-based financial organisations, for example. These community-based organisations focus on building trust in the shared vision of the collective, rather than battling with the inequities of the formal financial system. Dissent from outside of financial markets works differently, often attempting to insert *healthy* doses of mistrust into the financial system or its dysfunctional parts. Dissent from outside financial markets supports a clear divide between 'power' and 'resistance', with financial market interests pitched as 'power', while the key task for resistance becomes making use of the regulatory authority and international institutions to bring financial capital (the clearly identifiable enemy) under control (Langley 2008).

However, in tracing PR activity in alternative finance and the fringe economy, what emerges throughout this chapter is that financial dissent is ambiguous in nature. So in this chapter, I re-assert the theoretical argument from Chapter 2, that trust and power are ever-present in financial markets, but trust and power are fluid relations. As the preceding chapters should have made clear, one cannot find absolute forms of domination over financial markets. For the same reason, one cannot find absolute forms of financial resistance. Power and resistance in financial markets are not opposites, they are not autonomous, and cannot be completely separated (Langley 2008). If power is ambiguous, then resistance must be too. To this end, not only is financial resistance ambiguous, it is often contradictory or compromised (Langley 2008). Instead of financial resistance, I will therefore use the term 'financial dissent' throughout the chapter. The term 'dissent' also needs clarification, as it suggests organised, collective, public activity (Langley 2008). Yet financial markets have not been an obvious site for trade union-like organisation of dissent; on the contrary, financial markets are more typified by 'secretive crystallisations'[1] of governance and power (Roberts 1998, p. 129). In reality, financial dissent takes many forms, so it is important not to sideline dissent that does not fit the profile of oppositional politics, and may even form an intrinsic part of the financial status quo. While financial dissent is not always supported by strategic public relations activity, PR often becomes important in promoting the cause of financial dissenters through organised campaign activity.

Financial cooperatives: trusted operators, uncertain future

The first form of financial dissent encompasses a set of centuries-old financial organisations that predate the welfare state.[2] Financial cooperatives (e.g. credit unions) and financial mutuals (e.g. friendly societies, building societies and mutual life insurers) mushroomed during the industrial era as a means of protecting more vulnerable groups – impoverished workers and the burgeoning working class – when there was no social safety net available (Simpson 2001, Lewin 2002). They constituted an early form of financial dissent by giving some financial control to the working class. Both are owned by a defined group of members, and while the terms 'cooperative' and 'mutual' are sometimes used interchangeably, cooperatives are expected to have a common purpose which they put into practice. For the purpose of this discussion,

I will refer to both cooperatives and mutuals as the *cooperative model*. Financial cooperatives were traditionally counted among the most trusted financial institutions, a reputation developed during the industrial era as many fly-by-night operators aggressively competed for workers' savings breeding mistrust in financial services. The financial sector had two options for resolving the problem of mistrust: accept restrictive government regulation or carve a space for certain suppliers to acquire a particular reputation for trustworthiness (Simpson 2001). Financial cooperatives and mutuals fulfilled the latter option, resolving the problem of impersonal trust-at-a-distance by engendering closer customer relationships through consumer democracy: each customer became a 'member' and thus an owner of the cooperative.

As a form of dissent, cooperative membership is both 'intimate and voluntary' as well as 'mutual and collective', argues Langley (2008 p. 220). Small wonder the cooperative movement spread successfully throughout almost every corner of the world. PR and marketing have helped to promote the cooperative model and consumer democracy as a productive form of financial dissent. But contemporary financial cooperatives cannot compete with the vast marketing budgets controlled by international banks and insurers. Nor can cooperatives garner the level of media attention that large listed companies attract.

So long as membership remains reasonably homogenous, representing common interests, the cooperative model is a manageable one. However, financial cooperatives have been squeezed into a corner by market developments. First, decades of liberalisation policies in Western markets led many cooperatives and mutuals to 'de-mutualise', becoming publicly listed financial institutions now pressured to deliver shareholder value year-on-year. The declining number of cooperatives struggle to compete with the shareholder model, where financial institutions grow rapidly, extend into new countries and markets and diversify product ranges. The cooperative model cannot expand as easily: operating across national borders is difficult, as many mutual-type organisations are small, designed to work in the vicinity of their members and may even be restricted by charter to a locality or region. Cooperatives also have less access to investment capital and run the risk of making ownership and voting structure unwieldy if they accept non-members into their customer base (Lewin 2002). Consequently, the cooperative model as financial dissent is wavering in certain markets. France, Finland and the Netherlands are home to Europe's largest financial cooperatives (Cocalina 2016). However, some European countries do not permit mutual-type structures, or restrict their activities (Broek et al. 2012). In the UK, the largest financial cooperative struggled to regain trust after revelations of fraud at the highest levels of its banking operation. In the US, financial cooperatives do not feature as strongly in everyday saving and borrowing (Langley 2008). Even in developing countries where the cooperative model continues to grow, PR and marketing messages now de-emphasise consumer democracy and empowerment (Burke 2016).

Above all, the financial cooperative model has struggled to comply with rising capital requirements, a situation exacerbated by new regulations since the global financial crisis. This regulatory pressure has led many financial coop-eratives to merge, and in some jurisdictions their future is unclear. If these centuries-old organisations are to play a role in supporting the financially marginalised, what role can PR play? The cooperative sector is represented by various trade associations at both the global and international level. These associations engage in lobbying and maintain a presence. In the aftermath of the global financial crisis, the UK government temporarily touted coopera-tive saving and lending as the solution to the moral turpitude of the banking sector. Government speeches and reports incorporated cooperatives into plans to address financial exclusion. Yet policy intentions are not enough to change consumer behaviour without a large (and costly) public education campaign. If cooperatives themselves are de-emphasising cooperative education in their own PR campaigns, and if the annual general meeting loses its role in coopera-tive democracy, these organisations may continue to cede their role to more contemporary forms of financial dissent.

Consumer organisations – trusted but compromised

A more modern form of financial dissent is the consumer organisation, the supposedly disinterested scrutineers of market behaviour. Consumer organisa-tions range from government-funded agencies and charities to profit-making companies, but all aim to fill an important gap in financial markets by pro-viding consumer education, self-help and advice. Well-funded for-profit con-sumer organisations also carry out product testing, ranking and publicising best and worst products. However, evaluating consumer finance is more complex than researching 'best buys' on automobiles or household goods. With so many financial brands, only select products can be monitored. These products are intangible, and often modified, copied or withdrawn too quickly to monitor (Aldridge 1997), while problems generally emerge years after purchase. Yet this is precisely what makes consumer organisations such important trust mecha-nisms in financial markets. Applying the trust practice framework, consumer groups simplify the bewildering range of financial products. They may not offer guarantees on which products work best, but they are good at singling out financial products that do *not* work.

To be effective as trust mechanisms, consumer organisations must use active PR approaches, not just to demystify financial products and services through consumer education programmes, but to resist PR activity by financial institu-tions, by disentangling 'objective information' from financial institutions' pro-motional hype (Aldridge 1997). For example, consumer organisations often resist financial providers' issues-based PR activity, insisting that consumers sim-ply want to be told what to buy or not to buy (Kellaway 2015). Consumer organisations also provide effective financial dissent through mistrust campaigns against financial services providers. The UK consumer website Moneysaving-expert.com, founded by a former financial PR executive, has led the way in media campaigning. In 2006–8, the site campaigned against bank overcharging on TV and in the tabloid press, providing a template letter for consumers to demand refunds (Burton 2008). More than a million letters were downloaded, while the financial ombudsman received some 5,000 enquiries a week at the height of the campaign (Hickman 2007).

Consumer organisations are undoubtedly vital in leading financial dissent. However, given that power is exercised and realised *through* resistance (Langley 2008), consumer organisations' resistance is both ambiguous and compromised. First, the most successful campaigning consumer organisations in financial markets only target the financially *included*. Consumer organisations also construct 'mythical' financial consumers who are rational, disciplined and risk-averse. This leaves little room for the emotions which often drive financial decision-making (Aldridge 1997), and little room for the adventure and allure attached to investments (discussed in Chapter 4). Furthermore, the championing role of consumer organisations is often compromised by contemporary funding models. Profit-making consumer organisations increasingly depend on promoting in-house products and services such as credit cards, magazines and shopping discounts. This undermines the rational anti-promotional ethos espoused by most consumer groups (Aldridge 1997). The highly successful Moneysavingexpert.com is no exception: the site was sold for more than £80 million to a price comparison site, a potentially compromising move considering the opaque practices these sites engage in (see Chapter 7). In reality, the number of consumer organisations acting as trusted 'consumer champions' for the financially excluded is limited. Where they exist, such consumer organisations are small, with limited resources for high-visibility PR campaigns.

Government PR turns to financial 'literacy'

In some countries, governments assume responsibility for providing consumer education to marginalised financial consumers, offering increased attention to financial literacy as a response to the global financial crisis. Since 2008, international summits have echoed resolutions on financial inclusion. The US government launched the President's Council on Financial Literacy, while several major US cities formed the Cities for Financial Empowerment Coalition (*Economist* 2008). Increasingly, such campaigns appear to support market ideology rather than social welfare. This is particularly true of public education campaigns which present universal participation in financial markets as a *natural* condition, one in which consumers ought to be able to buy as many financial products and services as they like. In these campaigns, the obstacles faced by marginalised consumers – whether geographical exclusion, price exclusion, marketing exclusion, even self-exclusion – can somehow be overcome through financial education (Marron 2013). Financial exclusion is therefore attributed to inadequate financial self-management rather than lapses in public policy, social mobility or financial market structures. PR supports this ideology in public education campaigns encouraging the financially excluded to change their conduct and adapt to their economically disadvantaged position by practising 'correct' financial practices of thrift, precaution and self-reliance (Marron 2013). Government-backed financial literacy campaigns are potentially compromised on two levels: first, where such campaigns' aim is to reduce the state's burden by shifting marginalised consumers to commercial financial options that may be unsuitable, while encouraging more-included financial consumers to enhance their material welfare by embracing speculative forms of financial risk (Marron 2013). Second, these campaigns have the unfortunate effect of mitigating financial institutions' bad behaviour, while placing the onus on consumers not to be misled by inappropriate financial products again.

Microfinance: successful financial spin

In several countries, governments once played a more purposive role in poverty reduction by backing microfinance organisations, providing tiny loans to poor individuals to establish or expand a simple income-generating activity (Bateman 2010). Microfinance became an evangelical movement with altruistic motives, as cooperatives were decades before. However, the original ethos of microfinance has long disappeared; these organisations have become re-purposed as 'appropriate' finance for the financially excluded. Many development experts attribute this to PR campaigning by Grameen Bank, the world's best-known microfinance organisation. Based in Bangladesh, Grameen was established to lend to women in Bangladesh's conservative, rural male-dominated society. Social trust plays no part in Grameen's model; lending is based on social coercion, peer-group monitoring is used to reduce lender's risk, with women designated most suitable for this form of social pressure. In self-selected groups, if one member defaults, all group members lose access to finance (Rogaly 1996, Mallick 2002). Founder Muhammad Yunus built an international profile as the 'pioneer[3] of microfinance' through countless PR-orchestrated media appearances, and books promoting the gospel of social business. Thousands travelled to Bangladesh to learn the Grameen 'way' (Mallick 2002). Grameen went 'international', launching Grameen America, backed by the Clinton Global Initiative, while the Grameen Foundation supports microcredit across other continents. Yunus and Grameen received the Nobel Peace Prize in 2006.

Critics point to the role played by Grameen's 'feel-good PR and marketing' in constructing myths around microfinance (Bateman 2010, p. 2). The critics' principle concern is with the astonishing levels of trust built in the Grameen model's impact on poverty reduction. Development experts argue that microfinance primarily benefits those hovering below the poverty line rather than the poorest, who in some cases are made worse off (Rogaly 1996). They argue that Grameen even impoverished the very women it set out to help, as these women did not necessarily benefit from loans disbursed in their names. Experts are particularly concerned that repayments based on social coercion have resulted in physical abuse (Rogaly 1996), and even suicide (McKeen-Edwards and Porter 2013). However, Grameen's PR blitz should be seen as a joint campaign. Quite simply, Grameen needed to be a success story to justify hundreds of millions donated or invested by the many organisations which promoted their association with Grameen. These include the United Nations, the Bill and Melinda Gates Foundation and George Soros (Mallick 2002, Bateman 2010, Muhammad 2015). Where Grameen once positioned itself as a voice of financial dissent, it now facilitates global corporate expansion through joint ventures which compromise its earlier altruism (Muhammad 2015). Danone now manufactures yogurt in Bangladesh in a joint venture with Grameen to promote the fight against malnutrition in children. The benefits to Danone are clear since Bangladesh was also the only country where Danone did not sell yogurt (Coster 2010). A joint venture with Veolia to supply water is similarly popularised in the name of the poor, despite no direct ownership by Grameen's members (Muhammad 2015). Grameen's PR edifice has served the bank well, particularly following charges of malfeasance, under-reported repayment rates and problem loans (Bhagwati 2011, Bernhardt 2012). 'Friends of Grameen' launched a well-funded defensive campaign, employing global PR firm Burson-Marsteller. In an ironic move, the US State Department interfered via a press release reprimanding Bangladesh's government for intervening in Grameen's affairs (Bhagwati 2011).

Grameen's well-funded international PR helped build visibility for microfinance. The sector has cemented its credibility by forming trade associations which have in turn mounted PR campaigns to defend collective interests (McKeen-Edwards and Porter 2013). PR also attracted the interest of Western investors, drawn by the prospect of low default levels in microfinance and its capacity to charge interest rates as high as 100 per cent in some developing countries (Ross 2013). The United Nations and the World Bank now promote microfinance as a form of 'universal financial inclusion' (Bateman 2012, Muhammad 2015). Bateman (2012) contends that Western investors and international development agencies have colluded in a cynical PR exercise which has effectively shut down financial dissent by claiming to give financial tools to the poor. The worldwide promotion of microfinance through regular international summits and conferences has permitted lenders to abandon the small and medium-sized enterprise (SME) sector, and enabled development agencies to divert funds from healthcare, education or infrastructure. Bateman (2010) maintains that 'new wave' microfinance is the opposite of financial dissent. He concludes that the microfinance industry's PR machine has led citizens to yield further power to global markets by positioning microfinance as *better* than collective action (e.g. trade unions or social movements), and a *better* welfare model than universal healthcare, public sector employment, or even radical redistribution of wealth and power.

PR's role in predatory lending

Despite its problems, the microfinance model is simply not as widespread as the 'fringe economy' which exists in all countries (Karger 2005). Subprime lending and other fringe economic activity are as old as the hills. Traditional subprime lending even had an element of low-level trust generated through regular contact between borrowers and lenders (Leyshon et al. 1998). Few moneylenders used credit scoring, relying on the knowledge of local agents to identify good and bad customers, and conducting weekly visits to exert discipline and control (Burton 2008). However, the modern fringe economy is very different, very large and very profitable. Its phenomenal growth is partially driven by mainstream lenders moving in to take advantage of subprime lenders' low start-up and running costs, and the tremendous profits to be made in the very same market spaces mainstream lenders had once deserted (Karger 2005, Burton 2008). In the US, banks such as Citi, JPMorgan Chase, Morgan Stanley, the former Banc of America Securities, Wachovia and Wells Fargo all had banking relationships with subprime lenders before the financial crisis (Karger 2005). Today, many high street lenders operate in the 'grey' area between the prime and sub-prime market, offering 'impaired mortgages' with higher rates for customers who are discharged bankrupts or have liens against their names (Burton et al. 2004).

Newer modes of subprime lending are not relationship based at all. Where traditional banks serve low-income communities, they are frequently as predatory as fringe economy businesses (Karger 2005). Large mainstream lenders can run subprime institutions more efficiently by offering large buffers and credit lines, yet they can be just as predatory as backstreet lenders, arguing that their high charges reflect the risks of doing business with economically unstable customers (Karger 2005). In reality, the real profits in the fringe economy come from customers who do *not* pay off loans (Karger 2005). As predatory lenders gain more legitimacy, more and more marginalised consumers gravitate towards them. Some take the plunge out of desperation, others out of ignorance, while many are simply unable to meet the criteria of lower-risk alternative lenders, such as credit unions, which often require community-based membership and regular savings.

The growing legitimacy of many predatory lenders has been achieved through intensive marketing and PR. On the one hand, many subprime lenders are now the biggest spenders on advertising in consumer finance, using direct marketing, and advertising in tabloids, television infomercials and websites (Burton et al. 2004). Advertising material promotes overly positive images and the liberating effects of credit, facilitating dreams and fantasies, while obscuring the grave consequences and language of debt. (Burton 2008). PR's role is many tentacled, not just supporting aggressive marketing campaigns but also building trust in subprime lending brands by aligning them with worthy causes such as children's charities, education and financial literacy (Karger 2005). Since the global financial crisis, PR's role has intensified, mounting crisis communications and defensive PR campaigns for subprime lenders as they came under increased attack from politicians and activists. Larger subprime lenders now have dedicated public affairs teams lobbying policymakers and regulators for a continued industry foothold, while retained PR consultants argue the benefits of the subprime business model to investors.

UK payday lender Wonga has been a lightning rod for financial dissent. In 2012, Wonga earned more than £1 million a week, from loans offering interest rates as high as 5,000 per cent. Wonga's international operations made total profits of £62.5 million, up 36 per cent on the previous year (Armitage and Watts 2013, p. 2). The National Union of Students accused Wonga of targeting vulnerable young people. Politicians attacked Wonga in parliament for using puppets in its advertising to groom children into future borrowers. Consumer groups uncovered Wonga's practice of sending debt recovery letters to customers under the names of fictitious law firms[4] (R. Jones 2015). The Anglican church locked horns with Wonga over its exorbitant loan rates, but had to climb down when it was revealed that the church had indirect investments in Wonga (R. Jones 2015). Wonga fought back through advertising and PR. It launched a brand refresh, repositioning the firm for middle class and 'hard working' customers, with new advertising campaigns and a documentary featuring stories about 'real' Wonga customers. While Wonga was voted one of the UK's most-improved brands of 2015, activist PR had the last word. Protest groups not only succeeded in regulating all payday lenders, they then pressured the regulator to cap predatory interest rates, causing Wonga's profits to plummet.

Financial dissent against predatory lending is a battle with moving targets. Attempts to curtail profits in the 'getting-into-debt' industry simply drive investors to back the highly lucrative 'getting-out-of-debt' industry (Karger 2005). The 'getting-out-of-debt' industry covers debt collection agencies offering a variety of services, including credit scoring, door-to-door collection, computerised dialling systems, bailiffs, car recovery, surveillance and absconder tracing (Burton 2008). The sector thrives on financial institutions' ability to sell their debt on to any number of organisations. PR and marketing have helped the 'getting-out-of-debt' market to grow, by first besieging the financially marginalised consumers with messages about getting 'more and cheaper credit', followed by messages about how to 'get out of debt' (Karger 2005). There are serious issues of ethics and trust associated with consumers accepting loans from one lender, then having to repay another (Burton 2008). But the debt recollection industry operates below the radar, unlike high-visibility getting-into-debt operators like Wonga. Consequently, financial dissent against debt collection is harder to mobilise. Meanwhile, the getting-out-of-debt industry has formed trade associations in order to build credibility with wholesale customers, regulators and investors. Nevertheless, the growing acceptance of debt resale has successfully attracted the attention of various activist groups, whose grassroots PR campaigns will be discussed in the final section of the chapter.

PR and financial activism

Mainstream PR theory has situated corporate PR and political activism as polar opposites, framing activists adversarially, as a growing threat to legitimate corporate activity (Demetrious 2013). This view is generally supported by corporate PR advisers who often take a 'socially autocratic' stance toward activists when corporate strategies are challenged (Demetrious 2013, p.1). Corporate communicators have even developed their own matrixes for 'dealing' with activists, choosing which groups to engage and which to marginalise (Pitcher

2003). In considering the relationship between PR and activism in shaping trust discourses in financial markets, I have incorporated Demetrious's theorising of PR, activism and dominant discourses. Applying Demetrious (2013, p. 30), I position corporate PR advisers as representatives of the status quo in financial markets, carefully policing the borders of trust discourses, assembling 'fences' around 'trust' where necessary, while looking out for breaks and tears in need of restoring. Extending Demetrious's work further, financial activists resist the efforts by PR's boundary riders, focusing on finding breaks and tears in trust discourses or deliberately constructing 'rifts' in those discourses, as well as contesting trust strategies employed by powerful financial institutions.

If activism is often pitched as antithetical to capitalist-led corporate PR, activists and corporate PR practitioners alike seem entirely comfortable with this dichotomy. However, financial activism is multidimensional, and while activist groups may be suspicious of PR and marketing practices, they use these same practices regularly. Some authors even argue that some of the earliest forms of PR were perfected by activist groups (Coombs and Holladay 2014). The complexity deepens when looking at activists' campaign activities. Organisations often start out using grassroots techniques and community-based responses on minimal resources (Demetrious 2013). But the most successful activist organisations often grow into international corporate entities in their own right, through sophisticated marketing, strategic alliances and 'cheque book activism' (Hensby, Sibthorpe and Driver 2012). To discuss the implications of activist PR as financial dissent, I will look at organisations associated with 'prosocial PR' such as relationship building, educating and seeking cooperation (Adi and Moloney 2012), as well as those opting for 'protest PR' through confrontation, occupations, demonstrations, strikes etc. (Adi and Moloney 2012). Both forms seek to highlight financial inequality and long-term damage wrought by credit and debt on society, as well as damage to consumers' personal relationships and individual health (Burton 2008).

Prosocial PR

As a form of financial dissent, prosocial PR faces the problem of impact; its approach is slower and more centred on relationships, often with policymakers. Many such groups are focused on achieving real financial inclusion for the poor. Prosocial groups include US charity Operation Hope, which empowers the poor in Los Angeles through a mixture of financial literacy, advice and basic banking services. Prosocial groups in the UK include The James Gibb Stuart Trust in Glasgow and the Financial Inclusion Centre in London, which focus on reducing debt levels through public education. The Financial Inclusion Centre also campaigns for banking reform, a new financial regulatory architecture and development funding through social investment bonds, using communications tools such as in-depth reports and white papers (McAteer and Harrison 2009). Other vocal lobby groups include Finance Watch, a Brussels-based lobby group set up by Members of the European Parliament to champion the needs of EU citizens. Finance Watch advocates for a financial system committed to 'a plural, inclusive democracy' where citizens' voices are not 'drowned out by powerful, private actors' (Finance Watch 2014).

Protest PR

Unlike prosocial PR, protest PR is loosely organised around emerging issues. Protest PR in financial markets has existed for decades, gaining visibility through anti-globalisation demonstrations in the 1990s, and subsequent annual protests at the World Economic Forum and G14 meetings. The anti-globalisation movement found new energy following the 2007 credit crunch and the ensuing global financial crisis. The Robin Hood Tax campaign, now an international movement, emerged in direct response to the financial crisis. Robin Hood Tax campaigns for a 'tiny tax' on financial transactions to be rerouted to fight poverty and climate change. However, the biggest single-issue for financial activists in the post-crisis period is escalating consumer debt, identified by some as the next potential global crisis (T. Jones 2015). US-based website www.ihatedebt. com exposes the unseen market where debts are sold, warning consumers of industry tactics. The Jubilee Debt Campaign takes a more direct approach to effect change. The Jubilee movement emerged in the 1990s, campaigning to abolish external debts owed by developing nations. A decade later, the movement finally achieved some debt cancellations, but many promises made by the international community remained unfulfilled. In the post-crisis era, a small-scale education project for debt relief called the Rolling Jubilee penetrated the murky debt resale market, purchasing and eliminating some US$15 million in consumer debt.

The Jubilee Debt Campaign is also associated with the high-profile Occupy movement, which rose to prominence in the summer of 2011. Ironically, Occupy Wall Street was inspired by Canadian anti-consumerist magazine Adbusters, calling for Wall Street to pay for causing the financial crisis. Yet some Occupy groups were known to employ sophisticated PR strategies. The movement spread quickly; within its first six months, 6,500 people were arrested and Occupy groups were set up in more than 1,000 cities, attracting diverse groups and causes (Kavada 2015). The largest Occupy movements operated through General Assemblies, the sovereign decision-making bodies responsible for forging Occupy's key messages and foundational texts (Pitcher and McNern 2011, Kavada 2015). Assemblies were the antithesis of corporate PR functions, since they rejected established hierarchy or even designated spokespeople. PR's legitimacy only came from participation in the General Assemblies. Despite the presence of experienced PR practitioners in Occupy's press teams and a rota for dealing with the media (Pitcher and McNern 2011, Kavada 2013), Occupy's PR activities triggered suspicion with the media. Not only were there multiple press teams competing with each other, while Occupy's spokespeople adopted the long-established activist technique of concealing real names, presenting themselves as 'someone-as-anyone' (Kavada 2013, Kavada 2015). Occupy Wall Street was further accused of hypocrisy when it received an unsolicited boost from Workhouse Publicity Publicity, a Manhattan PR firm (Chen 2011).

Workhouse Publicity entered its Occupy campaign work in the prestigious PRSA Silver Anvil awards, embittering Occupy's internal press teams (Roberts and Argetsinger 2012). Such hazy connections between Occupy's genuine grassroots activists and corporate PR firms contravened the movement's claims to be horizontal and leaderless (Kavada 2013).

After years of activism, many supporters were disappointed that while Occupy had mobilised and energised thousands of street protesters, and millions of supporters via social media, the movement had fizzled without achieving concrete change in the financial sector. Some identified Occupy's diffuse communications its amorphous structure and its lack of collective voice as contributing factors, together with Occupy's meandering list of demands and its focus on preaching to the converted (Cartmell 2011, Adi 2015). Sadly, the many creative engagements between Occupy and the financial sector – e.g. the 'Bank of Ideas' which welcomed bankers and fund managers to join daily discussions, and the Bank Transfer Day which encouraged customers to switch bank accounts to credit unions (Ross 2013) – gained little traction and limited media attention (Pitcher and McNern 2011).

Conclusion

So in thinking about financial inclusion, the exploration of trust, power and public relations in financial markets takes a different turn. Financial inequality is the most crucial issue arising from the global financial crisis, and remains an issue that PR should tackle from all the positions it represents throughout financial markets. If PR experts who work in financial markets could unite on this issue and take action, this might well lay the foundation for the PR profession to associate itself with building and managing trust. While financial inclusion has become a global discourse itself, PR represents many different and conflicting viewpoints. Governments wrestle with balancing current account obligations with societal demands for social welfare. International aid agencies grapple with development fatigue, chasing any 'new' ways to end poverty, even if traditional approaches remain unattained. Financial institutions argue that the way to achieve equality is to offer more financial education, and enable *more* people to access financial services. Increasing market access offers an easier alternative to governments and international agencies. This market ideology permits governments to remove welfare cushions while nudging the marginalised toward inappropriate financial products. Market ideology permits leading international agencies to abandon subsidised models of microfinance in favour of commercialised models that crowd out other development programmes. Meanwhile, despite periodic lip service to financial education, financial institutions avoid making it a perennial part of their PR and marketing. Indeed, financial institutions continue to be financially illiterate themselves by failing to provide affordable products that marginalised consumers want and deserve.

Activist groups remain focused on the correlation between debt and inequality, but financial dissent against debt is not easy, argues Ross (2013). Protest groups continue to highlight the irony that the banking sector, which has racked up the greatest debts, remains in a position of global trust, while the world's poorest debtors remain capitalism's most untrustworthy constituents. These are destructive myths to which PR inevitably contributes. There is a further inconsistency which the PR industry must address when laying claim to trust relations in global markets. PR professionals are happily transparent regarding their contribution to financial education campaigns or 'feel good' initiatives connected with finance. However, the industry masks its substantial involvement in promoting subprime products and financial exclusion. PR's troubling relationship with secrecy and opacity in financial markets is the subject of the next chapter.

Notes

1 I discuss these secretive crystallisations in more detail in Chapter 9.
2 Self-help mutual societies in the West can be traced back to the craft guilds of the Middle Ages (Shaw 2013).
3 Although Yunus assumed this title, the microfinance movement most likely began in India in the early 1970s, while state-run microcredit existed in Bangladesh as far back as the 1930s (Mallick 2002, Bhagwati 2011).
4 High street banks and even the Student Loan Company were found to be using similar tactics.

References

Adi, A. (2015). 'Occupy PR: An analysis of online media communications of Occupy Wall Street and Occupy London', *Public Relations Review*, 41, pp. 508–514.

Adi, A. and Moloney, K. (2012). The importance of scale in Occupy movement protests, *Revista Internacional de Relaciones Publicas*, 2 (4), pp. 97–122.

Aldridge, A. (1997). 'Engaging with promotional culture: Organised consumerism and the personal financial services industry', *Sociology*, 31 (3), pp. 389–408.

Armitage, J. and Watts, J. (2013). 'Payday loans making £1m a week for Wonga', *Evening Standard*, 3 September, p. 2.

Bhagwati, J.N. (2011) 'Grameen vs Bangladesh', *Project Syndicate*, 24 March. Retrieved from: http://www.cfr.org/bangladesh/grameen-vs-bangladesh/p24492

Bateman, M. (2010). *Why Doesn't Microfinance Work?* London: Zed Books.

Bateman, M. (2012). 'Let's not kid ourselves that financial inclusion will help the poor', *The Guardian*, 8 May. Retrieved from: http://www.theguardian.com/global-development/poverty-matters/2012/may/08/financial-inclusion-poor-microfinance

Bernhardt, R. (2012). 'The time to defend Grameen bank is now', *Grameen Foundation Insights Blog*, 4 August. Retrieved from: http://www.grameenfoundation.org/blog/time-defend-grameen-bank-now#.Vb9xa_lVhBc

Broek, S., Buiskool, B., Vennekens, A. and van der Horst, R. (2012). *Study on the Current Situation and Prospects of Mutuals in Europe*, The Netherlands: Panteia-EIM, Zoetermeer.

Burke, M. (2016). 'Cooperative democracy being eroded', *Jamaica Observer*, 28 April. Retrieved from: http://www.jamaicaobserver.com/columns/Co-operative-democracy-being-eroded_59158.

Burton, D. (2008). *Credit and Consumer Society*, Abingdon: Routledge.

Burton, D., Knights, D., Leyshon, A., Alferoff, C. and Signoretta, P. (2004). 'Making a market: The UK retail financial services industry and the rise of the complex sub-prime credit market', *Competition & Change*, 8 (1), pp. 3–25.

Burton, D., Knights, D., Leyshon, A., Alferoff, C. and Signoretta, P. (2005). 'Consumption denied? The decline of industrial branch insurance', *Journal of Consumer Culture*, 5 (2), pp. 181–205.

Cartmell, M. (2011). 'Revealed: Protestors' media moves', *PR Week*, 4 November, p. 3.

Chen, A. (2011). 'Occupy Wall Street gets much-needed help from PR firm', 3 October. *Gawker.com*. Retrieved from: http://gawker.com/5846154/occupy-wall-street-gets-much+needed-help-from-pr-firm.

Cocalina, C.Q. (2016). *Cooperatives Europe Key Figures 2015*, Brussels: Cooperatives Europe.

Coombs, T. and Holladay, S. (2014). *It's Not Just PR* (Second Edition). Chichester: Wiley and Son.

Coster, H. (2010) 'Danone and Grameen bank: Partners in CSR and marketing', *Forbes.com*. Retrieved from: http://www.forbes.com/sites/csr/2010/05/21/danone-and-grameen-bank-partners-in-csr-and-marketing/

Demetrious, K. (2013). *Public Relations, Activism and Social Change*. London: Routledge.

Economist. (2008). 'Getting it right on the money', *Economist*, 5 April, p. 83.

Finance Watch. (2014). *Annual Report 2014*. Retrieved from: http://www.finance-watch.org/press/press-releases/1098

Hensby, A., Sibthorpe, J. and Driver, S. (2012). 'Resisting the 'protest business': Bureaucracy, post-bureaucracy and active membership in social movement organizations', *Organization*, 19, pp. 809–823.

Hickman, M. (2007). 'The customers' revolt over high charges; revolt on bank fees', *The Independent*, 26 February, p. 2.

James, D. (2015). *Money from Nothing: Indebtedness and Aspiration in South Africa*, Stanford: Stanford University Press.

Jones, R. (2015) 'Wonga relaunch targets 'hard-working' people', *The Guardian*, 19 May. Retrieved from: https://www.theguardian.com/business/2015/may/19/wonga-relaunch-targets-hard-working-people-1509-percent-apr-brand-to-stay

Jones, T. (2015) *The New Debt Trap*, London: Jubilee Debt Campaign.

Karger, H. (2005). *Shortchanged: Life and Debt in the Fringe Economy*, San Francisco: Berrett-Koehler Publishers Inc.

Kavada, A. (2013) 'Communicating Protest Camps: Politics and Communication in the Occupy Movement and Beyond', *Conference Paper. 63rd Annual ICA Conference*, Hilton Metropole, London, 17–21 June.

Kavada, A. (2015). 'Creating the collective: Social media, the Occupy movement and its constitution as a collective actor', *Information, Communication & Society*, 18 (8), pp. 872–886.

Kellaway, L. (2015). 'Martin Lewis, the money saving expert, talks to Lucy Kellaway', *Financial Times*, 30 October. Retrieved from: https://next.ft.com/content/53bd0dd4-7cea-11e5-98fb-5a6d4728f74e

Langley, P. (2008). *The Everyday Life of Global Finance*, Oxford: Oxford University Press.

Lewin R. (2002). 'Investigating the benefits of mutuality: A discussion of the demutualisation trend', *Pensions International Journal*, 7 (4), pp. 313–336.

Leyshon, A., Thrift, N. and Pratt, J. (1998). 'Reading financial services: Texts, consumers, and financial literacy', *Environment and Planning D: Society and Space*, 16, pp. 29–55.

Leyshon, A. and Thrift, N. (1999). 'Lists come alive: Electronic systems of knowledge and the rise of credit scoring in retail banking', *Economy and Society*, 28 (3), pp. 434–466.

Mallick, R. (2002). 'Implementing and evaluating microcredit in Bangladesh', *Development in Practice*, 12 (2), pp. 153–163.

Marron, D. (2013). 'Governing poverty in a neoliberal age: New Labour and the case of financial exclusion', *New Political Economy*, 18 (6), pp. 785–810.

McAteer, M. and Harrison, D. (2009). 'Democratic deficit', *Financial World*, June, p. 27.

McKeen-Edwards, H. and Porter, T. (2013). *Transnational Financial Associations and the Governance of Global Finance*, Abingdon: Routledge.

Muhammad, A. (2015). 'Bangladesh, a model of neoliberalism: The case of microfinance and NGOs'. *Monthly Review*, 1 March. Retrieved from: http://monthlyreview. org/2015/03/01/bangladesh-a-model-of-neoliberalism/

Pardoe, A., Lane, J., Lane, P. and Hertzberg, D. (2015). *Unsecured and Insecure? Exploring the Mountain of Britain's Unsecured Personal Debt*, London: Citizens Advice.

Pitcher, G. (2003). *The Death of Spin*, Chichester: Wiley & Sons.

Pitcher, G. and McNern, R. (2011). 'Occupy London protests: Interview with Sarah Luca', *PR Week Podcasts*, 11 November. Retrieved from: http://link.brightcove.com/services/ player/bcpid8883627001?bckey=AQ~~,AAAAAFn2Wf0~,IAYAUTS64mVDmk9VmU VxV99ZpYXx1qiD&bctid=1269287394001.

Roberts, R. and Argetsinger, A. (2012). 'Occupy Wall Street and a battle over PR prize for the protest movement', Reliable Source blog, *The Washington Post*, 12 June. Retrieved from: http://www.washingtonpost.com/blogs/reliable-source/post/occupy-wall-street-the-battle-over-pr-prize-for-the-protest-movement/2012/06/11/gJQAuqCiVV_blog.html

Roberts, S. (1998). 'Geo-governance in trade and finance and political geographies of dissent'. In Herod, A., Tuathail, G. and Roberts, S. (eds) *An Unruly World? Globalization, Governance, and Geography*. London, Routledge, pp. 116–134.

Rogaly, B. (1996). 'Micro-finance evangelism, 'destitute women', and the hard selling of a new anti-poverty formula', *Development in Practice*, 6 (2), pp. 100–112.

Ross, A. (2013). *Creditocracy and the Case for Debt Refusal*, New York: O/R books.

Shaw, M. (2013). 'Making it mutual: Insurance and mutuality', *Respublica*, 5 April. Retrieved from: http://www.respublica.org.uk/disraeli-room-post/2013/04/05/mak ing-mutual-insurance-mutuality/

Simpson, D. (2001). 'Trust in life assurance', *Economic Affairs*, 21 (1), pp. 23–28.

9 Organising silence

PR in financial silos

While trust issues extend to every corner of financial markets, public scrutiny remains focused on the trustworthiness of visible financial institutions – those directly engaged with the public, such as high street banks, stock markets, retail investment funds, financial advisers and general insurers. The problem with concentrating on what 'the eye can see' is that most financial activity takes place in wholesale and business-to-professional markets. Not only does wholesale finance operate away from the public eye, deliberate strategies are also employed to make sure these spaces *remain* concealed.

I argue in this chapter that the elites who control large tracts of power in financial markets are less preoccupied with strategies for organising trust than they are with strategies for organising and controlling invisibility, space and silence (Clair 1998, Achino Loeb 2005, Wedel 2013). The success of these strategies can be seen in popular metaphors used to depict wholesale finance – from 'silos' and 'icebergs' to 'dark pools' and 'shadow banking'. Equally, experts in wholesale financial markets are sometimes portrayed as financial 'wizards' or 'high priests', engaged in assorted forms of financial 'alchemy'. These hidden spaces barely attract the spotlight until a financial crisis. Only then do we realise just how deep some central parts of financial markets are buried.

By contrast, public relations activity is often seen as a route to *visibility*, helping organisations to be 'heard above the noise'. It is possible to detect PR campaigns on behalf of more visible financial institutions, while assuming that the hidden areas of finance – wealth managers, private equity firms, investment banks, hedge funds etc. – avoid PR altogether. In reality, PR experts are very active in wholesale markets, where they support various groups of financial experts in promoting products and services to *each other*. Confusion often arises when 'detecting' PR because of the difference between PR roles. Many junior PR professionals are tasked with achieving visibility for organisations – through increased press mentions, greater social media presence, TV and radio appearances, photo opportunities, publicity stunts, high-profile events, industry awards or celebrity tie-ins. By contrast, senior PR advisers are frequently valued for their ability to organise silence. Acting invisibly and leaving no fingerprints (Davis 2002), senior PR consultants regularly support social restrictions to financial silos on behalf of client-organisations (Preda 2009).

This chapter highlights the role of public relations in organising silence and invisibility, strategies largely ignored in communications research (Dimitrov 2015). It is particularly important to uncover PR strategies in concealed areas of finance, given that these hidden spaces have done more to destroy public trust in finance than to build it. The chapter will draw on a range of interdisciplinary work to explore how silence and invisibility are organised (Eisenberg 1984, Clair 1998, Achino Loeb 2005, Christophers 2009, McGoey 2012a, Wedel 2013, Dimitrov 2015). The discussion yields a set of five overlapping discursive strategies used by PR experts to support the social restrictions protecting financial silos. These communicative strategies include the use of complexity, selective visibility, numerical facades, strategic ambiguity and enforced silences.

Controlling financial spaces: financial elites, PR and the media

Financial silos are part of a cycle of competition. New, unregulated spaces are created through innovation. Deliberate strategies are then used to conceal these spaces from the competition, as increasingly complex financial instruments are created and pushed underground to manipulate earnings and avoid regulatory scrutiny (Partnoy 2009). Once regulation is introduced, financial actors try to avoid exposure by moving to one side of the regulatory boundary. This cycle of competition produced 'shadow banking', encompassing the unregulated activity carried out by visible, regulated organisations such as investment banks, commercial banks and pension funds, in concealed, 'shadowy areas' via complex offshore vehicles. This never-ending cycle of boundary-building and concealment is the hallmark of wholesale financial markets where many processes are commoditised, thus easily replicated.

Financial boundary work is dependent on trust relations within and between elites (Preda 2009). These elites constitute a tightly defined 'aristocratic small world network' (Olsen 2008) of corporate lawyers, private equity partners, hedge fund managers and investment bankers, operating at the nexus of global finance. The trust relations within elite networks are based on social networks, cultural patterns and, most of all, a shared expert language required to choreograph hidden spaces and operate as architects of abstract financial products (Hall 2009). Financial elites then present a collective face to outsiders, diverting external attention and access away from hidden spaces and proprietary financial expertise (Preda 2009). Financial elites are able to engage with and divert external attention through the legitimate social positions they hold outside their respective silos, spanning multiple spheres such as politics, public policy, technology or infrastructure. Elite group members can often claim positions as writers, educators, scientists and philanthropists (Preda 2009, Wedel 2013). These extended social positions enable financial elites to provide the trusted 'voice' of financial markets as opinion leaders, making recommendations, and influencing market decisions, thus organising a layer of system trust, while simultaneously organising what is and is *not* discussed (Olsen 2008, Tett 2009).

The layer of collective trust possessed by elites gives PR the ability to divert attention from wholesale market activity by controlling the flow of information, what is spoken and unspoken (Davis 2002). These social restrictions around wholesale market silos are tacitly supported by the mainstream media which prefers financial storytelling connected with visibility, everyday relevance and 'human interest' (Davis 2002, Tett 2009). Naturally, assiduous business journalists will be inquisitive about activity within silos, but their occupational curiosity rarely counterbalances the substantial control wielded by financial elites over commercial media as official spokespeople, covert sources, advertisers, consumers of business and financial news, and as the main purchasers of PR services (Davis 2002). Hence financial silos, such as the debt, credit and derivatives markets, barely merit a mention in the general media despite their vast size (Tett 2009). Likewise, debates and conflicts within these silos are only reflected in the media within limited parameters (Davis 2002). In good economic times, the mainstream media, and by extension the public, tend to leave financial silos unscrutinised (Rogers 2008).

Of course, there is extensive media coverage of market silos within the specialist financial media. However, they also control the flow of financial information since the specialist media exist to support communication by elites with *other* elites, not with the public. This results in the 'capture' of business news within 'closed discourse networks' (Davis 2002, p. 70). Elites communicate with each other within and between financial silos through a web of specialist financial conferences and events, as well as niche publications such as *Euromoney* magazine, the flagship publication of the bond markets; *Citywealth* magazine which represents private bankers; or hedge fund publications such as *AltAssets*. *Bloomberg* newswire has a reputation for strong debt market coverage, resourced by Bloomberg's subscription service providing real-time market information to market professionals via proprietary keyboards and monitors. It is via these specialist media that elite financial debates and conflicts might be revealed, but the general public is rarely able to access these discussions. PR professionals are very active within these silos, providing stories to specialist media and, more importantly, staunching the flow of information outside of silos. The rest of the chapter digs more deeply into the PR techniques used to control the flow of market information. Specifically, I unpack deliberate communicative strategies used to organise and mobilise silence, thus perpetuating hidden spaces and concealing power. On the one hand, organising silence would appear to contravene efforts to build trust. On the other hand, the degree of deliberate mystery and obfuscation which surrounds financial silos helps to compel public trust and belief in the abstract, 'unseeable' nature of finance.

Silence and invisibility as discursive strategies

Before I examine the discursive strategies used to protect the hidden spaces of finance, I will first explore silence and invisibility as interconnected forms of discursive power. I frame the discussion by drawing on Foucault, whose body of work also shapes my trust practice framework (see Chapter 2). Foucault maintained that silence – 'the thing one declines to say, or is forbidden to name' (1976/1998, p. 27) – is less the absolute limit of discourse than an element that functions alongside the things said, and in relation with other strategies. Foucault argued that there is 'not one but many silences' (p. 27) underlying and permeating discourses (p. 27). Achino-Loeb (2005) builds on this perspective, adding that silence is a vehicle for the exercise of power in 'all its modalities', while the very power of silence lies in its inherent ambiguity (2005, p. 2). Public relations advisers regularly employ silence as a discursive strategy (Dimitrov 2015). PR has obvious links with silence in its capacity to express some stories while sequestering others. But the ambiguity of silence stems from its dual powers; not only does communication have the power to silence, but silence itself can communicate (Clair 1998). Equally, silence can not only repress, it also transforms (Foucault 1976/1998). To this end, discourses can silence certain people, special issues or particular interests, while silence in discourses can distort power relations, disguise inequity, sequester resistance and even close emancipatory forms of communication (Clair 1998).

Furthermore, silence is interwoven with *invisibility* so as to obscure hidden spaces. Together, silence and invisibility increase opacity and reduce scrutiny, thus conferring power on financial elites who safeguard the ability to 'pierce the veil' (Tett 2009, p. 10). 'Piercing the veil' of financial markets is particularly challenging since the real discursive power of finance is its representation as abstract, 'seeking to be everywhere and claiming to be nowhere' (Ho 2009, p. 37). Money's particular formlessness and abstractness further perpetuate financial markets' secrecy through the invisibility and silence of most monetary exchanges (Simmel 1978). Money transactions further perpetuate the veil of modern finance, characterised by complex financial products, digital money transfers and high-frequency trading. In the next section of the chapter, I set out five sets of discursive techniques used in PR to achieve silence and invisibility in financial markets. Many of these strategies appear designed to build mistrust rather than trust, and range from *complexity as exclusionary discourse*, *selective visibility*, *numerical facades*, as well as the associated practices of *strategic ambiguity* and *strategic ignorance*, and, finally, *enforced silences*. All five techniques are outlined in the section below.

1. Complexity as exclusionary discourse

Perhaps the most commonly accepted means of organising silence in financial markets is the creation of technical jargon and complexity around financial products. This is especially true of wholesale financial markets, where complexity and information asymmetry are considered vital in preventing competitors from replicating products (House of Commons 2004). The bias toward complexity in wholesale finance governs the distinct contrast between the financial communication targeting the general public, versus communication targeting other financial elites. In retail markets, stock markets are often portrayed as 'adventure and excitement', banking as 'careful money management', and insurance as 'caring for your family'; whereas in wholesale markets, arcane language renders finance incomprehensible to all but other elites. This is why debt capital markets were barely discernible to the public even though debt markets had long ago usurped equities markets in size and scale. The mainstream press labelled debt markets 'too dull' despite the wave of innovation taking place in this financial silo.

Experts promoting derivatives and structured products in debt markets avoided the use of emotional language, despite the high risks associated with these products, and experts definitely avoided references to 'grubby cash' (Tett 2009, p. xx). Instead, structured products were promoted using technological wizardry and abstract mathematical language: Greek letters or phrases such as 'Gaussian copula', 'standard deviation', 'delta hedging' or 'first-to-default basket' – terms grasped only by a small elite (Tett 2009, p. xx). Even when complex financial jargon makes a great deal of noise, it will always communicate a form of silence to those unable to make sense of it. The specialist financial media spews a steady stream of financial jargon to those who seek it out. In fact, there is such a vast supply of specialist financial information, it can be overwhelming. Many bankers, regulators, investment advisers and financial journalists struggled to make sense of excessively complex finance (Rogers 2008, Das 2010).

The use of complex financial language in contemporary markets replicates the medieval church's use of 'priestly incantations' to evoke fear and ignorance among the pious (Fulton 2010). Indeed, Christophers (2009) argues that money and finance are *made* to seem much more complex than they actually are. The inference of complexity not only confers cultural and economic capital on the high priests of finance, but the more complex finance is made to *appear* to be, the less likely those outside financial markets can actively question market actors or call them to account. So, where the trust practice framework identifies making visible and simplifying trust strategies, complex financial jargon does nothing of the kind. This is not to say that jargon specifically produces mistrust. Rather, complexity makes it difficult for customers to assess whether it is safe to trust or not.

2. Selective visibility

Making financial products and processes visible and transparent is considered an increasingly important aspect of building trust, as illustrated in the trust practice framework in Chapter 2. However, in both retail and wholesale financial markets, selective visibility – a sense of exclusivity, even elusiveness – can prove a vital promotional tool. There are many instances where PR enables only qualified or restricted visibility of finance, and many places within financial markets that strive to remain hidden. For instance, many financial consultants (e.g. in private equity or corporate finance) value the ability to promote their company services as a 'well-kept secret'. This encourages prospective clients to regard the advice they receive as distinctive and exclusive. In PR, mystery can be far more effective than transparency (Horton 2010). The simple act of *avoiding* the media often increases editorial appetite and market curiosity. Similarly, investment houses can choose selective invisibility by marketing products categorised as 'For professional clients only. Not appropriate for retail clients.' This regulatory stamp of exclusion can create customer appetite for investments.

Too many financial institutions still regard financial media as a tap they can simply turn on and off whenever they are thirsty for favourable publicity. Many private equity firms, investment banks and corporate financiers strive to stay out of the press in order to conceal transactions and other negotiations taking place behind closed doors. A mere whiff of public attention can scupper a billion-dollar deal that was months in the making. PR advisers still help financial experts avoid 'on the record' quotes about their own transactions, while trading off-the-record information about other companies as *quid pro quo*. Periodically, PR advisers might be permitted to give 'select outsiders' a peek behind the organisational curtain. Alternatively, PR might be required to engage only with 'tame' media outlets willing to secure access by writing what is dictated. PR also helps financial institutions to 'manage down stories', thus avoiding negative press coverage: this element of PR work can account for 50 per cent of the job (Davis 2002). Financial institutions also engage in selective visibility through lobbying; even this is often masked by the more benign term 'public affairs'. Successful lobbying uses the cover of semi-social networking to do deals that crossover with the elite and semi-elite environment of politics (L'Etang 2008).

Wealth managers and private bankers are notorious for their limited press and public engagement. These very private firms rely heavily on strong inter-personal relationships with clients, focusing on elite-to-elite PR activities offering a personal touch (e.g. wealth succession courses for children of wealthy families.) To this end, wealth managers avoid the mainstream press, reflecting the privacy and opacity desired by clients. The hedge fund industry (important to wealth management) has deliberately cultivated the image of the 'outlier'. Hedge funds have long operated outside of regulatory boundaries, clustered within geographical boundaries of London and New York. These jurisdictional silos allowed hedge funds to maintain secrecy around their strategies and proprietary trading platforms (Holmes 2009, Iliev 2010), using their 'outlier' status as a competitive selling point.

Tax havens are another important wealth management tool where invisibility is used as a marketing ploy. Tax haven customers seek invisibility for their assets, which they secure in 'hidden' financial places enabled by structural and territorial enclosures offered in tax havens such as Geneva, Luxembourg, the Cayman Islands or the Isle of Man. Offshore funds, now widely used, but typically promoted to professional investors only, are typically domiciled in tax havens. Ireland has even promoted its advantage as a domicile for the Special Purpose Vehicles (SPVs) used to package structured finance products often based on distressed assets. SPVs are an example of selective visibility, since they are often set up by mainstream financial institutions then kept 'off balance sheet'.

Blanket invisibility is unfeasible in a digital era, while visibility is increasingly 'foisted' on certain wholesale market financial institutions. For example,

Goldman Sachs, the global investment bank, was forced to rescind a long-standing 'omerta' to 'stay out of the press' (Cohan 2012), after it went public in 1999. Many wealth management firms have had to open themselves up to the media gaze in the face of increased international competition and greater political scrutiny over tax avoidance. While wealth managers engage in more external communications, their tone remains cautious and sedate, presenting a calming, deliberately elitist image as trusted advisers to elites. Private equity firms were largely invisible to the public for decades, despite the number of employees working for companies backed by a private equity. Various crises have pressed the private equity industry to recognise that complete invisibility fostered a culture of distrust by regulators, and by investors disappointed with falling returns. Market crises and financial losses have imposed similar transparency on Lloyd's of London insurance market, now scrutinised by ratings agencies and a new regulatory regime. Even Switzerland's notoriously secretive banking sector has adopted a new communications strategy following concerns that offshore money would drain away to other financial centres if banking secrecy laws were compromised (Sudhaman 2010).

Hedge funds repeatedly lobby to protect their selective visibility, but even they are typically regulated, if only with a 'light touch'. The hedge fund industry has engaged in aggressive PR campaigns in order to maintain light touch regulation and secure its existence (see Chapter 4). But hedge funds can no longer truly promote themselves as outliers because they are firmly interwoven into mainstream finance – anyone in a pension scheme is probably indirectly invested in hedge funds. In reality, hedge funds never really were 'outliers' to begin with; they work closely alongside investment banks, which profit heavily by introducing hedge funds to new business. Hedge funds are also regular customers of mainstream financial institutions providing hedge funds with trading, execution, clearance and custody services (Kambhu et al. 2007).

Perhaps the most disquieting form of concealed financial space to be exposed in recent years are 'dark pools' of asset trading located in large global banks. Increased competition, market fragmentation and high visibility in stock markets has made it difficult for these institutional investors to trade large parcels of stock without competitors knowing. Banks created their own secret stock exchanges or dark pools to facilitate 'iceberg orders' from their institutional investor clients who were keen to keep their trading activity away from the stock market limelight. The existence of dark pools is a divisive issue for market elites. Their existence came to light, energised by an aggressive PR campaign by the World Federation of Exchanges, which argues that dark pools pose a threat to public stock exchanges. By contrast, the Security Industry and Financial Markets Association, which represents institutional investors, waged a defensive PR campaign in support of dark pools (McKeen-Edwards and Porter 2013). The existence of dark pools came as a surprise to many employees within the banks themselves. Were bank PR teams in the dark too? If so, can PR professionals really claim to be 'in charge' of trust if they are not privy to all an organisation's secrets?

3. Numerical facades

A third way that market elites organise silence and invisibility in financial markets is through facades constructed to help companies and products look better than they really are. In financial markets, facades are often constructed with numbers, used to seduce and provide financial certainty, and the illusion of financial strength. Public relations plays a vital role in 'selling' numbers, incorporating those numbers into compelling financial narratives that produce believable myths or outright misdirection. While numerical certainty helps to organise trust, numerical facades are a means of organising silence.

In debt markets, ratings symbols are just one set of numbers actively marketed as a means of certainty and trust. This numerical certainty ranged from AAA (trustworthy) through to DDD (untrustworthy). An entire structured credit edifice was built on the assumption that Triple-A was not only real but ultra-safe. The very certainty placed in their symbols enabled rating agencies to become a voluntary system of governance, thus reducing the cost of trust formation in unregulated markets (Yandle 2008). Yet rating agencies have been at the centre of repeated trust crises, notably the 2007 credit crunch. (See also Chapter 3.) Throughout the 2000s, rating agencies marketed their symbols to the thriving high-risk debt market. The trust created through heavily marketed Triple-A-rated structured finance contributed to the growth of a massive shadow banking system (McCulley 2009). Behind closed doors, rating agencies discovered their models were not accurately predicting the performance of securities tied to risky assets. Rating agencies failed to publish revised ratings until 2007, spreading and crystallising mistrust in high-risk debt instruments with global repercussions (Nomura 2006, US Senate 2011). The failure to publish ratings revisions implicates PR. Yet rating agencies' communications heads staunchly defended their sector, arguing that ratings had performed exactly as designed when put under stress, and that rating agencies had been made a scapegoat for market failures (Pulsepoint 2009).

The Libor price-setting mechanism held even more influence in financial markets. Libor is the most frequently used benchmark for interest rates globally, tied to some US$300 trillion in transactions (HM Treasury 2012). But despite Libor's integral role in marketing product performance against benchmark, the market elites behind Libor itself operated like a secret society. Participation by contributing banks was voluntary, and the panels setting the daily benchmark rates were small (HM Treasury 2012). No one could 'see' behind Libor to understand how rates were set. Libor's administrative body, the British Banking Association, was nearly destroyed by stubborn justification of its Libor oversight, both through defensive PR campaigns and failed litigation. (See also Chapter 4.)

In equity markets, the former energy company Enron[1] remains the posterchild for illusion and misdirection, with its crooked balance sheets fooling financial experts everywhere. The company's PR and investor relations experts actively promoted Enron's illusory financial performance. The resulting investment flows helped Enron become the seventh-largest company in the US. But

Enron didn't just use numbers, it used many conjurer's tricks to fool investors. For instance, Enron set up a 'pretend' trading floor designed to trick analysts into believing business was booming, even though no trades were actually made there (Westbrook 2014). Enron's implosion in 2001 erased US$11 billion in stockholder value, leaving tens of thousands out of work. After the collapse, the company's PR advisers claimed to have been in the dark all along (Hall 2003). Yet these PR advisers also witnessed and/or participated in Enron's extensive public affairs work in Washington DC. Enron's campaign contributions not only influenced public policy but also anesthetised congressional and senate oversight committees (Holmes 2002).

Spectacular illusions by listed companies are never far away. UK supermarket chain Tesco spent years promoting its incredible like-for-like growth, until 2014 when a whistle-blower revealed that the supermarket chain had been 'diddling' the books. (See also Chapter 5.) But PR and marketing also promote numerical certainty around retail financial products in everyday ways that go undetected. In retail fund management, for example, the most valuable marketing tool is a strong performance record, which helps to attract new funds. But fund management firms can create the illusion of financial strength by manipulating fund performance data. Even informal affinity schemes based on networks of community trust have been known to manipulate performance numbers, offering unbelievably high monthly returns to 'hook' new investors (Neves and du Toit 2012). Similarly, large investment houses often throw marketing budgets behind the launch of new funds at the expense of other funds in the family in order to establish a statistical record of high returns (Feuerborn 2001).

4. Strategic ambiguity, strategic ignorance

Strategic ambiguity is one of the most pervasive strategies for organising silence. It is a vital competitive mechanism, achieving multiple aims, all supported by PR. Through strategic ambiguity, a financial institution or association can allow divergent objectives or ideologies to coexist, hold strained relations together and reduce conflict, thus enabling financial elites to speak as a single voice (Eisenberg 1984). Ambiguity is directly stipulated by regulators for publicly-owned companies involved in a company sale or purchase, the departure and/ or appointment of a new CEO, the forging of a new commercial agreement with a supplier or competitor, intelligence gathering and new product development (Horton 2010). Companies can be reconciled to being mistrusted in order to prevent speculation and protect proprietary practices (Eisenberg 1984). Hence, for PR, silence is sometimes golden (Horton 2010). Company spokespeople practise strategic ambiguity when they are reluctant to have their views aired in the media so as to protect proprietary research, plans and products until they are executed. Strategic ambiguity also gives companies room to manoeuvre, allowing aggressive market players to talk their way swiftly and flexibly into areas they are not necessarily expert in (Eisenberg 1984). So strategic ambiguity is not always a 'bad thing', yet its purpose is often to obscure.

Strategic ignorance is a far more troubling means of organising silence. McGoey (2012b) defines strategic ignorance as mobilising the unknowns in a situation so as to command resources, deny liability in the aftermath of disaster, or assert expert control in the face of both foreseeable or unpredictable outcomes (2012b, p. 555). Knowing what *not* to know is one of the most indispensable forms of social and political knowledge, and is fundamental to professional jurisdiction (Eisenberg 1984, McGoey 2012b). Furthermore, ignorance is most convincing when exhibited collectively, not just at the level of a single financial institution but across a particular sector or market. Experts who *should* know something are particularly useful for *not* knowing it because their expertise becomes a 'knowledge alibi', helping to legitimate claims that a phenomenon is impossible to know (McGoey 2012b, p. 556). As Eisenberg argues, 'a source deemed credible who speaks ambiguously may be called a prophet, but a low-credible source speaking identically may be dubbed a fool' (1984, p. 13).

For the experts who make up financial market elites, ignorance – not knowledge – became the most indispensable resource throughout the global financial crisis. The sheer scale of experts claiming not to have seen the crisis coming – central bankers, financial regulators, economists, investment bankers, high street bankers, institutional investors, etc. – was somehow believable. The financial sector's collective ignorance became a useful alibi, deflecting accountability for those who precipitated the crash (McGoey 2012a, 2012b). Strategic ignorance protected central bankers' reputations, and allowed many of those involved in manufacturing or trading high-risk instruments to survive by suggesting that no one understood how derivatives worked, or that risks were unknowable or unpredictable in advance (Davies and McGoey 2012). However, ambiguity by its very nature makes it difficult to know the extent to which PR actively helps organisations perpetuate strategic ignorance. It is equally difficult to know the extent to which PR professionals engage in strategic ignorance themselves.

5. Enforced silences

The final strategy I propose involves the use of financial discourses to enforce silence. 'Enforcement' typically connotes coercive rather than discursive power. However, PR is also used to enforce silences in financial discourses, which has implications for trust production. Take, for example, financial education campaigns that divide consumers into financially 'literate' consumers versus financially 'illiterate'. These education campaigns effectively subdue, even silence, consumer resistance by suggesting that consumers who know enough about finance would avoid inappropriate financial products in the first place. If this were a suggestion from one source, offered once or twice, then silence might exist but would not be politically enforced. However, the dividing line drawn between the financially 'literate' and the financially 'illiterate' is a dominant discourse deployed by governments, regulators, financial providers and financial advisers alike. Their views are further propped up in education campaigns by not-for-profit organisations and consumer advice organisations. The collective silencing of the so-called financially illiterate is further enforced by the financial media.

Dimitrov (2015) argues that the exhaustive representation of silence is what transforms it into discourse. The notion of a 'pensions time bomb' has been exhaustively represented in several financial markets; it is a discourse that has privileged some consumer-citizens while silencing others. In the UK during the 2000s, several campaigns shamed and silenced public sector employees for receiving so-called gold-plated pensions while claiming that private sector workers worked harder, yet had less certainty in retirement provision. As more 'gold-plated pension' public and private sector schemes closed, this toxic discourse shifted tack. Pensions campaigns now focus on privileging the voices of 'baby boomers' (the generation which turned 55 from the year 2000) while silencing the voices of 'millennials' (the generation reaching adulthood around the same time). Companies in the pensions market are motivated to bring about policy changes that will reduce the costs of managing pensions while securing profits. This helps shape the presentation of pensions as a 'time bomb'. However, the various motivations of companies involved are hidden by opaque promotional techniques which silence consumer-citizens who do not know what to interrogate and how to resist.

Conclusion

Organisational silence is hard to see. Silence is a hidden barrier unless we observe it in motion, and/or engage in silence ourselves (Shockley-Zalabak et al. 2010). PR helps preserve this hidden barrier by itself acting invisibly and 'leaving no fingerprints'. PR's role in organising silence is not easily reconciled with PR's aspirational role in organising trust. Strategies for organising silence bear little resemblance to the trust practices as outlined in the framework in Chapter 2, and may even generate *mis*trust between the financial sector and its many publics. Participating in silence also puts PR at direct odds with the media, an important constituency (Dimitrov 2015). Specifically, silence strategies put corporate PR in antagonistic opposition against activist groups attempting to shake up financial markets and effect positive change. By participating in silence, PR also participates in barring other important and emancipatory forms of communication (Clair 1998).

The discussion in this chapter also raises the possibility that organising silence may be *more* important to financial elites than organising trust. While trust strategies may reduce the cost of business by negating the need for regulation, in an era where business is increasingly measured in terms of risk, trust strategies may be too soft, too intangible to measure up to market needs. It is not far-fetched to suggest that PR has enabled successive financial scandals and market crises by actively obscuring financial silos, and deliberately presenting numerical facades. Meanwhile, strategic ignorance seems to be a particularly important strategy in deflecting blame when crises do occur. As a means of organising silence, strategic ignorance is both simpler and less time-consuming to achieve than organising trust. In fact, a bias toward organising silence over organising trust is rational behaviour since the elites protecting the hidden places in financial markets are always seeking a way to retreat underground (Wedel 2013). The issues raised here and in the preceding chapters are now carried forward for a final discussion and conclusion. I return to the notion of the trust strategist in public relations, and consider the future for this aspirational role.

Note

1 See Chapter 5 for a more in-depth discussion of Enron.

References

Achino-Loeb, M. (2005). 'Introduction'. In Achino-Loeb, M. (ed) *Silence: The Currency of Power*. New York: Berghahn Books, pp. 1–42.

Christophers, B. (2009). 'Complexity, finance, and progress in human geography', *Progress in Human Geography*, 33 (6), pp. 807–824.

Clair, R. (1998). *Organizing Silence*, New York: State University of New York Press.

Cohan, W. (2012). 'The 'vampire squid' spills its ink', *Financial Times*, 14 March. Retrieved from: http://www.ft.com/cms/s/0/ee1c04b4–6deb-11e1-b9c7–00144feab49a.html#ax zz2B6XIxv4f

Das, S. (2010). *Traders, Guns and Money: Knowns and Unknowns in the Dazzling World of Derivatives*, Great Britain: Prentice Hall.

Davies, W. and McGoey, L. (2012). 'Rationalities of ignorance: On financial crisis and the ambivalence of neo-liberal epistemology', *Economy and Society*, 41 (1), pp. 64–83.

Davis, A. (2002). *Public Relations Democracy*, Manchester: Manchester University Press.

Dimitrov, R. (2015). 'Silence and invisibility in public relations', *Public Relations Review*, 41 (5), pp. 636–651.

Eisenberg, E.M. (1984). 'Ambiguity as strategy in organizational communication', *Communication Monographs*, 51, pp. 227–242.

Feuerborn, T.A. (2001). 'New mutual funds: Misplaced marketing through consumer misdirection', *Journal of Consumer Marketing*, 18 (1), pp. 7–11.

Foucault, M. (1976/1998). *The History of Sexuality Vol I*, (Trans: Hurley, R.), London: Penguin Books.

Fulton, S. (2010). 'One candle: Is the life industry failing the public', *CorpComms*, 11 March, Issue 44, p. 47.

Hall, C. (2003). 'Enron public relations exec tells what it's like at center of a storm', *Houston Business Journal*, 29 June. Retrieved from: http://www.bizjournals.com/houston/sto ries/2003/06/30/newscolumn5.html

Hall, S. (2009). 'Financialised elites and the changing nature of finance capitalism: Investment bankers in London's financial district', *Competition & Change*, 13 (2), pp. 173–189.

HM Treasury. (2012). *Wheatley Review of LIBOR*. Written Ministerial Statement, 17 October. London: HM Treasury.

Ho, K. (2009). *Liquidated: An Ethnography of Wall Street*, Durham, NC: Duke University Press.

Holmes, C. (2009). 'Seeking alpha or creating beta? Charting the rise of hedge fund-based financial ecosystems', *New Political Economy*, 14 (4), pp. 431–450.

Holmes, P. (2002). 'The Enron scandal impacts every aspect of PR – Part 2', *The Holmes Report*, 28 May. Retrieved from: http://www.holmesreport.com/latest/article/the-enron-scandal-impacts-every-aspect-of-pr-part-2

Horton, J. (2010). 'Silence', *Online-PR.com*. Retrieved from: http://www.online-pr.com/Holding/Silence.pdf

House of Commons. (2004). *Restoring Confidence in Long-term Savings*, House of Commons Treasury Committee Report, HC 71–1, 28 July.

Iliev, M. (2010). 'Court ruling could spell major power shift in hedge fund litigation', *FINalternatives: Hedge Fund & Private Equity News*, 11 November. Retrieved from: http://www.finalternatives.com/node/14521

Kambhu, J., Schuermann, T. and Stiroh, K.J. (2007). 'Hedge funds, financial intermediation, and systemic risk'. *Federal Reserve Bank of New York Staff Reports*. Report No. 291. New York: Federal Reserve.

L'Etang, J. (2008). 'Public relations, persuasion and propaganda'. In Zerfass, A., Amsterdamska, O. and Sriramesh, K. (eds) *Public Relations Research*, Wiesbaden: Vs Verlag für Sozioalwissenschaften, pp. 251–270.

McCulley, P. (2009). 'The shadow banking system and Hyman Minsky's economic journey'. *Global Central Bank Focus*, May. Newport Beach, CA: Pimco.

McGoey, L. (2012a). 'Strategic unknowns: Towards a sociology of ignorance', *Economy and Society*, 41 (1), pp. 1–16.

McGoey, L. (2012b). 'The logic of strategic ignorance', *The British Journal of Sociology*, 63 (3), pp. 553–576.

McKeen-Edwards, H. and Porter, T. (2013). *Transnational Financial Associations and the Governance of Global Finance*, Abingdon: Routledge.

Neves, D. and du Toit, A. (2012). 'Money and sociality in South Africa's informal economy', *The Journal of the International African Institute*, 82 (1), pp. 131–149.

Nomura. (2006). 'Rating shopping – now the consequences'. *Nomura Fixed Income Research*, 16 February. New York: Nomura Securities.

Olsen, R.A. (2008). 'Trust as risk and the foundation of investment value', *The Journal of Socio-Economics*, 37 (6), pp. 2189–2200.

Partnoy, F. (2009). *Infectious Greed: How Deceit and Risk Corrupted the Financial Markets*, New York: Public Affairs.

Preda, A. (2009). *Framing Finance*, Chicago: University of Chicago Press.

Pulsepoint. (2009). 'Chris Atkins on being a credit agency during the economic crisis'. Recorded interview. *Pulsepoint Group*. 1 July. Retrieved from: http://www.pulsepoint group.com/2009/07/chris-atkins-on-being-a-credit-agency-during-the-economic-crisis

Rogers, D. (2008). 'City firms need to place trust in comms', *PR Week*, 19 September, p. 20–21.

Shockley-Zalabak, P.S., Morreale, S.P. and Hackman, M.Z. (2010). *Building the High-Trust Organization*, San Francisco, CA: IABC/Wiley & Sons.

Simmel, G. (1978). *The Philosophy of Money*, Abingdon: Routledge Classics.

Sudhaman, A. (2010). 'Beleaguered Swiss bankers mount reputation fightback', *PR Week*, 16 April, p. 1.

Tett, G. (2009). 'Icebergs and ideologies', *Anthropology News*, October, p. 6–7.

US Senate. (2011). 'Wall Street and the financial crisis: Anatomy of a financial collapse', *US Senate Permanent Subcommittee on Investigations*, Washington DC: US Senate.

Wedel, J. (2013). 'How elite power brokers merge state and market and undermine democracy, government and the free market', *Conference Paper. Fractured Power: Elites in Our Time*, Goldsmiths: University of London, 29 May.

Westbrook, I. (2014). *Strategic Financial and Investor Communication*, Abingdon: Routledge.

Yandle, B. (2008). 'Lost trust: The real cause of the financial meltdown'. In George Mason University (ed) *Mercatus Center Working Papers*. Working Paper No. 09-02, February. Fairfax, VA: Mercatus Center, pp. 1–21.

10 Conclusion

Revisiting the trust strategist's role

Trust restoration campaigns take place in all sectors of public life, typically in response to public scandals. Strategic efforts to organise or restore trust are hardly new. However, trust campaigns appear to have intensified in conjunction with two developments: first, the increasing frequency of highly publicised market scandals, with news rapidly spread via international media; and second, the competing efforts by consulting professions such as HR, public relations and management consultancy, to position their services as integral management disciplines responsible for organisational-public relationships. Global PR firms and associations have done most to position trust as a pressing agenda for public relations. This agenda has been precisely tailored to establish a need, then offer a PR solution to global business in an era when trust is portrayed as a never-ending crisis.

However, professional claims to 'manage' trust need critical exploration. This is not just because PR professionals claim to organise trust in client-organisations, but because they also contribute strategically placed *mis*trust in the face of threats to client-organisations. More importantly, PR's 'trust strategist' aspirations must be questioned because purported trust restoration campaigns have done little to change corporate behaviour. After all, can anyone truly argue that the financial sector has become more trustworthy or even changed for the better in the past decade? On the contrary, with each crisis, finance continues to mutate into ever-larger spheres of activity, and ever-wider fields of control (Jameson 1997).

As I argued in **Chapter 1**, trust, and the need for it, has caused much angst in Anglo-Saxon markets since market deregulation in the 1980s, and this angst has intensified in subsequent years. The aftermath of the global financial crisis followed an established pattern in which politicians, consumer groups, think tanks and professional consultants talked incessantly about trust, producing numerous surveys and reports. **Chapter 1** mapped some of this discourse through its table of trust surveys, and examined the role of 'trust strategist' adopted by consultants in PR, HR and management consultancy. This critical, questioning approach underpinned the theoretical discussion in **Chapter 2**, where I adopted an interdisciplinary approach in considering how trust is organised in systems, specifically in financial markets. My primary objective in **Chapter 2** was to link trust with power, then reframe trust, power and PR. I positioned PR as a societal phenomenon, in which trust production is a systemic rather than an organisational process – part of a series of global discourses. Moving away from the bias toward organisational trust dominant in most PR studies, I emphasised Giddens's (1990) theory of abstract, faceless or system trust (Giddens 1990). Specifically, I positioned PR as discourse work, and developed a trust practice framework for thinking about how system trust is produced in financial markets. This framework guided the discussion in the ensuing chapters.

The rest of the book explored different sectors of financial markets, examining how trust is organised in proximity to PR. **Chapter 3** began at the apex of financial markets, examining promotional activity in state finance, particularly the dominant role of central banking communication in an era of 'radical transparency', as well as PR programmes by lending agencies such as the IMF and the World Bank. Applying the trust practice framework, I argued that while protecting assets is the most powerful trust strategy, protecting national assets assumes even greater power. With so much at stake, entire communities-of-practice are required to 'make' national economies (Smart 2006, Holmes 2014). While PR professionals participate in these communities-of-practice, they do not lead (Meyersson and Karlberg 2012). At the apex of financial markets, PR's trust strategist claim is substantially diminished.

Nonetheless, the 'trust strategist' role was arguably conceived to serve private sector interests. In **Chapter 4**, I moved from state interests to industry interests expressed collectively through financial trade associations or TAs, which also wield influence near the apex of financial markets where they provide a degree of voluntary governance. Whereas the international financial architecture polices financial markets from above, financial TAs primarily exist to protect market interests and fight tooth-and-nail for the right to police *themselves*. As such, financial TAs play an extensive role in the exercise of power over global financial markets, consistently producing and deploying power through collective influence (McKeen-Edwards and Porter 2013). Financial TAs cannot rely solely on tacit understandings or secret backroom deals. Collective power requires organisation to function, and organising processes are communication-driven (Conrad and Poole 2012, McKeen-Edwards and Porter 2013). Hence, the most effective TAs are full-time communications vehicles, investing substantially in member communication, public education, defensive PR campaigns and lobbying.

There are instances when TA activity looks like trust production, for example, when TAs mount public education campaigns to simplify complex industry issues. Despite this, many TA-led trust restoration campaigns are less about trust-building, and more about sowing the seeds of mistrust in policymakers and regulators, or in competing industries. **Chapter 4** concluded that financial TAs are focused on industry interests rather than the public interest, and that PR performs boundary work on their behalf, exerting control over space in financial markets through narratives supporting the status quo. I argued that such a focus makes it unfeasible to assign a trust restoration role to financial TAs or their PR advisers.

Chapter 5 moved to the world of stock markets, the iconic 'shop window' of global financial markets. PR traditionally earned its 'bread-and-butter' in stock markets by building trust between listed companies and long-term investors. PR also contributed more broadly to spreading the message of equity investing as a paradigm of the good society, and the best source of long-term investment returns (Aldridge 1997). Despite this prudent objective, stock market narratives are more stereotypically driven by myths of adventure and exploration. These myths help to stimulate trust-driven stock market 'bubbles'. The 'busts' in trust that inevitably follow are both dramatic and damaging. PR is also directly conflicted in single events such as manipulating market news around Facebook's flotation. Market manipulation is not a new phenomenon, nor are stock market bubbles. However, recent trends have shifted trust relations in the largest stock markets. First, more companies are turning to debt instead of equity capital markets for finance. Second, many asset managers and pension funds are undertaking large trades in the privacy offered by 'dark pools' hosted within large banks. Third, hedge funds, high frequency traders and other arbitrageurs now control the majority of global share capital. These arbitrageurs hold stocks for such short periods (often seconds), they simply have no need to trust the companies they invest in. Furthermore, activist hedge funds aggressively seek out company weaknesses, then plant mistrust among other investors, potentially winning enough support to 'muscle in' on company boards. PR supports both sets of combatants – arbitrageurs and target companies – in these battles of mistrust.

Chapter 6 explored trust communications *across* the banking system, and the intersection between everyday banking and wholesale banking. In the wake of the global financial crisis, no single area of financial markets faced a bigger trust conundrum than the banking sector. Structurally, the banking system sits high on the hierarchy of trust relations within nation states. Banks protect assets of millions of individual customers, small and large businesses, charities and governments. Protecting is the most powerful trust strategy in financial markets. However, trust in banks is illusory, based on the assumption that our money is readily accessible whenever we need it. We do not give much thought to the degree of trust we have in banks because we are compelled to deal with them. However, what banks fail to share with everyday customers is that the real business of modern banking is not lending money to everyday consumers and businesses, but arranging and spreading risks, and that our money is not readily accessible, but tied up in long-term loans of securitised instruments.

Not only has the focus of contemporary banking shifted from everyday lending, banks' relationships with retail customers are governed by whether the *customer* is deemed trustworthy, not whether customers trust the bank (Burton 2008). The customer's trustworthiness has always been a foundation of retail banking, but new surveillance technologies now screen customers with ever-more detail. Customers deemed unprofitable or unsuitable can find themselves 'sacked' by their banks. However, the global financial crisis exposed the banking sector's most significant trust dilemma. The banking system cannot function if wholesale banks do not trust each other. This veneer of trust between banks is thin, even though wholesale banks deal with each other daily. Curiously, the banking sector has addressed neither of these trust dilemmas in its decade-long trust restoration campaign. The sector's PR efforts seem misaligned with its real trust issues. **Chapter 6** concluded that trust restoration campaigns have acted as smokescreen while banks scurry to rejig their business models in the face of 'fintech' disruptors threatening their payments business, credit cards and other revenue lines.

Chapter 7 focused on insurance, investment and pensions. This is a broad area of finance where products are complex. Hence many of the sales take place through 'middlemen', especially in the largest markets where there is excessive choice, so financial intermediaries are common 'trust access points'. I argued in **Chapter 7** that consumers are increasingly expected to become more financially enterprising, using financial markets to meet core needs such as protection, cover and retirement income as governments retreat further from welfare provision, and as financial providers retreat further from unprofitable customers. The imperative to be 'enterprising' about finance is happening amidst widespread industry change. New regulation has increased the cost of doing business and, significantly, increased the cost of accessing financial advice. Meanwhile, new technologies have made it easier for customers to select even complex products online with the help of 'robo-advisers'. Many consumers are happy to place their trust in robo-advice. While some financial advisers have embraced 'robo' assistance, many smaller advisory firms have been driven out of business by this new technology. While robo-advice may improve trust levels in financial services, the truth is that robo-advice caters only for consumers who can afford the service. Enterprising or not, many consumers are left out 'in the cold' when it comes to managing their own financial needs.

Chapter 8 picks up on the issue of marginalisation and persistent exclusion from financial services. The chapter highlights the *real* crisis of trust in financial markets: as more citizens are excluded from mainstream finance, they are increasingly driven toward inappropriate, high-risk products and a spiral of mounting debt. The touted remedy for this crisis is 'financial inclusion', incorporating PR-led financial education campaigns. While these campaigns may seem benign, they often press consumers to become ever-more enterprising by purchasing ever-more financial products. Even less benign is the global promotion of microfinance, a highly problematic industry riddled with untrustworthy practices. **Chapter 8** also explored grassroots financial activism and its use of PR techniques in protesting against debt and inequality. Financial activism provides a vital voice of resistance in financial markets, as illustrated by groups such as Occupy, the Robin Hood Tax campaign and the Jubilee Debt Campaign. Financial dissent against debt may not be easy (Ross 2013), but these groups have been joined by mainstream economists in highlighting consumer debt as the potential source of the next global financial crisis.

Where Chapter 8 highlighted the marginalised subjects of finance, **Chapter 9** shone the spotlight on elites who control large tracts of power in financial markets. **Chapter 9** set the 'trust strategist' concept on its head entirely, proposing that financial elites invest in PR not so much to organise trust, but to organise silence (Clair 1998, Achino-Loeb 2005, Wedel 2013). PR contributes to strategies for organising silence in financial markets in ways that bear little resemblance to trust practices, even generating *mis*trust in finance. Public scrutiny focuses on trustworthiness of visible 'main street' finance – retail banks, stock markets, mutual funds, financial advisers and general insurers. However, most financial activity takes place out of sight in wholesale and professional financial services, which work hard to ensure these spaces *remain* concealed. Wholesale finance vastly exceeds the geographic area of retail finance, and invests heavily in PR campaigns, but these too are concealed, as wholesale market PR typically targets other elites, not the general public. **Chapter 9** concluded that elite activity is central to understanding trust relations in financial markets, since organising silence may be *more* important to financial elites than organising trust..

Public relations and the trust practice framework

Throughout the book, I have conducted a vertical-horizontal exploration of PR activity throughout financial markets, from the apex of state finance to everyday financial transactions. I established that trust issues extend to every corner of financial markets, driving further inequalities as citizens are increasingly enticed into financial markets, while becoming increasingly marginalised from the best and safest financial products. I also highlighted the geography of global financial markets, where many spaces remain concealed in order to protect elite interests, with PR playing a central role within these spaces by organising invisibility and silence. In this next section, I assemble my main conclusions regarding PR's role in organising trust in financial markets, working through each of the five strategies for organising trust, proposed in my trust practice framework – protecting, guaranteeing, aligning, opening up and simplifying.

First trust practice: protecting assets

I identified *protecting* assets as the most powerful trust practice in financial markets. From the outset, I argued that PR practitioners have no direct involvement in protecting financial assets, a fact which automatically establishes some distance between PR and organising trust. Banks occupy the highest position of trust in the financial market hierarchy. Central banks are foremost, since they protect national assets and guarantee trust in the rest of the banking system. Commercial banks come next in the pecking order of trust, with responsibility for protecting both public and private assets. I argued that the abstract trust placed in banking is problematic since it is based on a weak understanding of how the contemporary 'banking' system operates. The transformations currently underway are regularly discussed among financial experts via the specialist financial media. However, a real debate about the future of banking has yet to be stimulated in the public sphere. Until the public's understanding of modern banking aligns with reality, there are moral questions about whether trust in this sector should be restored at all.

Governments and industry leaders recognise the inherent issues with modern banking and its originate-to-distribute lending model. This is why post-crisis PR campaigns have promoted the trustworthiness of financial cooperatives such as credit unions, building societies and mutual insurers. The cooperative model is centuries old, designed to protect more vulnerable groups, and represent the financially marginalised. However, cooperatives can never replace banks in everyday banking relationships as global competition and changing legislation severely test the cooperative model. Financial advisers, the 'middlemen' for insurance, investment and pensions products, are periodically put forward as the best trust access points for everyday finance. Financial advisers often have responsibility for protecting assets, but their structural power in the financial hierarchy is weak, hence the fluctuating support they receive from financial providers and policymakers. Financial advisers' influence has been further weakened by conflicts over commission payments and the regulatory-mandated shift to fee-based advice. However, my greatest concern with protecting as a trust practice is that financial markets seem more interested in protecting their *own* interests than in protecting customer interests and assets. PR has supported efforts to protect industry interests, such as London and New York's campaigns to defend trust in their geographic positions as international financial centres (see **Chapter 4**), and the British Banking Association's efforts to protect member interests in the face of Libor manipulation.

Second trust practice: guaranteeing

The second trust practice in the framework is *guaranteeing*, a common practice throughout the finance industry. Central banks guarantee trustworthiness of a nation's financial system (Lapavitsas 2007). Rating agencies guarantee the trustworthiness of corporate and state debt repayments. Insurers regularly use terms like 'protected' and 'guaranteed' in their PR and marketing material to build trust in long-term savings products. As non-financial professionals, PR advisers are not the arbiters of financial promises made to customers. However, PR certainly plays a role in promoting the financial guarantees on offer. On the strength of central bank guarantees, PR helps governments to promote trustworthiness of their currencies, seek endorsement from credit rating agencies and raise funds in debt capital markets. However, developing countries' promotional efforts will forever be stymied by their weaker politico-economic status. PR also promotes credit ratings; however, Malsch and Gendron (2009) argue that financial experts, while openly supportive of ratings and other quantitative tools, are privately sceptical of them. It would seem that PR's contribution here is in propping up the myth of credit ratings as a form of trust-by-proxy, rather than as a genuine trust mechanism.

Guarantees play a crucial role in organising trust in retail finance. PR professionals regularly seek third party endorsement for financial offerings including industry rankings and awards, kitemarks and industry memberships. However, the guarantees offered in retail finance can be just as problematic as whole-sale market guarantees such as credit ratings or sovereign finance. For example, when PR professionals promote guarantees on insurance and investment products they are promoting the impossible, since investment return (except perhaps ultra-low returns) are impossible to guarantee (Simpson 2001). In any case, problems with long-term savings products generally emerge years after purchase, making it difficult for consumers to question financial guarantees at the point of purchase. Consumer organisations are therefore important trust mechanisms in financial markets. They may not offer guarantees on which products work best, but they often use PR campaigns to single out financial products that do *not* work. Consumer group campaigns are once instance when PR is used to contest the promises behind financial guarantees.

Third trust practice: aligning with other trust bodies

The third trust strategy, *aligning*, opens up further debates over PR's support for questionable financial behaviour. In state finance, there remains a stubborn dividing line between richer versus poorer nations. It has never mattered whether debtor nations trust the IMF, since the Fund's legitimacy has always owed more to disciplinary power than it is has to trust. After a period of declining prestige, the IMF worked hard to restore the trust of its OECD creditor nations. The IMF's PR 'playbook' has always masked inequality in the Fund's trust relations with states, casting debtor countries as 'unruly' children, while deflecting attention away from the harmful policies of industrialised nations (Popke 1994, De Goede 2005). The launch of new lending institutions by China and the BRICs is an attempt to redress the prevailing Western bias in inter-state lending by building alignment between borrowers and *non*-Western creditor nations.

While the IMF was never intended as a trust-based alliance, the eurozone's currency alliance was. For years, eurozone nations were able to maintain trustworthiness in the euro, their collective financial brand. This trustworthiness was based on the eurozone's transparent criteria for admission to the currency alliance. But the eurozone broke its own rules, allowing new and existing member states to bend criteria. Today, nations at the 'core' of the eurozone are deemed more trustworthy than those at the periphery, e.g. Greece and Portugal. Likewise, London, an international financial centre (IFC), appears more closely aligned with its financial sector interests than with other London-based commercial activities or individual residents. This compromises London's social pact (a form of trust) with its own citizens, and with the rest of the UK. In shifting trust relations, the financial industry's interests and the *public* interest only rarely align. Likewise, in stock markets, listed companies must demonstrate alignment with market regulation, and demonstrate even closer alignment with investor interests and shareholder value. However, trust will always be compromised where shareholder interests overpower other stakeholder interests.

Fourth trust practice: opening up

The fourth practice is *openness* and *transparency*. Much of the normative PR literature on trust places transparency at the very centre of trust-building efforts, with PR directly associated with this fourth practice. PR activity is often seen as a route to openness, helping organisations to build visibility and be 'heard above the noise'. However, I have argued throughout the book that it is difficult for PR to take the lead on transparency. For example, 'radical transparency' in state finance has been largely illusory, since states are just as able to tell lies about their liabilities as companies are (Resche 2004, Mason 2009). Furthermore, while the international financial architecture aims to 'speak with one voice', treasuries and central banks are more likely to speak in unison while the global economy is growing. During extended economic stagnation, state interests become heavily-biased toward national interests once again. In this construct, PR exists to represent competing national and regional interests, rather than build overall trust in the global financial system. In Chapter 4, for example, I explored efforts by the trade association AIMA to promote increased hedge fund transparency with institutional clients (Bourne and Edwards 2012). However, the industry's efforts were less about trust-building than they were a tactic to stave off further regulation. In other words, hedge funds conceded a degree of semi-transparency as the cost of doing business, while ensuring that transparency had its limits, through defensive PR.

Transparency as a trust mechanism has also had a chequered history in the banking industry. The British Banking Association steadfastly refused to investigate the transparency of Libor's little-understood calculative process, then launched a PR campaign to defend its supposed ignorance of Libor's manipulation by member banks. Equally, many global banks kept quiet about hosting 'dark pools' of secret equities trading until an energised PR campaign by world stock exchanges to defend the transparency offered by public stock markets. As I argued in **Chapter 9**, PR is more frequently enlisted to organise mistrust and silence. PR has contributed to pervasive issues of hidden costs and poor transparency in retail investment, providing scant detail on where pooled funds actually invest their money. Similarly, PR has helped private banks and private equity to protect their silos. These 'invisible' areas of finances remained secretive for many years, only opening up when forced to do so by global competition and regulatory scrutiny. PR has consistently enabled financial elites to divert attention from hidden areas of finance by controlling the flow of information, what is spoken and unspoken about finance, through strategies for organising and controlling silence (Clair 1998, Davis 2002, Achino Loeb 2005, Wedel 2013).

Fifth trust practice: simplifying

The fifth strategy, *simplifying*, is most closely associated with PR. Communicators play a pivotal role in selecting and rejecting messages about financial institutions, explaining and clarifying these messages, and contesting statements deployed by other financial actors. However, financial markets seem (deliberately) unsure how simplicity should be defined. For example, PR's historical role within central banks was to 'translate' monetary policy and economic value to financial markets, while maintaining a high degree of opacity, saying as little as possible, and saying it cryptically (Blinder et al. 2001). If communications officers attempted to simplify these utterances, they were told that plain language 'dumbed down' texts (Meyersson and Karlberg 2012, p. 119). Although state finance attempts simpler communication in an era of 'radical transparency', central banking remains a cryptic language to the average citizen. In retail finance, a major indictment on PR has been its failure to build trust by appropriately simplifying the industry's jargon. Financial advisers and other intermediaries who become straight-talking consumer champions win trust by translating complex jargon about insurance, pensions and savings into easily understood messages. Consumer groups and price comparison sites simplify the bewildering array of financial products, using PR campaigns to bifurcate 'good' products from 'bad'. Yet there are instances when financial markets over-simplify with destructive results, for example, when distilling an entire country's economic endeavours down to a single credit rating.

Application of the trust practice framework throughout the book demonstrates that links between PR and trust are more limited than imagined by normative PR theories. As I have underscored in previous work (see Bourne 2012, 2013, 2015), much of the responsibility for organising trust in financial services rests with financial experts, not with PR professionals. PR practitioners are not responsible for the act of protecting assets, nor are they in a position to make guarantees, although PR may promote the existence of such guarantees. PR professionals do not assign credit ratings, develop investment research, design bank accounts or underwrite insurance policies. PR does not set interest rates or determine that central banks should focus myopically on inflation targeting. PR is most closely associated with the discursive trust practice of simplifying – selecting and rejecting messages about financial institutions, explaining and clarifying these messages, and contesting statements deployed by other financial actors. Yet, PR's close association with this one trust practice in no way mitigates PR's role as an accessory to concealment and obfuscation in financial markets.

While various PR campaigns have been mounted to 'restore trust' in finance in the post-crisis period, the financial systems we are being asked to 'trust' again are themselves undergoing radical change, driven by new regulation and digital technologies. A decade after the global crisis, finance has *not* become more trustworthy, even though trust in financial services has reportedly been on the rebound for several years (Edelman 2016). Financial market actors are not as worried about public trust as the public might like them to be, because money and finance are always uncertain, so trust will never truly be 'banished' (Pixley 2012). Trust in financial markets will always be required . . . with or without PR.

Organising trust as strategic professional power

If PR is not the fulcrum for organising trust in financial markets, how important is it for PR professionals to be trust strategists? In this closing section of the book, I argue that 'trust' is not as important a term on the PR professional's business card as the term 'strategist' is. An organisation's strategy is deemed important with internal decision-makers and external stakeholders (Knights and Morgan 1991). Hence, strategists have power conferred on them since they facilitate and legitimise the organisation's exercise of power by developing and transforming organisation/market rules and practices (Knights and Morgan 1991). PR professionals, like other corporate advisers, yearn for strategic identity (Allard Poesie 2010). The 'strategist' designation brings with it a sense of professional security and destiny (Knights and Morgan 1991), justifying communication departments' efforts at empire-building (Pitcher 2003).

Unfortunately for the PR profession, communicators' efforts to be strategic have generally consisted of two activities. First, PR professionals typically manage 'soft' areas such as organisational-public relationships and positive media and stakeholder impressions. The second customary role for PR is that of 'cheerleader' for corporate strategy, communicating corporate vision and plans *after* someone else has devised them. Small wonder PR professionals identify one of the challenges of the job as 'convincing management that communications is a strategic function' (Louhiala-Salminen et al 2013, p. 147). Low professional status has long-plagued PR as an occupation, and this reality contributes to PR's never-ending struggle for legitimacy, relevance, status and influence (Bourne 2015). Trust restoration is appealing as a route toward strategic power, because while PR struggles to be seen as strategic in its everyday tasks, the struggle ends temporarily when there is a crisis, and particularly, when there is a crisis of trust. During times of crisis and uncertainty, PR's role transforms from technician, cheerleader and chamberlain to strategic decision-maker (Gambetti et al. 2013). Small wonder that the rapid escalation of trust crises during the twenty-first century has been an unprecedented opportunity for PR to grasp strategic power.

However, the severity and frequency of trust crises in global markets may have been the trust strategists' undoing. In a world of short-termism, shareholder value, 24/7 news cycles, the rapid spread of financial news and rumours, and the instantaneous transfer of financial payments and trades, trust restoration simply takes too long. In the midst of crisis, there is no time to 'restore' trust – it is the sort of emotional labour which may (or may not) take place after the crisis is over. In industries such as banking, insurance and fund management, which are being heavily disrupted by financial technology, trust campaigns merely act as a 'holding pattern' while financial institutions scramble to decide on their next real strategic step. The flood of trust surveys since the 2000s should also be taken with a pinch of salt. Trust surveys never measure trust satisfactorily, since public perceptions of trust are not the same as measuring an organisation's actual trustworthiness (O'Neill 2002).

So the trust strategists' moment may have passed, while another corporate language – one of risk and corporate value – has taken over (Klewes and Wreschniok 2009). Risk management was once a back-office operation. It is now fundamental to business models, and integral to business strategy and value creation (Power 2004). Risk officers seek to embed risk management as 'gospel' within broader organisational culture. Unlike PR professionals, risk officers offer the 'hard' skills required for strategic success, recruiting from accountancy, actuarial science, finance, corporate law or compliance. This reality has forced a broader rethink, particularly in global PR consultancy. Where trust is nebulous, risk – by contrast – is recognisable, measurable, quantifiable and an established part of accountancy and audit procedures. By recasting themselves as 'risk managers', senior-level PR consultants gain a more powerful remit and access to all areas, and vital earnings streams from crisis and reputation risk management (Burt 2012).

Revisiting the trust strategist's role

PR has helped to define the boundaries of trust discourses, functioning as a tool of elite conflicts at the expense of other stakeholders (Davis 2000). As such, the PR field bears some responsibility for understanding trust processes better than it currently does. PR's narrow focus on organisational trust has left organisations unable to visualise patterns of trust production within and across the systems in which they operate. The PR profession may have surveyed trust levels 'to death', but Phillips (2015, p. 46) is right in his assertion that the PR industry has continued to treat trust as a message rather than an outcome of an organisation's trustworthy behaviour. It is my belief that the PR profession's focus on restoring trust after corporate failures has happened at the expense of understanding power relations and, notably, understanding the deliberate production of mistrust (Welch 2006). PR's real value as a field of expertise, therefore, may not be in managing trust but in managing *mis*trust (Welch 2006). This skill seems particularly appropriate for contesting experts in highly specialist, competitive markets, as well as for managing relationships with the state. In other words, managing mistrust may be more important than rebuilding trust, since people still do business with all sorts of companies in various markets without trusting them 'an inch'. Furthermore, organisations have long been reconciled to being mistrusted in order to prevent speculation and protect proprietary practices (Eisenberg 1984).

Rather than thinking about mistrust as a dangerous and destructive force, PR experts might introduce a more benign understanding of mistrust as a natural mechanism, a 'caveat emptor' for customers and an important means of exerting checks and balances on power elites and maintaining system order (Kasperson et al. 1999). Equally, there is such a thing as too much trust. Trust can breed complacency, becoming a comforting measure, which can deceive PR advisers that all is well with their organisation or brand (Nairn 2007). Too much trust can encourage incremental change or 'baby steps' where there should be revolution or root-and-branch reform. Too much trust can also breed recessive campaigns rather than innovation (Nairn 2007). At the same time, I do not set aside the 'trust strategist' claim altogether: the PR profession is itself discursively constituted, as well as producing trust discourses and contesting them. The future is therefore open to the possibility that new expert trust roles can be discursively constituted within the PR discipline, and that these new experts can contribute to new social relations of trust.

References

Achino-Loeb, M. (2005). 'Introduction'. In Achino-Loeb, M. (ed) *Silence: The Currency of Power*. New York: Berghahn Books, pp. 1–42.

Aldridge, A. (1997). 'Engaging with promotional culture: Organised consumerism and the personal financial services industry', *Sociology*, 31 (3), pp. 389–408.

Allard-Poesi, F. (2010). 'A Foucauldian perspective on strategic practice: Strategy as the art of unfolding'. In Golsorkhi, D., Rouleau, L., Seidl, D. and Vaara, E. (eds) *Cambridge Handbook of Strategy as Practice*. Cambridge: Cambridge University Press, pp. 168–182.

Blinder, A., Goodhart, C., Hildebrand, P., Lipton, D. and Wyplosz, C. (2001). *How Do Central Banks Talk?* Geneva: International Center for Monetary and Banking Studies.

Bourne, C. (2012). 'Rating agencies as a corporate governance mechanism: Power and trust production in debt capital markets'. In Tench, R, Jones, B. and Sun, W. (eds) *Corporate Social Irresponsibility: Issues, Debates and Case Studies*. Bingley: Emerald Books, pp. 135–156.

Bourne, C. (2013). 'Reframing trust, power and public relations in global financial discourses: Experts and the production of mistrust in life insurance', *Public Relations Inquiry*, 2 (1), pp. 51–77.

Bourne, C. (2015). 'Thought leadership as a trust strategy in global markets: Goldman Sachs' promotion of the 'BRICs' in the marketplace of ideas', *Journal of Public Relations Research*, 27 (4), pp. 322–336.

Burt, T. (2012). *Dark Art: The Changing Face of Public Relations*, London: Elliot & Thompson.

Burton, D. (2008). *Credit and Consumer Society*, Abingdon: Routledge.

Clair, R. (1998). *Organizing Silence*, New York: State University of New York Press.

Conrad, C. and Poole, M.S. (2012). *Strategic Organizational Communication in a Global Economy* (Seventh Edition), Chichester: Wiley-Blackwell.

Davis, A. (2000). 'Public Relations, business news and the reproduction of corporate elite power', *Journalism*, 1 (3), pp. 282–304.

Davis, A. (2002). *Public Relations Democracy*, Manchester: Manchester University Press.

De Goede, M. (2005). *Virtue, Fortune & Faith*, Minneapolis: University of Minnesota Press.

Edelman. (2016). *2016 Edelman Trust Barometer*, New York: Edelman.

Eisenberg, E.M. (1984). 'Ambiguity as strategy in organizational communication', *Communication Monographs*, 51, pp. 227–242.

Gambetti, R., Giovanardi, M. and Brioschi, E.T. (2013). 'Exploring the professional identity of the corporate communication officer'. In Gambetti, R. and Quigley, S. (eds) *Managing Corporate Communication: A Cross-Cultural Approach*. Basingstoke: Palgrave-Macmillan, pp. 115–134.

Giddens, A. (1990). *The Consequences of Modernity*, Oxford, UK: Polity Press/Blackwell.

Holmes, D.R. (2014). *Economy of Words: Communicative Imperatives in Central Banks*, Chicago: University of Chicago Press.

Jameson, F. (1997). 'Culture and finance capital', *Critical Inquiry*, 24 (1), pp. 246–265.

Kasperson, R.E., Golding, D. and Kasperson, J.X. (1999). 'Risk, trust and democratic theory'. In Cvetokovich, G. and Lofstedt, R. (eds) *Social Trust and the Management of Risk*. London: Earthscan Publications, pp. 22–41.

Klewes, J. and Wreschniok, R. (2009). 'Introduction'. In Klewes, J. and Wreschniok, R. (eds) *Reputation Capital: Building and Maintaining Trust in the 21st Century*. Berlin-Heidelberg: Springer-Verlag, pp. 1–7.

Knights, D. and Morgan, G. (1991). 'Corporate strategy, organization and subject: A critique', *Organization Studies*, 12 (2), pp. 251–273.

Lapavitsas, C. (2007). 'Information and trust as social aspects of credit', *Economy and Society*, 36, pp. 416–436.

Louhiala-Salminen, L., Kankaanranta, A. and Uusi-Rauva, C. (2013). 'Communications professionals in the 2010s: What knowledge – what skills?' In Gambetti, R. and Quigley, S. (eds) *Managing Corporate Communication*. Basingstoke: Palgrave-Macmillan, pp. 135–152.

Malsch, B., and Gendron, Y. (2009). 'Mythical representations of trust in auditors and the preservation of social order in the financial community', *Critical Perspectives on Accounting*, 20, pp. 735–750.

Mason, P. (2009). *Meltdown: The End of the Age of Greed*, London: Verso.

McKeen-Edwards, H. and Porter, T. (2013). *Transnational Financial Associations and the Governance of Global Finance*, Abingdon: Routledge.

Meyersson, P. and Karlberg, P.P. (2012). *A Journey in Communication: The Case of Sveriges Riks Bank*, Stockholm: SNS Förlag.

Nairn, A. (2007). 'Beware the trust trap', *Marketing Week*, 29 November, p. 31.

O'Neill, O. (2002). *A Question of Trust*, Cambridge: Cambridge University Press.

Phillips, R. (2015). *Trust Me, PR Is Dead*, London: Unbound.

Pitcher, G. (2003). *The Death of Spin*, Chichester: John Wiley & Sons.

Pixley, J. (2012). *Emotions in Finance: Booms, Busts and Uncertainty* (Second Edition), Cambridge: Cambridge University Press.

Popke, E.J. (1994). 'Recasting geopolitics: The discursive scripting of the international monetary fund', *Political Geography*, 13 (3), pp. 255–269.

Power, M. (2004). *The Risk Management of Everything*, London: Demos.

Resche, C. (2004). 'Investigating 'Greenspanese': From hedging to 'fuzzy transparency'', *Discourse & Society*, 15 (6), pp. 723–744.

Simpson, D. (2001). 'Trust in life assurance', *Economic Affairs*, 21 (1), pp. 23–28.

Smart, G. (2006). *Writing the Economy: Activity, Genre and Technology in the World of Banking*, London: Equinox Publishing.

Wedel, J. (2013). 'How elite power brokers merge state and market and undermine democracy, government and the free market', *Conference Paper. Fractured Power: Elites in Our Time*, Goldsmiths, University of London, 29 May.

Welch, M. (2006). 'Rethinking relationship management: Exploring the dimension of trust', *Journal of Communication Management*, 10, pp. 138–155.

Index